Elizabeth P. Cramer
Editor

D0029623

Addressing Homophobia and Heterosexism on College Campuses

Addressing Homophobia and Heterosexism on College Campuses has been co-published simultaneously as *Journal of Lesbian Studies*, Volume 6, Numbers 3/4 2002.

Pre-publication
REVIEWS,
COMMENTARIES,
EVALUATIONS . . .

"A RESOURCE THAT WILL HAVE WIDE APPEAL to university faculty, staff, and students of all sexual orientations who are involved with addressing LGBTQ issues on campus. There is no person involved in sexual orientation issues on today's campuses that will not find several chapters relevant to their work or personal experiences."

James M. Croteau, PhD
Professor of Counselor Education
and Counseling Psychology
Western Michigan University

Harrington Park Press

Addressing Homophobia and Heterosexism on College Campuses

Addressing Homophobia and Heterosexism on College Campuses has been co-published simultaneously as *Journal of Lesbian Studies*, Volume 6, Numbers 3/4 2002.

The *Journal of Lesbian Studies* Monographic "Separates"

Below is a list of "separates," which in serials librarianship means a special issue simultaneously published as a special journal issue or double-issue *and* as a "separate" hardbound monograph. (This is a format which we also call a "DocuSerial.")

"Separates" are published because specialized libraries or professionals may wish to purchase a specific thematic issue by itself in a format which can be separately cataloged and shelved, as opposed to purchasing the journal on an on-going basis. Faculty members may also more easily consider a "separate" for classroom adoption.

"Separates" are carefully classified separately with the major book jobbers so that the journal tie-in can be noted on new book order slips to avoid duplicate purchasing.

You may wish to visit Haworth's website at . . .

http://www.HaworthPress.com

. . . to search our online catalog for complete tables of contents of these separates and related publications.

You may also call 1-800-HAWORTH (outside US/Canada: 607-722-5857), or Fax 1-800-895-0582 (outside US/Canada: 607-771-0012), or e-mail at:

getinfo@haworthpressinc.com

Addressing Homophobia and Heterosexism on College Campuses, edited by Elizabeth P. Cramer, PhD (Vol. 6, No. 3/4, 2002). *A practical guide to creating LGBT-supportive environments on college campuses.*

Femme/Butch: New Considerations of the Way We Want to Go, edited by Michelle Gibson and Deborah T. Meem (Vol. 6, No. 2, 2002). *"Disrupts the fictions of heterosexual norms. . . . A much-needed examiniation of the ways that butch/femme identitites subvert both heteronormativity and 'expected' lesbian behavior." (Patti Capel Swartz, PhD, Assistant Professor of English, Kent State University)*

Lesbian Love and Relationships, edited by Suzanna M. Rose, PhD (Vol. 6, No. 1, 2002). *"Suzanna Rose's collection of 13 essays is well suited to prompting serious contemplation and discussion about lesbian lives and how they are–or are not–different from others. . . . Interesting and useful for debunking some myths, confirming others, and reaching out into new territories that were previously unexplored." (Lisa Keen, BA, MFA, Senior Political Correspondent, Washington Blade)*

Everyday Mutinies: Funding Lesbian Activism, edited by Nanctte K. Gartrell, MD, and Esther D. Rothblum, PhD (Vol. 5, No. 3, 2001). *"Any lesbian who fears she'll never find the money, time, or support for her work can take heart from the resourcefulness and dogged determination of the contributors to this book. Not only do these inspiring stories provide practical tips on making dreams come true, they offer an informal history of lesbian political activism since World War II." (Jane Futcher, MA, Reporter,* Marin Independent Journal, *and author of* Crush, Dream Lover, *and* Promise Not to Tell)

Lesbian Studies in Aotearoa/New Zealand, edited by Alison J. Laurie (Vol. 5, No. 1/2, 2001). *These fascinating studies analyze topics ranging from the gender transgressions of women passing as men in order to work and marry as they wished to the effects of coming out on modern women's health.*

Lesbian Self-Writing: The Embodiment of Experience, edited by Lynda Hall (Vol. 4, No. 4, 2000). *"Probes the intersection of love for words and love for women. . . . Luminous, erotic, evocative." (Beverly Burch, PhD, psychotherapist and author,* Other Women: Lesbian/Bisexual Experience and Psychoanalytic Views of Women *and* On Intimate Terms: The Psychology of Difference in Lesbian Relationships)

'Romancing the Margins'? Lesbian Writing in the 1990s, edited by Gabriele Griffin, PhD (Vol. 4, No. 2, 2000). *Explores lesbian issues through the mediums of books, movies, and poetry and of-*

fers readers critical essays that examine current lesbian writing and discuss how recent movements have tried to remove racist and anti-gay themes from literature and movies.

From Nowhere to Everywhere: Lesbian Geographies, edited by Gill Valentine, PhD (Vol. 4, No. 1, 2000). *"A significant and worthy contribution to the ever growing literature on sexuality and space. . . . A politically significant volume representing the first major collection on lesbian geographies. . . . I will make extensive use of this book in my courses on social and cultural geography and sexuality and space." (Jon Binnie, PhD, Lecturer in Human Geography, Liverpool, John Moores University, United Kingdom)*

Lesbians, Levis and Lipstick: The Meaning of Beauty in Our Lives, edited by Jeanine C. Cogan, PhD, and Joanie M. Erickson (Vol. 3, No. 4, 1999). *Explores lesbian beauty norms and the effects these norms have on lesbian women.*

Lesbian Sex Scandals: Sexual Practices, Identities, and Politics, edited by Dawn Atkins, MA (Vol. 3, No. 3, 1999). *"Grounded in material practices, this collection explores confrontation and coincidence among identity politics, 'scandalous' sexual practices, and queer theory and feminism. . . . It expands notions of lesbian identification and lesbian community." (Maria Pramaggiore, PhD, Assistant Professor, Film Studies, North Carolina State University, Raleigh)*

The Lesbian Polyamory Reader: Open Relationships, Non-Monogamy, and Casual Sex, edited by Marcia Munson and Judith P. Stelboum, PhD (Vol. 3, No. 1/2, 1999). *"Offers reasonable, logical, and persuasive explanations for a style of life I had not seriously considered before. . . . A terrific read." (Beverly Todd, Acquisitions Librarian, Estes Park Public Library, Estes Park, Colorado)*

Living "Difference": Lesbian Perspectives on Work and Family Life, edited by Gillian A. Dunne, PhD (Vol. 2, No. 4, 1998). *"A fascinating, groundbreaking collection. . . . Students and professionals in psychiatry, psychology, sociology, and anthropology will find this work extremely useful and thought provoking." (Nanette K. Gartrell, MD, Associate Clinical Professor of Psychiatry, University of California at San Francisco Medical School)*

Acts of Passion: Sexuality, Gender, and Performance, edited by Nina Rapi, MA, and Maya Chowdhry, MA (Vol. 2, No. 2/3, 1998). *"This significant and impressive publication draws together a diversity of positions, practices, and polemics in relation to postmodern lesbian performance and puts them firmly on the contemporary cultural map." (Lois Keidan, Director of Live Arts, Institute of Contemporary Arts, London, United Kingdom)*

Gateways to Improving Lesbian Health and Health Care: Opening Doors, edited by Christy M. Ponticelli, PhD (Vol. 2, No. 1, 1997). *"An unprecedented collection that goes to the source for powerful and poignant information on the state of lesbian health care." (Jocelyn C. White, MD, Assistant Professor of Medicine, Oregon Health Sciences University; Faculty, Portland Program in General Internal Medicine, Legacy Portland Hospitals, Portland, Oregon)*

Classics in Lesbian Studies, edited by Esther Rothblum, PhD (Vol. 1, No. 1, 1996). *"Brings together a collection of powerful chapters that cross disciplines and offer a broad vision of lesbian lives across race, age, and community." (Michele J. Eliason, PhD, Associate Professor, College of Nursing, The University of Iowa)*

Addressing Homophobia and Heterosexism on College Campuses

Elizabeth P. Cramer, PhD, MSW, LCSW, ACSW
Editor

Addressing Homophobia and Heterosexism on College Campuses has been co-published simultaneously as *Journal of Lesbian Studies*, Volume 6, Numbers 3/4 2002.

Harrington Park Press
An Imprint of
The Haworth Press, Inc.
New York • London • Oxford

Published by

Harrington Park Press®, 10 Alice Street, Binghamton, NY 13904-1580 USA

Harrington Park Press® is an imprint of The Haworth Press, Inc., 10 Alice Street, Binghamton, NY 13904-1580 USA.

Addressing Homophobia and Heterosexism on College Campuses has been co-published simultaneously as *Journal of Lesbian Studies*™, Volume 6, Numbers 3/4 2002.

The development, preparation, and publication of this work has been undertaken with great care. However, the publisher, employees, editors, and agents of The Haworth Press and all imprints of The Haworth Press, Inc., including The Haworth Medical Press® and The Pharmaceutical Products Press®, are not responsible for any errors contained herein or for consequences that may ensue from use of materials or information contained in this work. Opinions expressed by the author(s) are not necessarily those of The Haworth Press, Inc. With regard to case studies, identities and circumstances of individuals discussed herein have been changed to protect confidentiality. Any resemblance to actual persons, living or dead, is entirely coincidental.

Cover design by Jennifer M. Gaska

Library of Congress Cataloging-in-Publication Data

Addressing homophobia and heterosexism on college campuses / Elizabeth P. Cramer, editor.
    p. cm.
    "Co-published simultaneously as Journal of lesbian studies, volume 6, numbers 3/4, 2002."
    Includes bibliographical references and index.
    ISBN 1-56023-304-4 (hard : alk. paper)– ISBN 1-56023-305-2 (pbk : alk. paper)
    1. Homophobia in higher education–United States. 2. Heterosexism–United States. I. Cramer, Elizabeth P. II. Journal of lesbian studies.
LC212.862 .A33 2002
378.1'982664–dc21
                                       2002012900

Indexing, Abstracting & Website/Internet Coverage

This section provides you with a list of major indexing & abstracting services. That is to say, each service began covering this periodical during the year noted in the right column. Most Websites which are listed below have indicated that they will either post, disseminate, compile, archive, cite or alter their own Website users with research-based content from this work. (This list is as current as the copyright date of this publication.)

Abstracting, Website/Indexing Coverage......... Year When Coverage Began

- **Abstracts in Social Gerontology: Current Literature on Aging**... 1997

- **CNPIEC Reference Guide: Chinese National Directory of Foreign Periodicals**.................................... 1997

- **Contemporary Women's Issues** 1998

- **e-psyche, LLC <www.e-psyche.net>** 2001

- **Family & Society Studies Worldwide <www.nisc.com>** 2001

- **Feminist Periodicals: A Current Listing of Contents**.............. 1997

- **FINDEX <www.publist.com>** 1999

- **Gay & Lesbian Abstracts <www.nisc.com>**...................... 1997

- **GenderWatch <www.slinfo.com>** 1999

- **HOMODOK/"Relevant" Bibliographic database, Documentation Centre for Gay & Lesbian Studies, University of Amsterdam (selective printed abstracts in "Homologie" and bibliographic computer databases covering cultural, historical, social, and political aspects of gay & lesbian topics)** 1997

(continued)

Special Bibliographic Notes related to special journal issues (separates) and indexing/abstracting:

- indexing/abstracting services in this list will also cover material in any "separate" that is co-published simultaneously with Haworth's special thematic journal issue or DocuSerial. Indexing/abstracting usually covers material at the article/chapter level.
- monographic co-editions are intended for either non-subscribers or libraries which intend to purchase a second copy for their circulating collections.
- monographic co-editions are reported to all jobbers/wholesalers/approval plans. The source journal is listed as the "series" to assist the prevention of duplicate purchasing in the same manner utilized for books-in-series.
- to facilitate user/access services all indexing/abstracting services are encouraged to utilize the co-indexing entry note indicated at the bottom of the first page of each article/chapter/contribution.
- this is intended to assist a library user of any reference tool (whether print, electronic, online, or CD-ROM) to locate the monographic version if the library has purchased this version but not a subscription to the source journal.
- individual articles/chapters in any Haworth publication are also available through the Haworth Document Delivery Service (HDDS).

To my partner, Jewel, and to our daughter, Karen, for providing me with daily reminders about what is truly important in life.

ABOUT THE EDITOR

Elizabeth P. Cramer, PhD, MSW, ACSW, LCSW, is Associate Professor of Social Work at Virginia Commonwealth University in Richmond. Her primary practice and scholarship areas are lesbian and gay issues, domestic violence, and group work. She has published extensively on educational strategies to reduce the homophobia of social work students and has also presented on the topic at national conferences. For the past two years, she has facilitated a group on sexuality and gender issues for lesbian, bisexual, trans, and questioning women at a residential substance abuse treatment program. Dr. Cramer has served as peer reviewer for the *Journal of the Gay and Lesbian Medical Association* and *Criminal Justice and Behavior.* As a commissioner on the Council on Social Work Education's Commission on Sexual Orientation and Gender Expression, Dr. Cramer developed and is responsible for a mentorship project that matches lesbian, gay, bisexual, and trans (LBGT) senior faculty members with LGBT junior faculty members and doctoral students.

Addressing Homophobia and Heterosexism on College Campuses

CONTENTS

PART II: ATTITUDE ASSESSMENT AND CHANGE

PART III: PRACTITIONER TRAINING PROGRAMS

PART IV: PEDAGOGY AND CLASSROOM INTERVENTIONS

PART V: FEATURE FILMS AND DOCUMENTARIES

Acknowledgments

I would like to thank Virginia Commonwealth University School of Social Work for providing me with a semester of faculty scholarly leave to work on this project. I am grateful for four colleagues at Virginia Commonwealth University School of Social Work who were second reviewers on many of the manuscripts: Dr. Kia Bentley, Professor, Director, PhD program; Ms. Randi Buerlein, Director, Student Services; Dr. Humberto Fabelo, Associate Professor and Interim Director, Baccalaureate Social Work Program; and Dr. Jaci Miller, Associate Professor and Director, Feild Instruction.

Introduction

Elizabeth P. Cramer

When I distributed a call for abstracts and outlines on the theme "approaches to addressing college students' heterosexism and homophobia," I did not know how many I might receive. I was overwhelmed when 50 abstracts arrived. Needless to say, I had a difficult task before me. A considerable number of the abstracts seemed promising, yet I had to limit the number of persons invited to submit manuscripts. Then came the second round of hard decisions–determining which of the manuscripts would be accepted among so many interesting and well-written papers. The final project, I am pleased to say, is a blend of 19 conceptual and empirical papers that are thought provoking, informative, and fascinating. Along the way, I decided to modify the title slightly to "Addressing Homophobia and Heterosexism on College Campuses." Homophobia and heterosexism impact the entire academic community, not just the students.

There are no uniform definitions for homophobia and heterosexism. The word "homophobia" appeared in the scholarly literature in the early 1970s. The oft-cited definition by George Weinberg (1972) is "the dread of being in close quarters with homosexuals" (p. 4). Other early definitions of homophobia emphasized fear (phobia) of homosexuals. Later definitions expanded beyond fear (phobia, in a clinical sense, did not adequately explain the bases of antigay attitudes and behaviors) to include dislike (i.e., aversion, loathing, abhorrence, repugnance). Fone (2000) notes: "Adverse reactions to homosexuals and homosexuality, therefore, are founded upon fear and dislike of the sexual difference that homosexual individuals embody–stereotypically, effeminacy in homosexual men, mannishness in homosexual women" (p. 5). For purposes

[Haworth co-indexing entry note]: "Introduction." Cramer, Elizabeth P. Co-published simultaneously in *Journal of Lesbian Studies* (Harrington Park Press, an imprint of The Haworth Press, Inc.) Vol. 6, No. 3/4, 2002, pp. 1-6; and: *Addressing Homophobia and Heterosexism on College Campuses* (ed: Elizabeth P. Cramer) Harrington Park Press, an imprint of The Haworth Press, Inc., 2002, pp. 1-6. Single or multiple copies of this article are available for a fee from The Haworth Document Delivery Service [1-800-HAWORTH, 9:00 a.m. - 5:00 p.m. (EST). E-mail address: getinfo@haworthpressinc.com].

of utilizing a common definition for all authors in this collection, I supplied the following definition of homophobia: "Fear, disgust, hatred, and/or avoidance of lesbians and gay men. The behavioral manifestations of homophobic feelings and beliefs include antigay discrimination and antigay hate crimes." Related terms include biphobia (fear, disgust, hatred and/or avoidance of bisexuals) and transphobia (fear, disgust, hatred, and/or avoidance of transgendered persons).

The term heterosexism refers to "an ideological system that denies, denigrates, and stigmatizes any nonheterosexual form of behavior, identity, relationship, or community" (Herek, 1997-2001, p. 1). Heterosexist beliefs and practices permeate society. Herek reminds us that heterosexism "operates through a dual process of invisibility and attack. Homosexuality usually remains culturally invisible; when people who engage in homosexual behavior or who are identified as homosexual become visible, they are subject to attack by society" (p. 1). The definition for heterosexism that I used for authors in this collection is:

> The expectation that all persons should be or are heterosexual. The belief that heterosexual relations are normal and the norm. These expectations and beliefs occur on individual, institutional, and cultural levels. The behavioral manifestations of heterosexist beliefs include denying marriage licenses for same-sex couples and restricting health and retirement benefits to those in heterosexual marriages.

Related terms include compulsory heterosexuality, which Rich (1993, p. 232) defines as:

> the cluster of forces within which women have been convinced that marriage and sexual orientation toward men are inevitable–even if unsatisfying or oppressive–components of their lives. The chastity belt; child marriage; erasure of lesbian existence (except as exotic and perverse) in art, literature, film; idealization of heterosexual romance and marriage–these are some fairly obvious forms of compulsion, the first two exemplifying physical force, the second two control of consciousness.

Another term, heteronormativity, popular in critical pedagogy and queer theory, refers to the "normalization of heterosexuality" (see Yep's essay in this collection).

Both homophobia and heterosexism have been criticized as concepts (see Herek, 2000) and a new term "sexual prejudice" has been proposed. Herek defines sexual prejudice as "all negative attitudes based on sexual orientation, whether the target is homosexual, bisexual, or heterosexual. Given the current organization of society, however, such prejudice is almost always directed at people who engage in homosexual behavior or label themselves as gay, lesbian, or bisexual" (p. 19). An advantage of using this term is that sexual prejudice is comparable to other types of prejudices. The term sexual prejudice, however, could potentially be misinterpreted as prejudice based on any type of sexual behavior one fears or dislikes, such as prejudice against persons who engage in sadomasochistic acts.

Although there is merit to using alternative terms for heterosexism and homophobia, such as sexual prejudice, compulsory heterosexuality, and heteronormativity, I chose to use the more common terms homophobia and heterosexism. Much of the literature and most research instrumentation continue to use homophobia, and to a lesser degree, heterosexism. There are a few authors in this collection who prefer use of the term heteronormativity. Most authors used LGBT as an acronym for lesbian, gay male, bisexual, and transgender. Some also added a "Q" for questioning or queer.

Homophobia and heterosexism are of concern in the academic community. For faculty and staff members as well as administrators, homophobia and heterosexism may act as a deterrent to disclosure of one's sexual orientation. LGBT faculty and staff members may be at risk of losing their positions if their employers do not include sexual orientation in their nondiscrimination policies. LGBT faculty members whose scholarship includes LGBT issues may find a lack of support for their scholarship among their administrators and faculty colleagues. Heterosexist policies, such as offering health benefits only to married couples and their children, and informal procedures, such as inviting "spouses" to an office party, may make employees with same-sex partners feel alienated and angry (McNaron, 1997).

For college students who are LGBT, homophobia and heterosexism can potentially create a hostile and unsafe environment. LGBT students may experience harassment, discrimination, and intimidation (Berrill, 1996; D'Augelli, 1992; Herek, 1993; Human Rights Watch, 2001). Antigay harassment and violence are quite common on college campuses. In one study of heterosexual college students in the San Francisco Bay area, nearly one-quarter of the students admitted to antigay name-calling, while 1 in 10 had been physically violent or threatened violence toward persons they thought were gay (Franklin, 2001). LGBT college students are more likely than heterosexual college students to feel lonely and depressed (Westefeld, Maples, Buford, & Taylor, 2001).

In the classroom, LGBT students can face stereotyped portrayals of LGBT persons or omissions of the content on LGBT persons altogether. The instructor plays an important role in creating a classroom environment that LGBT students perceive as supportive, especially for those students who are beginning to identify as gay, lesbian, or bisexual (Lopez & Chism, 1993).

There are 5 parts in this collection. Part I focuses on addressing homophobia and heterosexism through campus-wide programs and policies. Draughn, Elkins, and Roy review the literature on Safe Zone or Allies programs on campuses, including their strengths and limitations. The authors provide a framework for development of Safe Zone/Allies programs. Garber describes the creation of a network of LGBTQ-friendly campus projects to combat homophobia. Evans and Broido present results of their qualitative study of the experiences of lesbian and bisexual female university students living in residence halls. The authors' review of the supportive and nonsupportive actions of residence hall staff members and other students will be helpful for residence hall staff members who are interested in creating a welcoming environment for lesbian and bisexual students. Part I concludes with Sausa's recommendations for campus policies to address issues of gender identity and gender expression.

Attitude assessment and attitude change is the focus of Part II. Three empirical studies and one case study of a classroom intervention to change homophobic attitudes are described. Using a Canadian sample of psychology students, Hewitt and Moore examine the correlation between beliefs about causes of homosexuality, "treatments" for homosexuality, and attitudes toward lesbians and gay men. This study expands to females the previous research in this area, which examined lay theories of homosexuality and attitudes toward gay men only. Moving to Australia, Jones, Pynor, Sullivan, and Weerakoon describe the results of their study of attitudes toward sexuality among students enrolled in health professions education. Research participants were asked about their level of comfort in: working with a lesbian client, working with a gay male client, and asking a client his/her sexual orientation. They were also asked whether they thought their academic programs adequately dealt with these issues. Analysis by gender was conducted. Next, Newman reports findings from her study of the relationship between religious affiliation, gender, and attitudes toward lesbians and gay men in a large U.S. sample of beginning graduate students in counseling and social work programs. Liddle and Stowe provide a practical example of an intervention designed to address homophobia in the classroom through the use of a lesbian/heterosexual teaching team. The Fantasy Exercise in their Appendix may be particularly useful for a classroom exercise.

Part III highlights unique considerations for professional schools. Lidderdale reviews training issues for mental health practitioners and presents a psychoeducational model to train students in counseling LGBT persons. Social work programs are the focus of Messinger's article. She covers several areas, including program policies, student recruitment, hiring practices, curriculum development, extracurricular activities, career placement, and program evaluation. In the final selection of Part III, Bennett discusses intersubjectivity in the classroom environment. Her classroom-based vignettes illustrate the application of intersubjectivity theory to homophobic and heterosexist classroom interactions.

Pedagogical considerations and specific teaching techniques to address homophobia and heterosexism are described in Part IV. Moshman applies principles of academic freedom as delineated by the Academic Freedom Coalition of Nebraska to address issues of homophobia and heterosexism in classes. Influenced by queer theory and critical pedagogy, Yep critiques existing models of antihomophobia education and proposes a teaching model based on heteronormativity and its relationship to issues of race, class, and gender. Lovaas, Baroudi, and Collins also use the concept heteronormativity to organize their review of pedagogical strategies to address trans issues. Their Appendix of recommended resources on trans issues is a valuable listing for instructors who wish to incorporate trans issues into the classroom. Three approaches to "giving voice" to LGBT issues in the classroom are presented by women's studies faculty members from different disciplines, Chevillot, Manning, and Nesbitt. Little and Marx argue that generating empathy for LGBT persons will create more accepting student attitudes toward this population; Taylor disagrees and asserts that classroom strategies to encourage empathy are doomed to fail. In essays by Rose and Zavalkoff, specific tools for classroom teaching are offered. Rose's family lecture illustrates a variety of household groups and familial relationships, which challenge students' assumptions about nuclear families and other types of households. Zavolkaff presents a conceptual tool she designed to teach about diverse sexual identities and behaviors based on Butler's concept of performativity.

Part V is a listing compiled by Little and Marx of feature films and documentaries on LGBT issues. These feature films and documentaries can be used on campus to raise awareness about the life experiences of LGBT persons.

This collection offers diverse theoretical frameworks (i.e., multiculturalism, critical pedagogy, intersubjectivity) and disagreements among authors about effective approaches to addressing homophobia and heterosexism in academic communities. In this way, it represents much of the current thinking on this topic. Attention to such variables as gender and religious differences among students is prominent in several of the essays; however, analysis by race and class, although present in some essays, is not incorporated to the same extent. In some previous studies on homophobia, the variables of race and class have been shown to have a correlation with attitudes toward lesbians and gay men.

It is my hope that the collection as a whole will motivate the reader to challenge some beliefs about how to go about the business of addressing homophobia and heterosexism on college campuses. It certainly has challenged mine.

REFERENCES

Berrill, K. (1996). Organizing against hate. In C.F. Shepard, F. Yeskel, & C. Outcalt (Eds.), *LGBT campus organizing: A comprehensive manual* (pp. 175-190). Washington, DC: National Gay and Lesbian Task Force.

D'Augelli, A.R. (1992). Lesbian and gay male undergraduates' experiences of harassment and fear on campus. *Journal of Interpersonal Violence, 7*, 383-395.

Fone, B. (2000). *Homophobia: A history*. New York: Henry Holt and Company.

Franklin, K. (2001). *Psychosocial motivations of hate crime perpetrators: Implications for prevention and policy*. Retrieved November 12, 2001, from American Psychological Association Website: (PsycNet): http://www.apa.org/ppo/issues/pfranklin.html.

Herek, G.M. (2000). The psychology of sexual prejudice. [Electronic version]. *Current Directions in Psychological Science, 19*(1), 19-22.

Herek, G.M. (1997-2001). *Definitions: Homophobia, heterosexism, and sexual prejudice*. Retrieved November 12, 2001 from Gregory Herek's Website: http://psychology.ucdavis.edu/rainbow/html/prej_defn.html.

Herek, G.M. (1993). Documenting prejudice against lesbians and gay men on campus: The Yale sexual orientation survey. *Journal of Homosexuality, 25*, 15-30.

Human Rights Watch. (2001). *Hatred in the hallways: Violence and discrimination against lesbian, gay, bisexual, and transgender students in U.S. schools*. New York: HumanRights Watch.

Lopez, G., & Chism, N. (1993). Classroom concerns of gay and lesbian students: The invisible minority. *College Teaching, 41*, 97-103.

McNaron, T. (1997). *Poisoned ivy: Lesbian and gay academics confronting homophobia*. Philadelphia: Temple University Press.

Rich, A. (1993). Compulsory heterosexuality and lesbian existence. In H. Abelove, M.A. Barale, & D.M. Halperin (Eds.), *The lesbian and gay studies reader* (pp. 227-254). New York: Routledge.

Weinberg, G. (1972). *Society and the healthy homosexual*. New York: St. Martin's Press.

Westefeld, J.S., Maples, M.R., Buford, B., & Taylor, S. (2001). Gay, lesbian, and bisexual college students: The relationship between sexual orientation and depression, loneliness, and suicide. *Journal of College Student Psychotherapy, 15*(3), 71-82.

PART I
THE CAMPUS ENVIRONMENT:
CAMPUS-WIDE PROGRAMS
AND POLICIES

Allies in the Struggle:
Eradicating Homophobia
and Heterosexism on Campus

Tricia Draughn
Becki Elkins
Rakhi Roy

SUMMARY. Providing a community that is committed to standards, diversity, and enhancement of the academic environment is often difficult. Offering an Allies or Safe Zone program is among of the first steps an institution can take to achieve a community that embraces diversity and creates a learning environment that is accepting of lesbian, gay, bisexual and transgendered individuals. While there are many opportunities in institutional group settings to address these issues, they often go either unnoticed or untapped. How can being an ally impact the greater institutional environment? This paper will discuss the campus environment for LGBT students, examine existing Allies and Safe Zone pro-

Tricia Draughn, MS, is Program Coordinator, Engineering Academic Programs Office, Look College of Engineering, Texas A&M University, MS 3127, College Station, TX 77843-3127 (E-mail: tricia@eapo.tamu.edu).

Becki Elkins, MS, is a doctoral student, Student Affairs Administration and Research, College of Education, The University of Iowa, N369 Lindquist Center, Iowa City, IA 52242 (E-mail: becki-elkins@uiowa.edu).

Rakhi Roy, MS, is Assistant Director of Administrative Services, Oakland University, 118 Oakland Center, Rochester, MI 48309-4401 (E-mail: roy@oakland.edu).

[Haworth co-indexing entry note]: "Allies in the Struggle: Eradicating Homophobia and Heterosexism on Campus." Draughn, Tricia, Becki Elkins, and Rakhi Roy. Co-published simultaneously in *Journal of Lesbian Studies* (Harrington Park Press, an imprint of The Haworth Press, Inc.) Vol. 6, No. 3/4, 2002, pp. 9-20; and: *Addressing Homophobia and Heterosexism on College Campuses* (ed: Elizabeth P. Cramer) Harrington Park Press, an imprint of The Haworth Press, Inc., 2002, pp. 9-20. Single or multiple copies of this article are available for a fee from The Haworth Document Delivery Service [1-800-HAWORTH, 9:00 a.m. - 5:00 p.m. (EST). E-mail address: getinfo@haworthpressinc.com].

grams, and offer a framework to assist program coordinators and participants in establishing comprehensive programs to change the campus climate and develop institutional environments that are gay affirmative. *[Article copies available for a fee from The Haworth Document Delivery Service: 1-800-HAWORTH. E-mail address: <getinfo@haworthpressinc.com> Website: <http://www.HaworthPress.com> © 2002 by The Haworth Press, Inc. All rights reserved.]*

KEYWORDS. Ally/Allies, campus climate, heterosexism, homophobia, safe zone

A student responds to a comment in class by blurting out "that's so gay." The class, including the faculty member, laughs and continues the discussion. . . . Students arrive on campus one morning to find the sidewalks chalked with such phrases as "fags, go home" and "death to queers." . . . A first-year female student who intends to major in engineering is told by her student orientation advisor that the odds of finding a boyfriend will be in her favor. . . . An English professor fails to include sexual orientation in contextual conversations for literary works. . . . The Student Activities Office uses an image of a woman and a man kissing to advertise its healthy dating program.

Countless incidents of heterosexism and homophobia such as these confront college students across the nation every day. Often perceived to be a safe haven for students, the college campus remains uninviting, at best, and treacherous, at worst, terrain for lesbian, gay, bisexual, and transgendered (LGBT) students (e.g., Berrill, 1996; Franklin, 1997, 1998). In response to this environment, "Allies" and "Safe Zone" programs emerged on campuses nationwide during the decade of the 1990s (Klingler, 2001). These volunteer programs generally provide visible support for campus members of the LGBT community. Though they hold enormous potential for addressing homophobia and heterosexism in group-level interactions, Allies and Safe Zone programs tend to focus on preparing participants to provide individual support to LGBT students, while failing to address homophobic and heterosexist institutional environments.

The purpose of this paper is to explore the potential role to be played by Allies and Safe Zone programs in the eradication of homophobia and heterosexism on campus. The paper begins with a discussion of the campus environment for LGBT students and an analysis of the existence of Allies and Safe Zone programs. Finally, the article attempts to create a framework to assist the coordinators and participants of such programs in establishing comprehensive programs that work to change the campus climate and develop institutional environments that confront homophobia and heterosexism.

THE CAMPUS ENVIRONMENT

To understand the impact of the campus environment on LGBT students, faculty and staff must first understand the background experiences and pressures faced by LGBT students. Many LGBT students arrive on college campuses having survived high school environments steeped in homophobia and heterosexism. A report by the Massachusetts Governor's Commission on Gay and Lesbian Youth (1993) found that 97 percent of high school students reported hearing homophobic remarks from their peers on a repeated basis; 53 percent reported hearing such remarks from members of the school staff. A study by Garafalo, Wolf, Kessel, Palfrey, and DuRant (1999) of 4159 randomly selected 9th-12th graders in Massachusetts schools revealed that, over the course of a month, 25.1 percent of gay, lesbian, and bisexual students reported being threatened with a weapon at school and 25.3 percent reported missing school out of fear.

As a result of these and other experiences, the emotional well-being of LGB students often suffers. As much as 80 percent of lesbian, gay, and bisexual youth reported experiencing severe social, emotional and cognitive isolation (Hetrick & Martin, 1987). Suicide represents a critical issue for LGB students, with recent research indicating that 35.3 percent of LGB youth report having attempted suicide as compared to 9.9 percent of their heterosexual peers (Garafalo, Wolf, Kessel, Palfrey, & DuRant, 1999).

Close examination of the social environment reveals that homophobia and heterosexism remain acceptable prejudices within the U.S. culture (American Psychological Association, 1998). Entering institutions of higher education, one might expect to find a more accepting environment, as colleges and universities emphasize non-discrimination statements and a "commitment to diversity." Yet, it is at educational institutions that 10 percent of all hate crimes occur (Federal Bureau of Investigation, 1999). In fact, evidence suggests that there has been a significant rise in the number of harassment and violence reports against LGBT individuals on campuses, indicating that "just as in the larger society, bigotry may be gaining ground on many college campuses" (Berrill, 1996, p. 175). While crimes reported as targeting the LGB population rank third highest in the FBI report, other research has indicated that crimes targeting sexual minorities may be the most socially acceptable and widespread among youth and young adults (Franklin, 1997 & 1998).

Though hate crimes are the most extreme manifestation of prejudice, the nature of the harassment varies greatly. LGBT students are subjected to offensive jokes, ugly graffiti, sexual harassment, hate mail/e-mail, verbal insults, and threats of physical violence to vandalism of personal property, having objects thrown, being chased, followed, spat upon, punched, kicked, beaten, and assaulted with weapons (e.g., Berrill, 1996; Herek, 1993). These experiences are not rare. A review of research indicates that between 40 and 76 percent of LGB students report having been verbally harassed, 16 to 26 percent having been threatened with violence, and nearly 5 percent having been the target of anti-gay physical assaults over the duration of their college careers (Berrill, 1996).

ALLIES AND SAFE ZONE PROGRAMS

In light of both the national and campus environments for LGBT individuals, many colleges and universities have developed "Allies" or "Safe Zone" programs. Conversations with students and faculty and staff members from different institutions provide anecdotal evidence of the existence of such programs on most types of campuses in most regions of the country. A review of the literature, however, reveals that there has been little documentation of the development or effectiveness of Allies or Safe Zone programs. The documentation that does exist generally focuses on case presentations of individual campus programs (e.g., Burns Hothem & Keene, 1998) or on steps individuals may take to become allies to members of the LGBT community (e.g., Broido, 2000; Washington & Evans, 1991). Although this information holds value for single programs and individuals, it fails to provide a comprehensive assessment of Allies or Safe Zone programs. Without such research, knowledge about the missions, objectives, processes, and outcomes of these programs remains restricted to that shared from individual to individual, either anecdotally or through program presentations.

To address this void in the literature and create a manual for developing such programs, Klingler (2001) collected information from programs at 21 institutions across the U.S. According to his research, the proliferation of Allies and Safe Zone programs occurred during the 1990s. Generally, these programs consisted of a network of faculty, staff, and students who identified as being supportive of LGBT students, who were willing to provide a safe haven for students in need of support, and who, as a result, displayed an "Ally" or "Safe Zone" sticker in their office or living space. Although individual programs differed, Klingler found a number of commonalities in purposes and goals. Program missions included providing confidential and visible support to LGBT individuals, fostering student development, creating an atmosphere of acceptance and support, and reducing the presence of homophobia and heterosexism on campus. While several of the institutions listed specific goals designed to address the campus environment for LGBT individuals (e.g., the elimination of homophobia/heterosexism on campus; support for campus equity and non-discrimination policies), the majority of program goals emphasized individual interaction. That is, goals for individual allies or safe zone participants included providing safe spaces for students to talk, being aware of and providing resource information to students in need, increasing visibility of support for the LGBT campus community, and working to create welcoming environments. All of these goals speak to the potential for individual members to have one-on-one interactions with LGBT students. Of the 21 programs reviewed, according to Klingler's research, only two programs specified that displaying the Allies or Safe Zone sticker represented an individual's commitment to confront specific incidents of homophobia or heterosexism on campus.

There are several limitations to Klingler's (2001) research, namely the number and types of institutions reviewed (predominantly mid- to large public colleges and universities). In addition, to date, his research does not specify whether the programs required participants to attend an educational or training seminar prior to displaying the Allies or Safe Zone sticker. Nonetheless, the results are instructive. Given that the majority of institutional and program goals focused on individual interaction, it could be argued that what training and educational requirements existed as prerequisites to participation emphasized aspects of individual interaction. These aspects often included general education about LGBT issues, such as vocabulary; examples of harassment, discrimination, and denial of rights; exploration of personal biases; awareness of campus and community resources; and how to assist an individual who is facing issues related to sexual identity.

Every day on campuses across the nation, allies, and potential allies, encounter multiple opportunities to effect societal change with regard to the treatment of LGBT individuals. Institutional issues include increased visibility, normalcy, and equity (Evans & Wall, 2000). Confronting homophobic comments, correcting misinformation, infusing the curricula with the histories and cultures of LGBT people, identifying and addressing incidents of harassment and discrimination, and including sexual orientation in diversity education efforts (Broido, 2000) represent a few of the opportunities that exist to effect institutional change. Many, if not most, of these opportunities occur in group settings, such as classrooms, faculty and staff meetings, student organization meetings and events, as well as collegial and peer gatherings. Often, however, these educational opportunities remain untapped, either as a result of a failure to identify them, or of a lack of knowledge as to how to address them, leaving institutional environments intact. As Broido suggests, "while providing support to students is necessary, it does not change the social structure that sustains homophobia and heterosexism" (p. 361). What appears to be missing from Allies and Safe Zone programs, then, is a comprehensive approach to confronting homophobia and heterosexism in the campus environment, including, in particular, how to respond in group-level interactions.

A FRAMEWORK FOR ALLIES AND SAFE ZONE PROGRAMS

Developing Allies and Safe Zone programs that successfully address homophobia and heterosexism in the campus environment involves numerous steps. First, both the institutional climate and the existing Allies or Safe Zone program should be assessed. From that assessment, participant recruitment and education methods as well as options for on-going training and development must be considered. Finally, in addition to preparing members to provide support to LGBT individuals in one-on-one interactions, strategies for confronting incidents of homophobia and heterosexism in group-level situations must be formulated. The following suggestions are drawn from the authors' experiences working with and coordinating Ally/Safe Zone programs at several public institutions.

Assessment

Prior to addressing the campus environment, an assessment of it is essential (Upcraft & Schuh, 1996). Formal assessment measures may include campus-wide or area-specific surveys, focus group interviews, and individual interviews conducted with faculty, staff, and students. While formal campus assessments have the potential to yield information critical to formulating effective strategies for addressing homophobia and heterosexism, the number of campuses conducting such research remains fairly small (Malaney, Williams, & Gellar, 1997).

In place of a formal campus climate assessment, individuals interested in improving the environment can conduct an informal assessment of their campus through reflection on personal experiences, conversations with others, review of campus policies and documents, and examination of campus culture. Questions to consider in determining, through informal means, the campus environment for LGBT students include, but are not limited to, the following:

1. To what extent are issues affecting LGBT individuals visible on campus? How are such issues represented in the campus media?

2. What support systems exist for LGBT members of the campus community? Does the institution have a designated LGBT Resource Center? An Allies or Safe Zone program?

3. Does the institution have a non-discrimination policy and, if so, is sexual orientation covered by it?

4. How, if at all, is intolerance of homophobia and heterosexism communicated to new members of the campus community?

5. Have incidents of homophobia received campus attention over the past few years? If so, what form did such attention take (e.g., news reports, open forums, educational programs). If not, is the lack of attention due to a lack of such incidents on campus or due to limited awareness or desire to deal with such incidents?

6. What aspects of institutional culture serve as potential barriers to an inclusive, safe environment for LGBT individuals? As suggested by Love (1998), questions to consider include what is the institutional culture, what external or peripheral constituencies influence the institution, and what are the culturally appropriate ways to discuss sexual orientation at the institution.

In a similar fashion, the campus Allies or Safe Zone network should also be assessed. Questions to consider include:

1. What is the nature of the organization? Is it an active, visible presence on campus or a presence in name only?

2. What is the stated purpose of the organization? Does the purpose adequately emphasize both providing support to LGBT individuals and working to confront homophobia and heterosexism in the campus environment?

3. Who are the members? Are faculty and administration involved? If not, why?

4. How does the organization support LGBT members of the campus community?

5. How does the organization confront homophobia/heterosexism in the environment?

6. What education do new members receive? What opportunities exist for further education, beyond initial training seminars? To what extent do these educational opportunities focus on working with individuals versus groups? To what extent are participants trained to address incidents of homophobia and heterosexism in group situations?

7. From what campus constituencies and community resources does the organization receive support?

Recruiting Members

Assessment of the campus environment and the existing Allies or Safe Zone program should provide information to assist with the recruitment of new members to the organization. As with assessment, recruitment should be an ongoing process. There are a number of items to consider in developing a recruitment strategy:

1. *Recruitment considerations.* Students, faculty and staff members have different needs and concerns that may affect their participation. For instance, given tenure concerns, new faculty members may feel limited in their ability to be involved with the organization while students may be hesitant to display the Allies or Safe Zone sticker out of fear of the reactions of other students. Successful recruitment must consider and address the differing needs and concerns of potential members.

2. *Inviting participation from the campus community.* Attracting a diverse group of members requires using a diverse set of strategies. Using a single approach may result in a narrowly defined group, making it more difficult to address issues in the broader campus climate. While it may be easier to appeal to, for example, faculty in liberal arts, having faculty allies in engineering is equally as important. Making use of a variety of advertising options (e.g., newspapers, displays, listservs, Websites, etc.) as well as a variety of campus professional and student organizations (e.g., faculty networks, human resource organizations, administrative groups, student governments, etc.) allows the program to reach a wide number and variety of people.

3. *Involving current members in recruitment.* Current participants of Allies and Safe Zone programs are often under-used in terms of what they can bring to the organization, particularly in the area of recruitment. Members may, in fact, be the best advertisers for the organization. Organizations can encourage members to simply share information with their colleagues and peers or can involve them through such activities as membership drives, college or department membership competitions, or phone-a-thons designed to welcome new faculty members, staff members, and students to campus and to invite them to become involved in the organization.

Ongoing Training and Development

Continued training for Allies and Safe Zone participants is important for various reasons. Most initial training sessions, typically lasting three hours or less, cover only basic information. Thus, one of the most vital reasons for providing ongoing training is the opportunity for continued education. Such opportunities serve other purposes as well. Given that the typical format for many Allies and Safe Zone programs involves attending a basic training session and then displaying a sticker, individual participants may feel distanced from the organization once their membership is finalized. Ongoing training sessions offer the potential for continued connection with other participants. This connection can provide a support system for individuals and, possibly, foster a greater commitment to address incidents of homophobia and heterosexism. Furthermore, these sessions may serve both as a way to foster more active participation in the organization and as a way to keep members informed about the campus environment and strategies to use in addressing that environment.

Potential training sessions and topics include, among others: refresher sessions covering basic ally information as needed, how to be a visible ally, moving beyond one-on-one conversations into group interactions, how to implement change in institutional policies, breaking down the LGBT acronym and engaging each topic individually for greater depth of understanding, examining the connection between all forms of oppression, identifying and addressing specific campus needs with regard to LGBT issues, and strategy brainstorming sessions. Making training sessions as convenient as possible, considering both time and location, as well as dynamic and interesting will foster higher participation. Finally, organizations may also want to consider creating an advisory board or leadership committee to give members greater ownership in the program.

Preparing Members to Address Group Situations

As suggested earlier, the primary downfall of many existing Allies and Safe Zone programs appears to be the failure to prepare individual members to confront homophobia and heterosexism in group settings. The potential exists, however, to provide such preparation, particularly through the use of on-going training and development sessions. To prepare individuals for group-level interactions, we suggest having members examine the types of groups with which they interact and evaluate their comfort level in specific group situations. Providing some basic group interaction skills and encouraging follow-up reflection after an interaction should also be key components of training.

Individuals differ in their comfort with group settings. Even for those who find group interaction to be comfortable and exhilarating, the idea of discussing LGBT issues or confronting homophobic or heterosexist incidents in a group setting may be daunting. Fear of conflict, fear of speaking up in groups, distaste for calling attention to oneself, and fear of not having the correct information are but a few of the reasons allies often remain silent in critical situations. Encouraging members, both those who identify as heterosexual or LGBT, to evaluate their personal comfort with group interactions serves as an initial step in preparing them to be proactive within group-level settings. Suggestions for individual reflection include:

1. Identify the groups with whom you most commonly interact (e.g., classes, student organizations, professional organizations, work environments, peer groups, etc.). Who are the formal and informal leaders in each group?
2. In terms of your comfort level in that particular setting, rate each of these groups on a scale from 1 (extremely uncomfortable) to 10 (extremely comfortable). Provide a brief rationale for each rating.
3. Re-rate each of these groups, using the scale above, in terms of your comfort level in discussing LGBT issues in that particular setting. Again, provide a brief rationale for each rating.
4. For each group, list occurrences of homophobic or heterosexist comments or actions. Do such incidents occur often, sometimes, rarely, or never? When they do occur, how does the group react?
5. Over the next two weeks, make note of homophobic or heterosexist language or comments when they occur. Make note of how you feel in each situation.
6. What fears do you have in speaking up in each group? What would help you feel safe to discuss and explore LGBT issues in each group?

These questions not only assist individuals in assessing their personal comfort level in various settings but also may be of use in helping them assess the climate of different groups. Both assessments are critical to helping allies determine their course of action in any given situation. The climate of the group and what is at stake, with regard to both personal costs and societal costs, may dictate the response. For instance, if, as an ally, Helen hears another student make a homophobic comment during class, she may perceive that she has more to lose in that situation than if she hears a similar comment at a basketball game. She may also perceive that, in the classroom, it is the faculty member's responsibility to address such incidents. As a result she may be less likely to respond to the incident in class than to the one at the game. It is important to note that because of differences in comfort levels, with both group interactions and LGBT issues, as well as differences of group climates, individuals confronted with similar situations may respond quite differently. The point is not to formulate and implement a single response but rather to assist individuals in identifying ways to respond that feel manageable to them but also challenge existing homophobia and heterosexism.

The second step in preparing allies for group-level interactions involves providing some basic skills to foster educational discussion. Training allies to be "guides" who pose questions, raise contradictions, and encourage self-reflection (Adams, Bell, & Griffin, 1997) can provide them with skills not only to confront homophobia or heterosexism but to do so in a way that enhances learning for all present. Giving allies basic response tools such as "I don't appreciate that comment"; "I am offended that you would say that about LGBT individuals"; "what do you mean by that statement"; "where did you get that information"; or "how did you come to believe that," to state a few, can be an essential, but often overlooked, beginning. Responding with "I" statements, posing questions, and providing accurate information creates opportunities for others to reflect on the incident. Role-playing can be a useful activity to simulate the types of group situations allies may encounter, giving allies the opportunity to explore, in a safe space, how they might best approach a situation.

After an incident, it is important that individuals take time to process and evaluate what happened as well as their response. Members should be encouraged to reflect on how the experience made them feel; what they would change about their response; what they would do again in responding; what information they needed but did not have; and what type of support they need from others, particularly other Allies or Safe Zone members. It is important to remind members that taking action does make a difference, even if the desired outcome was not achieved (Lopez & Chism, 1993). The authors assert that failing to respond is, in fact, a response, one that supports rather than challenges the existing environment.

CONCLUDING THOUGHTS

Although Allies and Safe Zone programs acknowledge issues of heterosexism and homophobia on campus, there is little in the literature to indicate that allies are being prepared to confront these issues in group-level settings. Education and support systems are critical to the improvement of the campus environment. For homophobia and heterosexism to be eradicated on campus, however, intervention in group settings (e.g., classrooms, organizational meetings, residence hall settings) must occur. Allies and Safe Zone programs should provide educational preparation for both one-on-one and group-level interactions. Training should focus on helping individuals assess and increase their comfort levels in group interactions, providing group intervention strategies, and avoiding a "one solution solves all" formula. Finally, celebrating institutional changes, regardless of how small, is crucial to motivating campus allies!

REFERENCES

Adams, M., Bell, L. A., & Griffin, P. (Eds.). (1997). *Teaching for diversity and social justice.* New York: Routledge.

American Psychological Association. (1998). *Hate crimes today: An age-old foe in modern dress.* Retrieved July 14, 2001 from www.apa.org/pubinfo/hate/.

Berrill, K. (1996). Organizing against hate. In C. F. Shepard, F. Yeskel, & C. Outcalt (Eds.), *LGBT campus organizing: A comprehensive manual* (pp. 175-190). Washington, DC: National Gay and Lesbian Task Force.

Broido, E. M. (2000). Ways of being an ally to lesbian, gay, and bisexual students. In V. A. Wall & N. J. Evans (Eds.), *Toward acceptance: Sexual orientation issues on campus* (pp. 345-369). Washington, DC: American College Personnel Association.

Burns Hothem, K., & Keene, C. D. (1998). Creating a safe zone project at a small private college: How hate galvanized a community. In R. L. Sanlo (Ed.), *Working with lesbian, gay, bisexual, and transgender college students: A handbook for faculty and administrators* (pp. 363-369). Westport, CT: Greenwood Press.

Evans, N. J., & Wall, V. A. (2000). Parting thoughts: An agenda for addressing sexual orientation issues on campus. In V. A. Wall & N. J. Evans (Eds.), *Toward acceptance: Sexual orientation issues on campus* (pp. 389-403). Washington, DC: American College Personnel Association.

Federal Bureau of Investigation. (1999). *Hate crimes report*. Available: http://www.fbi.gov/ucr/99hate.pdf.

Franklin, K. (1997, November). *Psychosocial motivations of hate crime perpetrators: Implications for prevention and policy.* Paper presented at a congressional briefing co-sponsored by the American Psychological Association and the Society for the Psychological Study of Social Issues. Washington, DC.

Franklin, K. (1998, August 16). *Psychosocial motivations of hate crimes perpetrators: Implications for educational intervention.* Paper presented at the 106th Annual Convention of the American Psychological Association at San Francisco, CA. (ED 423 939).

Garafalo, R., Wolf, R. C., Kessel, S., Palfrey, J., & DuRant, R. H. (1998). The association between health risk behaviors and sexual orientation among a school-based sample of adolescents. *Pediatrics, 101*, 895-902.

Governor's Commission on Gay and Lesbian Youth. (1993). *Making schools safe for gay and lesbian youth*. Boston, MA: Author.

Herek, G. (1993). Documenting prejudice against lesbians and gay men on campus: The Yale sexual orientation survey. *Journal of Homosexuality, 25 (4)*, 15-30.

Hetrick, E., & Martin, A. D. (1987). Developmental issues and their resolution for gay and lesbian adolescents. *Journal of Homosexuality, 14*, 26-44.

Klingler, D. L. (2001). *Safe zone manual*. Unpublished manuscript, University of Wisconsin-Milwaukee.

Lopez, G., & Chism, N. (1993). Classroom concerns of gay and lesbian students: The invisible minority. *College Teaching, 41*, 97-103.

Love, P. G. (1998). Cultural barriers facing lesbian, gay, and bisexual students at a Catholic college. *The Journal of Higher Education, 69*, 298-323.

Malaney, G. D., Williams, E. Z., & Gellar, W. W. (1997). Assessing campus climate for gays, lesbians, and bisexuals at two institutions. *Journal of College Student Development, 38*, 365-375.

Upcraft, M. L., & Schuh, J. H. (1996). *Assessment in student affairs: A guide for practitioners*. San Francisco: Jossey-Bass.

Washington, J., & Evans, N. J. (1991). Becoming an ally. In N. J. Evans & V. A. Wall (Eds.), *Beyond tolerance: Gays, lesbians, and bisexuals on campus* (pp. 195-204). Washington, DC: American College Personnel Association.

Weaving a Wide Net:
The Benefits of Integrating Campus Projects to Combat Homophobia

Linda Garber

SUMMARY. Any single approach to students' heterosexism and homophobia, however well conceived and executed, is most successful when supported by an integrated campus approach to the problem. Taking as a model the multifaceted efforts at California State University, Fresno–a large public institution located in what can be considered the state's Bible Belt–this essay discusses the strengths and logistics of a campus-wide program to address homophobia and alleviate LGBTQ students' feelings of alienation from the institution and their oppression in society. The efforts of CSUF take place at a number of different levels–classroom, academic department, student services, faculty networking–and can be considered a successful work in progress. *[Article copies available for a fee from The Haworth Document Delivery Service: 1-800-HAWORTH. E-mail address: <getinfo@haworthpressinc.com> Website: <http://www.HaworthPress.com> © 2002 by The Haworth Press, Inc. All rights reserved.]*

Linda Garber, PhD, is Associate Professor in the Department of English and the Program for the Study of Women and Gender at Santa Clara University. She is the author of *Identity Poetics: Race, Class, and the Lesbian-Feminist Roots of Queer Theory* (Columbia University Press 2001), editor of *Tilting the Tower: Lesbians/Teaching/Queer Subjects* (Routledge 1994), and author of *Lesbian Sources: A Bibliography of Periodical Articles, 1970-1990* (Garland 1993).

Address correspondence to: Linda Garber, PhD, Associate Professor, Department of English, Santa Clara University, 500 El Camino Real, Santa Clara, CA 95053-0280 (E-mail: lgarber@scu.edu).

[Haworth co-indexing entry note]: "Weaving a Wide Net: The Benefits of Integrating Campus Projects to Combat Homophobia." Garber, Linda. Co-published simultaneously in *Journal of Lesbian Studies* (Harrington Park Press, an imprint of The Haworth Press, Inc.) Vol. 6, No. 3/4, 2002, pp. 21-28; and: *Addressing Homophobia and Heterosexism on College Campuses* (ed: Elizabeth P. Cramer) Harrington Park Press, an imprint of The Haworth Press, Inc., 2002, pp. 21-28. Single or multiple copies of this article are available for a fee from The Haworth Document Delivery Service [1-800-HAWORTH, 9:00 a.m. - 5:00 p.m. (EST). E-mail address: getinfo@haworthpressinc.com].

KEYWORDS. Faculty network, integrated approach, LGBTQ studies, student alliance, student services, women's studies

Lesson plans, task forces, teach-ins, support groups, classes–all can play vital roles in combating homophobia on college campuses. During my seven years on the faculty at California State University, Fresno (1994-2001), I participated in various initiatives that, together, began a cultural change on the campus larger than any single effort could have achieved. Once enough projects and groups were started and, crucially, integrated, we were able to create LGBTQ-friendly community,[1] build coalitions, pool resources, increase visibility, provide more services and resources, and expand participation in antihomophobic efforts.

California State University, Fresno is a large (approximately 18,000 students), mostly commuter campus located in the major city of California's San Joaquin Valley, a large, mostly agricultural region. No single ethnic group makes up a majority of the student body, and over sixty percent of the students are in the first generation in their families to attend college. Socially, the region can be characterized as the state's Bible Belt. Fresno is the kind of small city that boasts a lesbian/gay film festival *and* subsidizes visits of the Promise Keepers (on university grounds, no less). Campus Christian groups and Greek societies dominate the campus "Free Speech Area," whose name sometimes seems its only connection to its sixties' roots. Unlike many outsiders' perceptions of California, most of the state is not politically liberal, and its conservatism is evident in the Central Valley and on the Fresno State campus. On the other hand, Fresno State has a stand-alone Women's Studies Program, with its own full-time faculty and a bachelor's degree. I was hired as an assistant professor by this program, which saw my lesbian studies scholarship and LGBTQ activism as an asset. While not the first openly lesbian or gay faculty member on campus, I was one of three when I was hired, and apprehensive of the wider university's embrace of LGBTQ-positive activities. I quickly became co-adviser (and then adviser) to the LGBTQ student group, and in my second year I taught my first LGBTQ studies course, Introduction to Lesbian/Gay Studies.

I became the de facto campus point-person on most things queer, so as more projects were developed, and as I became involved in most of them, it was relatively simple to pool resources and coordinate efforts. The integration of LGBTQ projects into an increasingly coherent program arose organically at Fresno State, at a time when national attention focused on homophobia because of ongoing efforts of activists and media attention to the murder of Matthew Shepard. Although my role as campus LGBTQ liaison was not officially recognized, I was supported in and rewarded for my efforts. I was protected by the univer-

sity's non-discrimination policy that includes sexual orientation (bespeaking
the power of being out on campus), supported by my faculty union (which allowed me to include my antihomophobic organizing and LGBTQ teach-
ing/scholarship in a straightforward tenure plan process), and aided by faculty
allies (openly gay, closeted, and straight) who wanted to see me and my
antihomophobic efforts succeed. My privilege was to hold a faculty position
allowing (even requiring) me to work on behalf of LGBTQ students and studies. My responsibility was to involve others, not only to share the considerable
workload, but also to insure success, creativity, diversity, and longevity of
antihomophobic efforts. At the end of seven years, when I accepted a position
at another university, I had implemented some personal projects, collaborated
on others, and (I hope) helped to plant seeds for future expansions, coalitions,
and action.

As faculty adviser to the Lesbian/Gay/Bisexual/Transgender Alliance
(LGBTA), I inherited a group whose membership and activity ebbed and
flowed, as is often the case. In its most active period the group staffed a rain-
bow colored information booth in the Free Speech Area and co-sponsored an
on-campus "Outfest" open to the wider community. At the least, the LGBTA
functioned as a social group for a small number of regular members. For
LGBTQ students, it was important to know that any kind of group existed. If
they didn't want to participate often, let alone publicly, they knew they had an
available safe haven, or merely a queer place to socialize, whenever they
wanted it. (The group had no space of its own, but the Women's Resource Center, where most meetings were held, served as a default center for LGBTQ student activity. Campus coalitions that developed in part through work on
LGBTQ issues may result in the inclusion of LGBTQ space in the campus
multicultural center that is now in development.) For the broader campus community, the LGBTA was larger than its actual life size, receiving numerous
calls each semester–from students looking for the group, from journalists
looking for "the gay perspective" on something newsworthy, from off-campus
folks looking for the gay community in town, and more.

The student group also provided two services to the campus that clearly
overlapped with other types of antihomophobic, pro-LGBTQ initiatives. First,
it participated in the curriculum by offering speakers to talk about their experiences for classes ranging from human sexuality to social deviance.[2] Because
the group was reasonably well funded by the student government, and as the
different arms of the antihomophobic campus effort began to develop and
work together, the LGBTA was able to co-sponsor academic and extracurricular events that no single group could have afforded alone.

The student group faced three persistent problems: inconsistent membership, paucity of "out" students, and difficulty of advertising. The third was re-

lated to the first two, in that a handful of students, many afraid to be recognized as gay, had difficulty getting their message to a student body that mainly lived off campus. With posters and in-class announcements the most effective means of advertising LGBTA events and meetings, the developing integration of antihomophobic projects was of utmost importance. Faculty members involved in the widening antihomophobic network could be counted on to announce events in their classes (often offering extra credit for attendance or otherwise integrating the events into course projects), and allied organizations such as the Women's Resource Center and the campus health educator's office routinely posted LGBTA fliers.

Where the transience of a student body poses problems for organizing, the relative stability of the university's faculty and staff should provide a strength. In this area, Fresno State was only beginning to organize at the end of my seven years. LGBTQ faculty and staff members socialized informally, but no activist group existed in the 1990s. In my last year, the first attempts at a monthly lunch gathering in the university restaurant were successful in bringing people together. In a relatively homophobic community, the importance of that open social gathering–as public statement as well as support group– should not be discounted. At one of its first lunch meetings, the group hosted women's studies students who presented findings on LGBTQ topics from their research methods class, and discussions were underway when I left to develop the group in several positive directions. The most obvious role for a faculty/staff group, beyond peer support and collegiality, might be political advocacy. We already had domestic partner benefits and nondiscrimination policies (fought for and won at the statewide system level), but other issues clearly could be addressed. If nothing else, a faculty/staff group could take public stands on LGBTQ issues, just as the student group does, and with more authority. For example, in Spring 2001 the incoming faculty adviser and LGBTA president were gearing up to tackle the issue of condoms and HIV information in dormitories. That effort would be much stronger with the well organized support of staff and faculty members.

The group could also provide vital intellectual community and pedagogy workshop opportunities. As a community of scholars, the faculty could organize brown-bag symposia to present ongoing LGBTQ research across the disciplines, providing a testing ground for new scholarly work, so crucial to publication, tenure, and promotion, and spurring the development of LGBTQ studies lessons and courses on campus. Faculty members voiced interest in meeting to share successful pedagogical tools and strategies. Pedagogy workshops would provide the opportunity for instructors to discuss real classroom problems and benefit from others' tried and true solutions (or at least advice and promise of some group solidarity).

These efforts do not need to depend upon LGBTQ faculty and staff members, of course–which is a good thing, because there were not very many of us who were both willing to be out and interested in participating regularly.[3] We began to organize with folks who were interested, regardless of their orientation, in a multifaceted program called the LGBT Allies Network. Modeled initially on the nationwide "safe zone" concept, the Allies Network rapidly grew beyond the basic concept of sympathetic faculty and staff members exhibiting stickers on their doors to indicate their offices were "safe space" for LGBTQ students. For starters, the core organizing group rejected the title "safe zone" because we felt it implied that other spaces were by definition unsafe, the exact opposite of the campus climate we aimed to promote. We also wanted the group to serve as a network for campus allies–faculty and staff members and administrators of any orientation–as well as a one-on-one support and referral service for students. Opening up the mission of the group served many functions, paramount among them creating, educating, and making visible a pro-LGBTQ campus community.

The network was initiated by a social work graduate student interning at the Women's Resource Center who researched "safe zone" projects nationwide, proposed the idea to the resource center director, and with her drafted the first grant to the Associated Students Diversity Awareness Project (which has granted the project $1500-2000 a year for three years running). The diversity of the organizing group–student, faculty, staff, African-American, white, disabled, lesbian, heterosexual–was crucial in forging lasting alliances that went beyond strictly LGBTQ concerns. These ties were important for initiatives like the campus multicultural center, groups like the President's Human Relations Council, and events like Stop the Hate Week, where we fought together for inclusion of a variety of groups and issues, not just our own.

Network goals that we achieved in at least some measure in the first year were to educate LGBTQ allies; make conspicuous an antihomophobic presence on campus, thereby creating a more queer-positive peer culture among faculty, staff and administrators; provide visible welcoming environments and offer resources and information to students; and cosponsor events with other pro-LGBTQ groups. The organizing group began by inviting people who we thought would be interested in the network to attend a three-hour training session. We decided against an open call for participants to avoid two pitfalls: that homophobic university employees might join the network in order to harass or proselytize students seeking assistance, and that colleagues might feel either obliged to join the network to prove their tolerance or resentful that their failure to join implied their intolerance (complaints we actually heard).

The allies' training, conducted by a professional who works with LGBTQ youth in San Francisco's public schools, was a sort of "Gay 101" intended to provide all allies with a common grounding and vocabulary, because several people were well meaning but not necessarily well educated on basic LGBTQ issues. The training used a mixture of video, small groups, role plays, games, and open discussion to cover common stereotypes, review current university policy, state and local laws, and legal precedents, suggest strategies for responding to homophobic incidents, and instruct allies how to refer students to appropriate resources. Only after completing the training session were people given the Allies Network sticker to post and the LGBTQ resource guide we compiled (which includes local LGBTQ organizations, national resources with 800 numbers, Internet resources, and a recommended reading list).

Beyond yearly trainings, the network initially planned to hold monthly meetings to discuss topics of interest to members and to cosponsor and organize larger semiannual events. The events were well attended (especially a widely advertised lecture/reading by Minnie Bruce Pratt, less so a screening of the documentary *A Litany for Survival*), but the monthly gatherings never got off the ground. Network members said they were interested but pleaded busy schedules. The organizing group discussed the need either to drop the meetings or to integrate them with another campus antihomophobic effort, such as the brown-bag symposia or pedagogy workshops planned by the faculty/staff group.

Clearly, the trainings, workshops, and events feed and are nourished by academic LGBTQ studies initiatives on campus. The most common of these are LGBTQ units or lessons in a variety of classes, from literature to women's studies. At best, LGBTQ issues and readings are integrated throughout such courses, treating LGBTQ people as a population; however, "homosexuality" often is treated as a distinct topic, as evidenced by the number of calls I received yearly to guest lecture or to organize a panel of student speakers. Like many universities, Fresno State also offers a few LGBTQ studies courses. One graduate course, Lesbian and Gay Issues in Counseling, was offered every two or three years and was in the catalog when I arrived. Within a few years, in Women's Studies we added Introduction to Lesbian/Gay Studies and Topics in Lesbian/Gay Studies. Other courses have been taught under generic topics course designations in Women's Studies and English, such as the Sexuality in Literature course offered in Spring 2001. LGBTQ courses have the support of departments and deans but face the daunting challenge of drawing high enough enrollment to be offered regularly. Low enrollments in the courses at Fresno State seemed to be a function of both homophobia and focus on career and degree requirements. Obviously, homophobic students would not take LGBTQ courses, but interested students also stayed away for fear of having "lesbian," "gay" or "queer" on their transcripts. One partial solution was to allow students to take the courses under the official designation of "Independent

Study," making clear when we advertised the option that we were doing so because of homophobia and its consequences. The other reason for low enrollment was that, with the exception of cross-listed classes, the courses within Women's Studies fulfill degree requirements only for the small Women's Studies minor and major.

The Women's Studies Program committed to offering one LGBTQ studies course per year, more or less regardless of enrollment, arguing successfully that high enrollments in General Education courses took up the slack. This allows Women's Studies majors and minors to pursue an LGBTQ studies track of sorts. We hoped to encourage the development of more LGBTQ courses across the university through participation in the planned working group on curriculum development and by inviting professors from different departments to teach their specialties under our Topics in Lesbian/Gay Studies designation, thus diversifying the course offerings. Low enrollments make the likelihood of an LGBTQ studies certificate or minor slight, at least in the near future. And low enrollment could threaten the future existence of the courses at all, even in Women's Studies, as more extreme budget problems develop, if LGBTQ studies passes from its current (relative) vogue, or if changes in faculty result in different expertise and priorities.

Curricular initiatives at Fresno State are helped by two programs instigated by donors in the community. The first is an annual scholarship competition that awards tuition, fees, and books to students who are active in the LGBTQ community or who are pursuing LGBTQ studies in some way. The second is a periodic donation that established and maintains an LGBTQ library in the Women's Resource Center, where students may feel more comfortable using books than in the campus library, and for which faculty and staff in the Allies Network choose the books directly. Courses aid the scholarship and library as well as being aided by them, since the existence of LGBTQ courses helps to identify students eligible for the scholarship and leads to assignments for which the library is useful.

In the end, our efforts at Fresno State can be viewed as a successful work in progress. Many of the people involved in individual LGBTQ projects are active in more than one, so the integration of the various components was unplanned, but since recognized it is being fostered intentionally. It helped, intangibly but truly in terms of campus climate, that the university president called for the campus Human Relations Commission to study homophobia on campus the same year that we started the LGBT Allies Network. It helped more concretely that one faculty member was able to participate in virtually all of the campus antihomophobic efforts, keeping them in communication with each other. Better still would be an officially designated staff position, or at least faculty release time, combined with university funded space for an

LGBTQ center or an office in a multicultural center. So far, there has been no significant backlash to the initiatives at Fresno State, but if and when it comes, institutionalization, a physical place on campus, could be key to continued progress. Given how much we accomplished in so little time with so few out faculty in such a conservative location, I am convinced that an integrated program to combat homophobia can be built virtually anywhere.

NOTES

1. I have seen LGBTQ defined as both "Lesbian, Gay, Bisexual, Transgender, Queer" and "Lesbian, Gay, Bisexual, Transgender, Queer and Questioning." Both definitions suit my intentions, and where one or the other is appropriate, I assume it is clear from context.

2. I have several reservations about the use of LGBTQ speakers' panels in classes. First of all, it is difficult to escape the sense of queers under the microscope, although this can be mitigated by including at least one heterosexual on the panel, so that the topic becomes sexual identity. (Notice how the dynamic shifts if a straight person answers questions like "How did you first realize you were heterosexual?") Courses that make use of panels often treat gays and lesbians as a topic rather than a diverse population to which all sorts of topics are relevant, and panels run the risk of replacing research with anecdote in a class, a tendency students are all too ready to indulge. Pertinent questions to ask an instructor who requests a student panel include whether the course includes LGBTQ readings throughout the term and whether the instructor has invited speakers' groups to represent other populations. Is the instructor using the panel as a way to cope with an issue, perhaps the one issue, that is too hot for her/him to handle personally? Given the homophobia of most general audiences, it is a good idea to develop with students some sort of training to equip speakers to handle the variety of questions they are likely to face in a classroom.

3. A critical mass was approached with the hiring of four out faculty in three different departments in my last two years at Fresno State, which should expand the organizing efforts in coming years as the new faculty members acclimate to the institution and become active.

The Experiences
of Lesbian and Bisexual Women
in College Residence Halls:
Implications for Addressing
Homophobia and Heterosexism

Nancy J. Evans
Ellen M. Broido

SUMMARY. In-depth interviews were conducted with ten lesbian and bisexual women university students to learn about their experiences living in college residence halls. Many of the women reported experiencing a hostile environment as a result of direct and indirect harassment and lack of support from roommates, resident assistants, and other residents. Participants also reported supportive factors that helped to make the environment more comfortable. In particular, these students appreciated residence life staff who actively confronted homophobic acts and showed

Nancy J. Evans, PhD, is Professor, Educational Leadership and Policy Studies, Iowa State University, N247D Lagomarcino Hall, Ames, IA 50011 (E-mail: nevans@iastate.edu).

Ellen M. Broido, EdD, is Assistant Professor, College Student Personnel and Higher Education Administration Programs, Bowling Green State University, 330 Education Building, Bowling Green, OH 43403 (E-mail: ebroido@bgnet.bgsu.edu).

This study was funded by a grant from the Association of College and University Housing Officers-International.

[Haworth co-indexing entry note]: "The Experiences of Lesbian and Bisexual Women in College Residence Halls: Implications for Addressing Homophobia and Heterosexism." Evans, Nancy J., and Ellen M. Broido. Co-published simultaneously in *Journal of Lesbian Studies* (Harrington Park Press, an imprint of The Haworth Press, Inc.) Vol. 6, No. 3/4, 2002, pp. 29-42; and: *Addressing Homophobia and Heterosexism on College Campuses* (ed: Elizabeth P. Cramer) Harrington Park Press, an imprint of The Haworth Press, Inc., 2002, pp. 29-42. Single or multiple copies of this article are available for a fee from The Haworth Document Delivery Service [1-800-HAWORTH, 9:00 a.m. - 5:00 p.m. (EST). E-mail address: getinfo@haworthpressinc.com].

their support by providing information on lesbian, gay, and bisexual topics. Interviewees provided suggestions for improving the climate in residence halls and for training residence hall staff to work more effectively with lesbian, gay, and bisexual students. Implications are offered for addressing homophobia and heterosexism in women's residence halls. *[Article copies available for a fee from The Haworth Document Delivery Service: 1-800-HAWORTH. E-mail address: <getinfo@haworthpressinc.com> Website: <http://www.HaworthPress.com>* © *2002 by The Haworth Press, Inc. All rights reserved.]*

KEYWORDS. Homophobia, college environment, residence halls, lesbian/bisexual college students

The research regarding the collegiate experiences of lesbian, gay and bisexual (LGB) students indicates that in general they experience a hostile and homophobic campus. This is evident both in research on (presumably) heterosexual students, faculty, and staff members' attitudes toward LGB students and issues, and in the reports of self-identified LGB students regarding their collegiate experiences. Eddy and Forney's (2000) summary of research on campus climates indicates that many college students report negative attitudes toward LGB students and topics, that LGB students are more frequently targets of violence and harassment than are heterosexual students, and that LGB students often fear for their safety.

Research consistently reveals that many students, faculty, and staff members hold negative attitudes about LGB students. For instance, 18.9% of entering students (and close to 30% of the men) at one large public institution reported no interest in having a lesbian or gay friend (Mohr & Sedlacek, 2000). Engstrom and Sedlacek (1997) reported that students demonstrated more negative attitudes toward people described as lesbian or gay than toward people whose sexual orientation was not identified. In a study of campus climate at two institutions, more than 60% of the students surveyed reported hearing derogatory comments about LGB classmates (Malaney, Williams, & Geller, 1997). At one large university, 25% of the employees expressed explicitly negative responses in a survey about LGB issues (Eliason, 1996). In the only existing study examining the attitudes of prospective resident assistants, D'Augelli (1989) reported that few future RAs had close relationships with lesbian or gay students, and more than 75% had made disparaging remarks about lesbians or gay men.

Not surprisingly, this hostile environment influences the students who experience it. LGB students report less of a sense of community on campus than do heterosexual students (Zapata, 2000). Experiencing homophobia increased LGB college students' ability to confront hate and fear but also led to feelings of anger, frustration, and sadness (Amato, 1997). Westefeld, Maples, Buford, and Taylor (2001) reported that LGB college students are more likely to report feelings of depression and loneliness than are heterosexual college students. In contrast, most respondents in a study of the climate in a special interest residence hall for LGBT students and heterosexual allies reported feelings of support, community, and security (Herbst & Malaney, 1999).

Very little research or literature on campus homophobia and heterosexism specifically documents the experiences of lesbian or bisexual college women. More often, data are presented without exploration of gender differences. In this study we intentionally investigated the experiences of lesbian and bisexual women. Three questions guided this study: (1) How do lesbian and bisexual women experience living in college residence halls? (2) What aspects of residence hall living were supportive for lesbian and bisexual women and what factors were not? (3) What strategies might enhance the residence hall climate for lesbian and bisexual women?

Lewin's (1936) interactionist perspective, which stresses that behavior is a function of the interaction of the person and the environment, provided the theoretical foundation for the study. Specifically, D'Augelli's (1994) life-span model of gay, lesbian, and bisexual development guided our thinking. D'Augelli views identity development as influenced by three factors: individual behavior and meaning-making, interactions with others, and the setting.

METHODS

The findings reported here are a subset of findings from a larger study of the experiences of 20 lesbian, gay, and bisexual students living in the residence halls at a large eastern research university (Evans & Broido, 1999). Discussed here are the responses of the ten women participants. Because so little is known about the experiences of LGB college students, and even less about residential students or about lesbian and bisexual women, we chose to utilize a constructivist approach (Schwandt, 1994). We asked participants to describe and make meaning of their experiences by using open-ended interview questions, avoiding predefined responses.

Setting

This study was conducted at a large eastern research university from fall of 1995 through fall of 1996. The university is located in a small, isolated, conservative town. The campus enrolls roughly 40,000 students; about 11,000 live on campus. All first-year students must live in residence halls. While an active and visible LGB student group existed on campus, few resources were available for LGB students beyond the campus, and there was neither an institutionally supported LGB student center nor any professional staff with primary responsibility to LGB students. The university did, however, include sexual orientation in its non-discrimination policy.

Participants

Five of the ten women who participated in this study identified as lesbian, and five as bisexual. Two of the ten were exchange students from England, the others were U.S. nationals; all were White. One was a first year student, two were sophomores, two were juniors, and five were seniors. Two were actively involved in LGB activities and organizations, three were somewhat involved, and five were not at all involved. Only one woman identified herself as extensively "out," while seven were selectively out, and two were out to only a few people. While the participants were not specifically asked how long they had identified as lesbian or bisexual, their comments suggested that they had come out after starting college and that their self-concepts were quite healthy. (See Evans and Broido, 1999, for discussion of their identity development in college.) The women lived on single-sex floors of coed halls or in single-sex halls. All participants currently were full-time students at the university, lived in a residence hall or had lived in one within the previous year, and currently identified as lesbian or bisexual.

Data Collection

Participants met with one of four trained interviewers in an interview lasting 1.5 to 2.5 hours. Interviewers followed an interview guide, but had freedom to ask follow-up questions and pursue issues raised by participants. Interviews were audio-taped and transcribed.

Data Analysis

The first author read and coded the interview transcripts and notes, utilizing both inductive coding (Strauss, 1987), identifying common themes across transcripts, and interpretive coding (Mishler, 1986), looking for themes within each participant's transcript. A taxonomy of themes was created, identifying factors related to feelings of support and non-support (see Table 1). The primary themes and patterns identified by the first author were reviewed by the second author, who participated in earlier analyses of these data and who conducted many of the interviews. This feedback was incorporated into the findings presented here. In order to support the trustworthiness of these findings, we have provided thick description of the setting, research methodology, and assumptions. Findings are supported with quotes from the participants. Although we were unable to solicit feedback from participants on the findings, we engaged in peer debriefing by presenting our analyses to numerous residence life professionals.

TABLE 1. Factors Influencing Perceptions of Climate Held by Lesbian/Bisexual Women

Factors Leading to Positive Perceptions	Factors Leading to Negative Perceptions
Characteristics of Hall	
Presence of LGB staff	Large numbers of sorority members, athletes, and/or first-year students
Academically oriented	Lack of community
Experiences	
Lack of negative experiences	Harassment/harassment of others
LGB programming	Homophobic comments/nonverbals
Visible signs of support	Defacement/graffiti
	Lack of visible support
	Lack of social activities
Interactions	
Supportive roommate	Nonsupportive roommate
Lesbian/bisexual roommate	Not feeling about to come out to roommate
Supportive or LGB RA	RA indifferent to issues
Supportive Res. Life staff	Nonsupportive people on floor
Supportive people on floor	
Student's Behaviors	
Selectively out	Not out
Involvement/interaction with floor members	Not involved on the floor

FINDINGS

Data were examined to determine the respondents' perceptions of the residence hall climate, factors that influenced those perceptions, suggestions the interviewees had for improving the climate, and suggestions they had for preparing resident assistants to address LGB issues. No major differences were identified between the lesbian women and the bisexual women with regard to experiences, behaviors, or perceptions of the environment.

Perceptions of the Climate

Perceptions of the residence hall climate ranged from supportive to hostile. A few of the women reported that other women on their residence hall floors were actively supportive. For instance, one woman had friends who were members of Allies, a group whose purpose was to improve the climate for LGB students on campus. Those who felt their floors were supportive, however, tended to define support as a lack of problems and few negative comments. Sharon (all names are pseudonyms) stated: "So far the climate has been pretty exceptional . . . I haven't had any real negative experiences. . . . Some people on my floor . . . have suspicions and they've said things to friends of mine; . . . they've come back and told me things, just nothing terrible."

More women, however, felt that the atmosphere on their floors was nonaccepting. While homophobia was not expressed openly, interviewees had a feeling that it would be unwise to be open about their sexual identity. For instance, Kay stated, "I don't remember any specific person saying anything negative. . . . But there were . . . times where I . . . knew I shouldn't say anything." One woman, Carrie, saw the climate on her floor as hostile: "I think for the most part women are less physically violent than men would be. Women tend to talk behind people's backs. They're more emotionally violent. . . . I think in a lot of ways, emotional violence is probably worse."

Factors Influencing Perceptions of the Climate

Factors that seemed to influence the women's perceptions of their residence hall climate included characteristics of the hall itself, the specific experiences of the women in their halls, their interactions with other people, and their own actions (see Table 1).

Hall characteristics. When they knew LGB resident assistants and professional hall staff members who were open about their sexual identity, students had a more positive perception of the climate. Halls that were more academically oriented, such as honors halls, were also viewed as having a more positive climate. Halls that lacked a sense of community or had large populations of sorority members, athletes, or first-year students were seen as more hostile.

Experiences. Positive perceptions, as noted earlier, were associated with a lack of negative events as well as the experience of positive ones, such as hearing people on the floor confront homophobic comments. The presence of programming and other visible signs of support, such as support network symbols or advertising for LGB events, also contributed to more positive perceptions of a floor. On the other hand, when women had experienced harassment or knew that other LGB people had been harassed, heard homophobic comments, saw defacement of LGB-related posters or signs, experienced a lack of visible support and a lack of LGB-oriented social activities, their perceptions were less favorable. Anna provided the following example: "Every now and then, people will look at me with this cold look in their eyes, like 'Oh, she's one of them.'" Carrie reported hearing women on her floor talk about another lesbian woman: "It was really hard to sit there and listen to them pound this girl in her absence."

Interactions. Interactions with roommates, student resident assistants, professional residence life staff, and other students in the hall also influenced students' perceptions of the climate. Because of the close contact students have with their roommates, the extent of support they received from these women was a critical factor in their overall perceptions of the hall. Those students whose perceptions were positive had actively supportive roommates who cared about them, introduced them to other LGB people, and welcomed the students' visiting girlfriends. Those women with more negative attitudes about their halls had less accepting roommates who were distant, held heterosexist attitudes, and made negative comments.

Resident assistants (RAs) also played an important support role for women who found their hall climates to be positive. In addition to offering individual support, these RAs discussed LGB issues on their floors, organized programs with LGB themes, advertised LGB events, and went to LGB events themselves. Carrie commented, "I never had a time that I needed something and [my RA] wasn't there." Students who viewed their halls as nonsupportive often had RAs who demonstrated an uncaring attitude. They did little to promote an accepting environment, never brought up issues related to sexual orientation, and did no programming on LGB topics.

Professional residence life staff also contributed to a positive perception of the residence hall by lesbian and bisexual women. Participants who held positive attitudes about their halls mentioned that the staff actively confronted homophobic behavior, helped LGB students meet each other, assisted with room changes when students were experiencing difficulty with their roommates, and actively reached out to LGB students. Women who held negative perceptions of their halls did not mention professional residence life staff at all.

Interactions with other students on their floors influenced perceptions. Some students showed support by wearing pins, asking questions to learn more, changing homophobic opinions, attending programs, discussing issues openly, and expressing displeasure at homophobic acts. Kay was surprised by the positive actions of her floor mates: "A lot of them were more open-minded than I had given them credit for." More often, however, other residents demonstrated a lack of awareness of issues, made negative comments about LGB people and programs, were hostile to attempts to discuss issues, and engaged in stereotyping. Sharon had this insight: "Most people are just happy to go on with their lives and . . . ignore things that don't directly affect them. . . . LGB issues, for a lot of heterosexual people, are just kind of someone else's problem."

Behaviors. Finally, a student's own actions with regard to identifying her sexual orientation and involving herself in the floor also influenced her perceptions. Those individuals who were not out to others on their floors and who were less involved on the floor had a more negative perception of the climate while those women who were selectively out and who were engaged with others on the floor were more satisfied with the climate. Anna shared this insight, "The more out I've become, the more comfortable I've been, because I'm not leading a double life any more." On the other hand, Carrie was not out to anyone and had distanced herself from the other women on her floor because she "was so terrified of anybody finding out or knowing."

Suggestions for Improving the Climate

Participants were asked for suggestions to improve the climate of residence halls for LGB students. The women suggested more educational efforts, including classes and extracurricular programs. Carrie stressed the importance of "awareness and education, because a lot of stereotypes are built on fears which are built on ignorance." Increased visibility for LGB issues was viewed as critical. Angie stated, "It would be nice if [LGB identities and topics] could be more visible. It just seems like it doesn't even exist." Audrey also noted the importance of giving "people an opportunity to talk and see different viewpoints." Increased verbal support from Residence Life and the university as well as active confrontation of homophobia were advocated. Finally, students pointed out the need for more social activities for LGB students. Susan was particularly insightful in discussing this need:

> I really think that there needs to be a social environment on campus before there's a political one, because the freshmen come up here and

they're looking for something and they just jump right into this whole political realm they don't know anything about. And they need a social environment before they can do that.

Suggestions for Preparing Resident Assistants

Given the important support role that participants ascribed to resident assistants, we also asked for their ideas concerning ways that RAs could be better prepared to work with LGB students. The women saw RAs as playing four important roles: providing support for individual LGB students, offering information on LGB topics to students on their floors, creating an accepting environment on their floors, and confronting homophobic comments and actions.

To carry out these roles effectively, the participants in our study suggested that RAs need to be provided with information about LGB issues during their training. They felt that specific units might be included in a RA course or RA candidates might be encouraged to take other courses about sexual orientation or diversity. Participants also felt that exposure to LGB people, rather than just reading about issues, was important. They suggested the use of panel presentations involving LGB students or RAs becoming friends with LGB people. Finally, they believed that RAs needed to be exposed to information about resources for LGB students.

DISCUSSION AND IMPLICATIONS

Several themes were apparent as we reviewed the statements made by our interviewees. Each of these conclusions expands the knowledge base with regard to the experiences of lesbian and bisexual women in residence halls, provides guidance for addressing homophobia and heterosexism, and has implications for residence life divisions (see Table 2).

Not all students experience the residence hall environment similarly. As Lewin (1936) suggested, both student characteristics and characteristics of the setting shape students' behaviors. In this study, many environmental factors, such as the balance between homophobic acts and statements and the amount of support present on the floor, influenced the women's perceptions and behaviors in their residence halls. However, the extent to which the women were open about their identity and comfortable with themselves also affected how they perceived the floor and how they interacted with others. It is important to remember that not every lesbian or bisexual woman will experience a setting similarly. D'Augelli (1994) stressed that identity development is influenced

TABLE 2. Suggestions for Creating Positive Residence Hall Climates

---

Staffing

Note importance of accepting attitudes in job descriptions and advertisements
Design interview procedures to identify LGB-supportive candidates
Recruit LGB staff

Staff Training

Include LGB topics in RA training
Address attitudes and feelings
Provide for exposure to LGB individuals

Establishing a Positive Climate

Stress the importance of building community and getting students involved in floor activities
Set behavioral norms during orientation meetings
Confront homophobic and heterosexist acts
Assist LGB students in identifying supportive roommates
Assist LGB students with room changes if they find themselves in hostile situations
Provide active programming on LGB topics
Use passive programming (e.g., visual displays) to reach more students
Provide support groups and social outlets for LGB students

by interactions with others, the setting itself, and how individuals make meaning of their experiences. All were significant factors for the women we interviewed.

Women often experience homophobia and heterosexism in subtle rather than direct ways. Existing research (see Eddy & Forney, 2000) indicates that LGB students are more frequently the targets of violence and harassment than heterosexual students. Our findings suggest that, for women, this harassment, described by one respondent as "emotional violence," is more subtle than direct. Given that the women responded by feeling afraid, distancing themselves from others, and hiding their true identities, similar to the negative reactions to homophobia reported by Amato (1997), this less obvious type of homophobic expression seems to have as powerful an impact as direct attacks and must be actively addressed in student residence halls.

Setting policies at the beginning of the year about appropriate behavior and about actions that will be taken if students engage in disrespectful or harassing behavior is necessary to create norms of acceptance and inclusion on residence hall floors. Equally important is taking immediate action when policies are violated. If lesbian or bisexual women find themselves in roommate situations that are hostile or uncomfortable, staff should expedite their moving into more comfortable situations. Proactively, staff can assist lesbian and bisexual women in identifying roommates who will be accepting and supportive.

Women perceive their environments as positive when negative acts are minimal. Our respondents seemed to expect homophobia and heterosexism to occur in their residence halls and were surprised and relieved when it was minimal. Students reported that their residence hall climate was positive even though they could not point to actual experiences that caused them to feel welcome or supported. These findings point to the pervasiveness of homophobia and heterosexism in society, which condition lesbian and bisexual women to expect the worst and to be relieved when "nothing bad happens." Residence life staff must be careful not to assume that all is well on a floor when they fail to hear negative reports from lesbian and bisexual women.

A sense of community helps to create a more positive residence hall climate for lesbian and bisexual women. Herbst and Malaney (1999) reported that LGB students living on special interest floors generally felt supported and secure, a finding echoed in our study. Respondents who lived on honors floors or special interest floors where students came to know each other well and shared common interests were more likely to report feeling comfortable than were women who lived in larger, less connected residence halls where a sense of community was not evident. When students have a chance to get to know each other on many levels, they come to see each other as individuals rather than as members of particular stigmatized or dominant groups. Building community should be a primary goal of residence life staff. Social outlets and support groups must also be provided specifically for lesbian and bisexual women students.

Residence hall staff play a significant role in establishing a positive floor climate. Professional staff who actively work to create positive environments through connecting lesbian and bisexual women with each other, addressing roommate issues, and being visible to the lesbian and bisexual community do much to help lesbian and bisexual women feel welcome. And as the women in this study indicated, having a supportive RA who was willing to confront homophobic and heterosexist actions was an important factor in their comfort level.

Most heterosexual residence life staff members lack knowledge about the issues facing LGB students and the resources available to the LGB communities. The women we interviewed indicated that most individuals with whom they came in contact, including residence life staff members, were unaware of the issues they faced. They stressed the importance of education and contact with LGB individuals in raising awareness and changing attitudes.

Many women in our study commented on the important role that LGB staff members played in helping them meet other LGB students and in providing a listening ear when they had concerns. The presence of LGB staff also sends a strong message to heterosexual students that the residence hall environment is inclusive. Lesbian and bisexual women should be actively recruited for residence life positions in order to serve the needs of all students more effectively.

Visibility is the key to creating a welcoming climate. Our respondents articulately stated that they felt invisible in their residence halls. Few efforts were made to educate students about sexual orientation issues and little was done to advertise events and services for LGB students. Many of the women felt that other students were not hostile as much as they were ignorant. They advocated education and exposure to LGB individuals.

Residence life programs play an important role in the overall education of students. Introducing students to LGB topics during orientation programs and educational sessions helps to educate heterosexual students on aspects of life to which they may have had little exposure, while sending lesbian and bisexual residents the message that their concerns are valid and important. Unfortunately, if given a choice, many students will avoid attending programs on topics that make them uncomfortable, such as sexual orientation. Preparing display cases, putting up bulletin boards, displaying LGB resource materials, and posting "safe zone" stickers are alternative ways to support LGB people. When all students must pass by such visual indicators of legitimacy and acceptance, their attitudes may shift or at least be called into question.

CONCLUSION

As with any qualitative study, caution must be used when generalizing to other students or settings. Our findings are based on the perceptions of ten women in an eastern research university. Additional research in other settings will help to provide a more complete picture of life for lesbian and bisexual college women. In addition, more research is needed to determine the process of attitude change with regard to issues of oppression. Case studies of exemplary environments would be one way to determine factors that contribute to supportive climates.

Nonetheless, our study indicated that lesbian and bisexual women often feel uncomfortable and threatened in college residence halls. While homophobic acts are not often directly hostile and attacking, a subtly unwelcoming atmosphere is common, and no less damaging. Residence life staff have a responsibility to actively confront all manifestations of homophobia and heterosexism, direct or indirect. Increased visibility and education are key factors in ensuring that lesbian and bisexual individuals will be fully accepted as members of the residence life community. As Julia reflected, "the support of Residence Life and the university in general carries a lot of weight." Residence life divisions and indeed, all educators, must use their weight to create positive, inclusive environments for all students.

REFERENCES

Amato, C. J. (1997). How do lesbian and gay university students perceive and describe the experience of homophobia? *Dissertation Abstracts International, B. 58*(8-B), (UMI No. AAT 9805535). Retrieved from UMI database.

D'Augelli, A. R. (1989). Homophobia in the university community: Views of prospective resident assistants. *Journal of College Student Development, 30*, 546-552.

D'Augelli, A. R. (1994). Identity development and sexual orientation: Toward a model of lesbian, gay, and bisexual development. In E. J. Trickett, R. Watts, & D. Birman (Eds.), *Human diversity: Perspectives on people in context* (pp. 312-333). San Francisco: Jossey-Bass.

Eddy, W., & Forney, D. S. (2000). Assessing campus environments for the lesbian, gay and bisexual population. In V. A. Wall & N. J. Evans (Eds.), *Toward acceptance: Sexual orientation issues on campus* (pp. 131-154). Lanham, MD: University Press of America.

Eliason, M. J. (1996). A survey of the campus climate for lesbian, gay, and bisexual university members. *Journal of Psychology & Human Sexuality, 8*(4), 39-58.

Engstrom, C. M., & Sedlacek, W. (1997). Attitudes of heterosexual students toward their gay male and lesbian peers. *Journal of College Student Development, 38*, 565-576.

Evans, N. J., & Broido, E. M. (1999). Coming out in college residence halls: Negotiation, meaning making, challenges, supports. *Journal of College Student Development, 40*, 658-668.

Herbst, S., & Malaney, G. D. (1999). Perceived value of a special interest residential program for gay, lesbian, bisexual, and transgender students. *NASPA Journal, 36*, 106-119.

Lewin, K. (1936). *Principles of topological psychology.* New York: McGraw-Hill.

Malaney, G. D., Williams, E. Z., & Geller, W. W. (1997). Assessing campus climate for gays, lesbians, and bisexuals at two institutions. *Journal of College Student Development, 38*, 365-375.

Mishler, E. G. (1986). *Research interviewing: Context and narrative.* Cambridge, MA: Harvard University Press.

Mohr, J. J., & Sedlacek, W. E. (2000). Perceived barriers to friendship with lesbians and gay men among university students. *Journal of College Student Development, 41*, 70-80.

Schwandt, T. A. (1994). Constructivist, interpretivist approaches to human inquiry. In N. K. Denzin & Y. S. Lincoln (Eds.), *Handbook of qualitative research* (pp. 118-137). Thousand Oaks, CA: Sage.

Strauss, A. L. (1987). *Qualitative analysis for social scientists*. New York: Teachers College.

Westefeld, J. S., Maples, M. R., Buford, B., & Taylor, S. (2001). Gay, lesbian and bisexual college students: The relationship between sexual orientation and depression, loneliness, and suicide. *Journal of College Student Psychotherapy*, *15*(3), 71-82.

Zapata, L. P. (2000). The relationship between students' sexual orientation and their psychological sense of collegiate community. *Dissertation Abstracts International, A. 61*(3-A), (UMI No. AAT 9964343). Retrieved from UMI database.

Updating College
and University Campus Policies:
Meeting the Needs of Trans Students,
Staff, and Faculty

Lydia A. Sausa

SUMMARY. This article gathers information not only from my own personal experiences, but also from the experiences of trans students, staff and faculty members with whom I have worked as a human sexuality educator and consultant, and from my current qualitative research on trans youth for my PhD dissertation. As the trans community becomes more visible, and people become more comfortable in asserting their gender non-conforming characteristics, a backlash of harassment and discrimination has been evident across our campuses. Colleges and universities are often ignorant or ill-equipped without accurate knowledge of trans people, and as a result isolate students and employees, or ignore them altogether. This article discusses the current challenges of trans stu-

Lydia A. Sausa earned an MS Ed in human sexuality education and is a PhD candidate in the Graduate School of Education at the University of Pennsylvania. She is also an educational sexuality consultant and is currently a Lecturer in the Human Sexuality Studies Department at San Francisco State University.

Address correspondence to: Lydia A. Sausa, 224 Douglass St., Apartment #2, San Francisco, CA 94114 (E-mail: lydiasausa@hotmail.com) (www.lydiasausa.com).

The author would like to thank Kathryn Wood and Michael Morrissey, PhD, for their editorial feedback and support in writing this article.

[Haworth co-indexing entry note]: "Updating College and University Campus Policies: Meeting the Needs of Trans Students, Staff, and Faculty." Sausa, Lydia A. Co-published simultaneously in *Journal of Lesbian Studies* (Harrington Park Press, an imprint of The Haworth Press, Inc.) Vol. 6, No. 3/4, 2002, pp. 43-55; and: *Addressing Homophobia and Heterosexism on College Campuses* (ed: Elizabeth P. Cramer) Harrington Park Press, an imprint of The Haworth Press, Inc., 2002, pp. 43-55. Single or multiple copies of this article are available for a fee from The Haworth Document Delivery Service [1-800-HAWORTH, 9:00 a.m. - 5:00 p.m. (EST). E-mail address: getinfo@haworthpressinc.com].

43

dents, staff and faculty members, as well as addresses specific ways in which schools can improve work conditions and provide access to a safe education for all students. *[Article copies available for a fee from The Haworth Document Delivery Service: 1-800-HAWORTH. E-mail address: <getinfo@haworthpressinc.com> Website: <http://www.HaworthPress.com> © 2002 by The Haworth Press, Inc. All rights reserved.]*

KEYWORDS. Transgender, transsexual, gender queer, college policies, discrimination

INTRODUCTION: WHAT DOES IT MEAN TO BE TRANS?

In the United States, sex and gender are commonly viewed as dichotomous categories. There is a shared belief by most members of U.S. society that there are only two sexes (female and male); that every person, most animals, and many things must be either one or the other; and that one cannot be both male and female, cannot be neither male nor female, and cannot change sex without the aid of surgery (Devor, 1989). Concomitant with this belief is that there are only two genders (women and men), and that whatever a woman does will somehow have the stamp of femininity on it, while whatever a man does will likewise bear the imprint of masculinity (Devor, 1989). Before I can begin to discuss the definition of *trans*, I would like to first establish a common language about the terms *sex, gender,* and *gender expression*.

The term *sex* traditionally refers to someone's biological status as having a certain set of primary sexual characteristics, i.e., genital, chromosomal, hormonal, and reproductive. One's sex can be categorized as male, female, or intersexed, among others. But sexual characteristics can vary even within one sex. Many people have moved away from this definition of sex, which focuses on very specific biology, since it can be viewed as limited when comprehending the vast differences of biological possibilities among people, such as different size genitalia, various chromosomal combinations, hormone levels, and abilities to produce offspring.

Simone de Beauvoir said it best, "One is not born, but rather becomes a woman" (Beauvoir, 1952, p. 249). She argued that *gender* is a socially rather than biologically constructed attribute, and that people are not born with but rather learn the behaviors and attributes appropriate to their sex. Sex is generally believed to determine gender, and thus these two terms are commonly, and incorrectly interchanged, and as a result, the conceptual differences between the two are rarely acknowledged. The term *gender* refers to a person's social status, which can be categorized as a man, woman, androgyne, etc. Gender has traditionally been viewed as stagnant, though some current scholars of gender, including noted gender theorist Judith Butler (1990), view gender as more malleable or performative. Some people can change their gender, and even "perform" a variety of genders, such as drag artists.

A person's *gender expression* is the actions, thoughts, behaviors, and beliefs that distinguish one as a member of a gender category, i.e., masculine or feminine. Not all individuals in society fit within the common patterns that presume that females will become girls and then women, and that males will become boys and then men. A significant number of people fall outside this standard formula. Not all males are masculine enough to entirely satisfy the gender expression demands of social stereotypes, nor are all females feminine enough to do so. Many people also blur, bend, or blend their gender(s) through their gender expression.

The *trans* population is a complex and multifaceted community. The word *trans* will be used in this article as an abbreviation, which includes both transgendered and transexual people. As the trans community continues to develop and become more visible, it challenges people to explore the distinction between a person's sex (female, intersexed, male), gender (woman, androgyne, man), and their gender expression (feminine, androgynous, masculine). Many trans people may identify their gender as male or female, though unlike non-trans people, trans people believe that the gender they were assigned at birth is incomplete or incorrect. Some trans people identify as both a man and a woman, or multiple genders. Some identify as neither gender; rather they believe that gender categories are dichotomous and rigid, or that their gender identity is fluid.

Trans people traverse, bridge, or blur the boundary of the sex and gender they were assigned at birth (Feinberg, 1996). For the purpose of this article, the trans community will be defined as including the following: People who reassign the sex they were labeled at birth, and/or people whose gender expression is considered "inappropriate" for their sex.

Trans is also an umbrella term referring to a diverse group of individuals who cross or transcend culturally defined categories of sex and gender. The term trans is inclusive of different sex and gender identities including: female-to-male transexual (FTM) or transman, male-to-female transexual (MTF) or transwoman, female crossdresser, male crossdresser, drag queen, drag king, androgyne, masculine female, feminine male, and gender queer.

Differences Between Sexual Orientation and Gender Identity

Sexual orientation is often confused with gender identity. The definition of *sexual orientation* is complex and variable. Throughout history and among cultures the definition of sexual orientation shifts and changes. A current working definition of sexual orientation is an attraction to someone of the same or different gender, including identities such as gay, lesbian, bisexual, and heterosexual (Human Rights Watch, 2001).

As stated above, the term gender refers to a person's social status, which can be categorized as a man, woman, androgyne, etc. *Gender identity* is one's internal or self-identification as a gender, or in the case of trans people, how they transgress or exist between or beyond societal gender boundaries.

One's sexual attraction to a person, thus one's sexual orientation, is not to be confused with one's personal gender identity. The problem lays in the complexity of the definition of sexual orientation and its assumption of a two-gender model. For example, a person who is gay or lesbian is attracted to the same gender, and someone who is bisexual is attracted to both men and women. But how do we define a trans person's own sexual attractions, as well as those of someone who is attracted to a trans person? What is that person's sexual orientation? What is the sexual orientation of a person who does not identify as a man or a woman, or is attracted to a person who does not define oneself as a man or a woman?

Current models of sexuality and language are slow to embrace the diversity in gender and gender identities, and to include trans people and their experiences. Additional sexual orientations that may speak to this are the terms: *omnisexual* (omni is from Latin origins meaning all), and *pansexual* (pan is from Greek origins meaning all) (Webster's New Universal Unabridged Dictionary, 1994). Thus, someone who is omnisexual or pansexual can be attracted to all genders, or a variety of gender identities. Though this is not to say that a trans person may not identify as one particular gender identity, have an attraction to one gender identity or gender expression, and therefore have a particular sexual orientation.

The trans community and the gay, lesbian, bisexual community are often linked, which further confuses this issue. Though there are trans people who define themselves as heterosexual, there are also many who define themselves as gay, lesbian, bisexual, and pansexual or omnisexual. And in many cases, trans people may have initially come out or found support for their identities within the gay, lesbian, and bisexual community, when unable to find trans specific support systems, resources, or any trans people to share common experiences. Both the gay, lesbian, and bisexual community and the trans community challenge societal conceptions of sex, gender, attraction, and behavior that are considered outside the heterosexual norm. Therefore, the gay, lesbian, bisexual community and the trans community are co-joined and connected because they not only share persons who may be both gay, lesbian, and bisexual, and trans, but also share many similar struggles, such as lack of equal rights protection, discrimination and harassment issues, lack of societal support and resources, and concerns about safety and visibility.

WHAT ARE THE CURRENT NEEDS AND CONCERNS OF TRANS STUDENTS, STAFF AND FACULTY MEMBERS?

Trans Students in Our Schools

In the book, *Transgender Care* (1997), Gianna E. Israel and Donald E. Tarver II, M.D. state that "no single group has gone more unnoticed by society, or abused and maltreated by institutional powers, than youth with transgender needs and feelings" (p. 132). Trans youth are likely to be victims of social stigma, hatred, hostility, isolation, and alienation, as are gay and lesbian youth (American Academy of Pediatrics Committee on Adolescence, 1993), and to experience higher rates of substance abuse and suicide ideation than their heterosexual, gender-conforming peers (Sember, 2000). Research literature has provided estimates that gay, lesbian, and bisexual youth attempt suicide at a rate 2-3 times higher than their heterosexual peers (Faulkner & Cranston, 1998; Fergusson, Horwood, & Beautrais, 1999; Remafedi, French, Story, Resnick, & Blum, 1998;), but some experts indicate that the rate of attempted suicide for trans youth is higher than 50% (Davis, 1997; Israel & Tarver; 1997).

Trans youth are the most vulnerable adolescent population to both violence by peers and harassment by adults (Human Rights Watch, 2001). Below are quotes from trans students who were interviewed as part of my dissertation research on the educational needs of trans youth (Sausa, 2001): Phoenix (age 19) states, "I was constantly running from people, because everyone wanted to fight me. I always stuck to myself, I was isolated. I loved school, but I couldn't take it. I dropped out." Amelia (age 21) reported, "I was robbed, I was viciously beaten up. . . . I was raped. I just wanted to graduate."

Students who identify as, or are even perceived to be, trans face relentless harassment and live with overwhelming isolation (Human Rights Watch, 2001). Schools are not safe for trans students, and many trans students are often forced to drop out due to the daily violence they face from peers, and an administration that chooses to look the other way or is unprepared to meet their needs.

Only six states explicitly prohibit harassment and discrimination in public schools based on sexual orientation or perceived sexual orientation: California, Connecticut, Massachusetts, Hawaii, Vermont, and Wisconsin. And even fewer states protect a student from harassment based on their gender identity or gender expression. Few schools have programs in place to address issues of harassment and violence, as well as training for staff and faculty members about trans youth. Only three universities include gender identity and/or gender expression in their non-discrimination policies, including the University of Iowa, Rutgers University, and the University of Minnesota (based on state law) (Transgender Law and Policy Institute, 2001). Trans students are entering schools ready to learn, but are met with harassment, violence, lack of support, and school systems that are unaware of their needs or how to meet them. In a recent interview, Jake (age 21), a trans college student stated, "When I applied I told them I was trans in my application. I still had problems with people in my residence hall, the school bathrooms, my school ID card, and people calling me by the wrong pronoun" (Sausa, 2001).

There are many issues facing trans students today. These include: concerns about discrimination if they come out in their applications; the application forms themselves which only allow for two sexes or genders; concerns about their safety in bathrooms and locker rooms; acceptance among roommates and peers in residence halls; problems with being called by one's birth name and inappropriate gender pronoun, instead of one's new name and preferred pronoun; administrative issues with name and gender changes, including school picture identification cards, school files, and school transcripts and degrees; the need for healthcare access and healthcare services from trans knowledgeable health service providers including counselors, nurses, nurse practitioners, and physicians; harassment and violence on campus; lack of support and resources; and overall the ability to attend a school without constantly worrying about one's personal safety, as well as the ability to access services and resources afforded others at the same educational institution.

Working Conditions for Trans Staff and Faculty

Conditions at universities and colleges are not much better for trans staff and faculty members. Only two states, Minnesota and Rhode Island, and thirty cities have a non-discrimination law that clearly prohibits discrimination against trans people in employment, housing, credit and public accommodations (Transgender Law and Policy Institute, 2001). Trans people are not protected under federal anti-discrimination laws, such as Title VII of the Civil Rights Act of 1964, which prohibits workplace sex discrimination. Though recently, New York, Massachusetts, New Jersey, and Connecticut are four states in which courts have interpreted state sex discrimination laws to include trans people (Transgender Law and Policy Institute, 2001). Not even the current Employment Non-Discrimination Act (ENDA), which is a bill that would, if enacted, prohibit job discrimination based on sexual orientation, protects gender identity or gender expression.

Many faculty members and staff have been able to successfully come out as trans in today's academic environments. Though others still face many challenges being trans or transitioning on the job, especially for staff without job security or faculty without tenure. Wynd D. Harris, a professor of marketing and international business at Quinnioiac College, asked to be recognized as a female (Wilson, 1998). Dr. Harris had been taking hormones but had not yet had genital surgery when requesting the change. Though many trans people choose not to have genital surgery, the university asked for proof that the professor was a woman. "They told me I had to have a physical exam," recalls Dr. Harris (p. A11). The professor refused, and the college suspended Dr. Harris and started termination proceeding against her. At Rutgers University, Ben Singer, a graduate student in English, said his advisor became angry when he told her he was having a sex change. "As a feminist, her perception was that I was giving up my womanhood," recalled Mr. Singer (p. A11).

The needs and concerns of trans staff and faculty members not only begin with the ability to keep jobs they love and have performed with excellence, but also to receive support from and work as a team with supervisors or department chairs on how to address issues that may arise in the workplace. Some of these issues may include: the visible signs of living as another gender (or transitioning), and reactions and questions from co-workers and students; concerns about name changes; usage of bathroom facilities; insurance and health care coverage; and working in an environment free of harassment.

Concerns for trans people already in staff and faculty positions or applying for positions may include: working in an environment that does not tolerate harassment based on gender identity or gender expression, as reflected in a school's anti-discrimination policy; confidentiality of their trans identity; and providing a safe and supportive working environment, which can include providing resources and support networks, and periodic staff and faculty educational trainings about trans students, faculty, and staff.

HOW DO WE MEET THE NEEDS OF TRANS STUDENTS, STAFF AND FACULTY MEMBERS?

Universities and college campuses are beginning to address concerns by including "gender identity and gender expression" in their anti-discrimination policies, and including trans as part of their resource centers, organizations, and programming events. Below is a list of ways to improve the educational and work environments of colleges and universities for trans students, staff, and faculty.

Updating Policies and Forms

- Be gender inclusive with all forms, including surveys, administrative forms, applications. Do not only have the categories "male" and "female," but also include "transgendered" or "trans" for students, staff, and faculty to check off. They may not always indicate they are trans or may check off more than one, but allow for possibilities. Another suggestion is simply to have the category say "gender identity," and then place a blank after it for them to fill in.
- Include gender expression and gender identity in your official university or college anti-discrimination policies. This helps to provide a safe educational and work environment for everyone.
- Create specific guidelines about how to record, document, and address issues of harassment and verbal and physical abuse dealing with gender expression or gender identity, from student to student, employee to student, employee to employee, and student to employee.
- Develop guidelines for assisting trans students, staff, and faculty in navigating your school system, including addressing concerns with bathrooms, locker rooms, residential living arrangements, school identification picture cards, name changes, requesting school transcripts after a name change, possible issues of harassment, etc.

Using Appropriate Language

- Provide workshops, guest speakers, and professional training to encourage students, staff, and faculty to use gender-neutral language and do not assume the sexual orientation of a trans person. For example, use *parent* or *guardian* instead of *mother/father*, use *partner* instead of *girlfriend/boyfriend*.
- Respect trans people by using appropriate pronouns for their gender expression, or simply use their preferred name. When in doubt, ask.

Creating a Safe Environment

- Include trans literature, brochures, books, magazines, art work, and posters in your lobby or office. This helps people to feel welcomed and more comfortable.

- Be an ally to and advocate for trans people. Create an atmosphere in which derogatory remarks regarding trans people are not acceptable. Challenge put-downs and dispel myths and stereotypes about the trans community.
- Hire openly trans people as staff and faculty who would provide valuable knowledge about trans needs and concerns, as well as help trans students, and other trans staff and faculty feel represented in your college or university.
- Encourage role models and mentors through special peer mentoring programs, and by having openly trans staff and faculty members or trans allies who are trained and designated as "safe" people to approach for information and support. This can be done for students, as well as staff and faculty members.
- Establish support and discussion groups that are specific to addressing gender diversity and trans experiences.
- Remove *MEN'S* and *WOMEN'S* restroom labels, or create additional gender inclusive restrooms. Many trans people have been harassed, even physically removed by security personnel, for entering the "wrong" bathroom. This is especially common for people who do not fit into the dichotomous gender norms of our society, such as a masculine or androgynous woman who has been mistaken as a "man" entering the *WOMEN'S* bathroom. To help create a safer atmosphere for trans students, staff, and faculty, universal gender inclusive *RESTROOMS* may be beneficial.

Increasing Awareness and Providing Educational Training

- Take a trans sensitivity inventory of your college or university. Schedule periodic educational workshops and in-service trainings to provide important current information and assist with concerns or questions about the needs of trans people for your students, as well as your staff and faculty members. Continual education is also helpful to address changes among staff and faculty members, as well as the ever changing student body, and keep everyone up-to-date.
- Ask for help from trans specific local and national organizations. Build collaborative relationships between your college and university and local centers, organizations, and support groups. If the resources at your college or university cannot meet the needs of a trans student, staff, or faculty member, put their best interests first, and refer them to someone who is better qualified or more experienced.

- Hire specific point people to be trans resources for students, staff, and faculty members. These people can be extremely advantageous in assisting with concerns or questions, providing in-services or workshops for the school, and effectively dealing with everyday challenges in updating and representing a university or college on trans issues.
- Have your campus Lesbian, Gay, Bisexual (LGB) Resource Center be inclusive of trans people as well. Please remember that simply adding the "T" at the end is not enough. Providing trans specific services, programs, resources, and creating a safe and welcoming space by a trained trans sensitive staff is essential for support, outreach, education, and advocacy. Encourage all LGB organizations, clubs, or school groups to be inclusive of trans people.
- Encourage staff and faculty members to include trans films, articles, books, guest speakers, and panels in their curricula to provide a place for open discussion, increased awareness, and education about the various issues affecting trans people (see Appendix for resources).

Establishing Resources

- Designate resource people in your college or university to update and provide trans specific resources for students, staff, and faculty. These resources may include hotlines, listings of local and national trans organizations, listings of local support groups and medical providers who specifically service trans people, recent articles, books, and brochures. Having an accurate and current base of information is helpful for making effective referrals and attaining vital knowledge. Please make sure your personal or office libraries, and especially your college or university libraries can provide current books and films on trans issues and experiences.
- Fund students to attend trans specific conferences to educate themselves and encourage them to present their findings, or share their information with campus organizations and others.
- Be aware of the variety of current listserve discussion groups, Web sites, and other electronic media for further information about trans people and their experiences. Also create special campus listserves as a way of providing support for students, staff and faculty members and building connections to share information.

CONCLUSION

We can no longer ignore the violence, harassment, and discrimination faced by trans students, staff and faculty members. If we work in institutions of learning that stand for providing a safe learning and working environment for everyone, we must be role models first of learners and then of educators. I advocate that we first educate ourselves on the concerns and experiences of trans people, then teach others in our schools what we have learned, including mutual respect and diversity. I have known too many trans students who have been beaten by ignorance and invisibility. I have seen colleagues avoid wonderful careers in education or avoid coming out as trans, because they feared discrimination. Trans people are here. They are in our schools. They are the students in our classrooms. They are the staff and faculty members with whom we work each day. They are our colleagues, our mentors, our friends. It is time to make some changes in our schools.

REFERENCES

American Academy of Pediatrics, Committee on Adolescence. (1993). Homosexuality and adolescence. *Pediatrics, 92,* 631-634.

Beauvoir, S. de (1952). *The second sex.* New York: Bantam.

Butler, J. (1990). *Gender trouble: Feminism and the subversion of identity.* New York: Routledge.

Davis, D. (personal communication, April, 1997). Executive Director of Gender Education Center. Minneapolis, MN.

Devor, H. (1989). *Gender blending.* Indianapolis, IN: Indiana University Press.

Faulkner, A. H., & Cranston, K. (1998). Correlates of same-sex sexual behavior in a random sample of Massachusetts high school students. *American Public Health Association, 88*(2), 262-266.

Feinberg, L. (1996). *Transgender warriors: Making history from Joan of Arc to Dennis Rodman.* Boston, MA: Beacon Press.

Fergusson, D. M., Horwood, L. J., & Beautrais, A. L. (1999). Is sexual orientation related to mental health problems and suicidality in young people? *Archives of General Psychiatry, 56,* 876-880.

Human Rights Watch (2001). *Hatred in the hallways: Violence and discrimination against lesbian, gay, bisexual, and transgender students in U.S. schools.* New York: Human Rights Watch.

Israel, G. E., & Tarver, D. E. (1997). *Transgender Care: Recommended guidelines, practical information, and personal accounts.* Philadelphia, PA: Temple University Press.

Remafedi, G., French, S., Story, M., Resnick, M.D., & Blum, R. (1998). The relationship between suicide and sexual orientation: Results of a population-based study. *American Journal of Public Health, 88*(1), 57-60.

Sausa, L.A. (2001). *HIV prevention and educational needs of trans youth.* Unpublished doctoral dissertation, University of Pennsylvania.

Sember, R. (2000). Transgender health concerns. In R. L. Sell & P. Dunn (Eds.), *Lesbian, gay, bisexual and transgender health: Findings and concerns* (pp. 37-48).

New York & San Francisco: Columbia University Joseph L. Mailman School of Public Health, Center for Lesbian, Gay, Bisexual, and Transgender Health & Gay and Lesbian Medical Association.

Transgender Law and Policy Institute (2001). *Non-discrimination laws.* Retrieved from http://www.transgenderlaw.org/#whoweare

Webster's new universal unabridged dictionary (1994). Avenel, NJ: Barnes & Noble, Inc.

Wilson, R. (1998, February 6). Transgendered scholars defy convention, seeking to be heard and seen in academe. *The Chronicle of Higher Education, 44*(22), A10-13.

APPENDIX

Please contact author for additional resources and information.

Organizations

The American Boyz, Inc.; 351 Pleasant Street, PMB 130, Northhampton, MA 01060; (413) 585-9059; E-mail: info@amboyz.org; Web site: http://www.amboyz.org

Female-To-Male International (FTMI); 160 14th Street, San Francisco, CA 94103; (415) 553-5987; E-mail: TSTGMen@aol.com; Web site: http://www.ftm-intl.org/

The International Foundation of Gender Education (IFGE); P.O. Box 540229, Waltham, MA 02454-0229; (781) 899-2212; E-mail: info@ifge.org; Web site: http://www.ifge.org/

The Renaissance Transgender Association; 987 Old Eagle School Road, Suite 719, Wayne, PA 19087; (610) 975-9119; E-mail: info@ren.org; Web site: http://www.ren.org

TGNet Arizona; 2818 N. Campbell, PMB 315, Tucson, AZ 85719; (520) 566-4591; E-mail: info@tgnetarizona.org; Web site: http://www.tgnetarizona.org

Web Sites

http://www.tgfmall.com/
http://www.geocities.com/WestHollywood/park/6484/
http://www.tgnetarizona.org/tgwp1.htm
http://members.aol.com/SOFFAUSA/index.html

Books

Bornstein, K. (1998). *My gender workbook: How to become a real man, a real woman, the real you, or something else entirely.* New York: Routledge.

Cromwell, J. (1999). *Transmen and FTMs: Identities, bodies, and sexualities.* Champaign, IL: University of Illinois Press.

Feinberg, L. (1996). *Transgender warriors: Making history from Joan of Arc to Ru Paul.* Boston, MA: Beacon Press.

Jacobs, S. (Ed). (1997). *Two-spirited people: Native American gender identity, sexuality, and spirituality.* Urbana-Chicago; IL: University of Illinois Press.

Sanlo, R. (Ed.) (1998). *Working with lesbian, gay, bisexual, and transgender college students: A handbook for faculty and administrators.* Westport, CT: Greenwood Press.

Walworth, J. (1998). *Transsexual workers: An employee's guide.* Los Angeles, CA: Center for Gender Sanity.

PART II
ATTITUDE ASSESSMENT AND CHANGE

The Role of Lay Theories of the Etiologies of Homosexuality in Attitudes Towards Lesbians and Gay Men

Erin C. Hewitt
Leslea D. Moore

SUMMARY. Previous research has demonstrated that those who believe that homosexuality is genetically or biologically caused have less negative attitudes towards gays and lesbians than those who believe it is acquired, learned, or chosen. This study, utilizing an undergraduate and graduate Psychology student sample, found significant relationships between attitudes towards lesbians and gay men and beliefs about causes and "treatments" for homosexuality. Level of personal contact with lesbians and gay men and demographic factors also influenced attitudes toward and beliefs about homosexuality. These results suggest that educational attempts to change attitudes towards lesbians and gay men

---

Erin C. Hewitt, BA, MA, PhD, is Associate Professor, Department of Psychology, Atkinson Faculty of Liberal and Professional Studies, York University, 4700 Keele Street, Toronto, ON, Canada M3J 1P3 (E-mail: echewitt@yorku.ca).

Leslea D. Moore, BA, MA, is a PhD candidate, Department of Psychology, York University, 4700 Keele Street, Toronto, ON, Canada M3J 1P3 (E-mail: ldmoore@yorku.ca).

This research was supported by a research grant from the Atkinson Faculty of Liberal and Professional Studies. The authors would like to thank M. E. Ross for her editorial contributions.

[Haworth co-indexing entry note]: "The Role of Lay Theories of the Etiologies of Homosexuality in Attitudes Towards Lesbians and Gay Men." Hewitt, Erin C., and Leslea D. Moore. Co-published simultaneously in *Journal of Lesbian Studies* (Harrington Park Press, an imprint of The Haworth Press, Inc.) Vol. 6, No. 3/4, 2002, pp. 59-72; and: *Addressing Homophobia and Heterosexism on College Campuses* (ed: Elizabeth P. Cramer) Harrington Park Press, an imprint of The Haworth Press, Inc., 2002, pp. 59-72. Single or multiple copies of this article are available for a fee from The Haworth Document Delivery Service [1-800-HAWORTH, 9:00 a.m. - 5:00 p.m. (EST). E-mail address: getinfo@haworthpressinc.com].

59

should consider the role played by beliefs about the etiologies of homosexuality. *[Article copies available for a fee from The Haworth Document Delivery Service: 1-800-HAWORTH. E-mail address: <getinfo@haworthpressinc. com> Website: <http://www.HaworthPress.com> © 2002 by The Haworth Press, Inc. All rights reserved.]*

KEYWORDS. Lesbians, gay men, attitudes, causes of homosexuality

In the ever burgeoning research literature that addresses factors related to attitudes towards lesbians and gay men is a small number of studies that have demonstrated that people who believe that homosexuality is learned or chosen tend to have less positive attitudes towards lesbians and gay men than those who believe it is biological, genetic or innate (Aguero, Bloch, & Byrne, 1984; Ernulf, Innala, & Whitham, 1989; Furnham & Taylor, 1990; Gallup, 1994; Matchinsky & Iverson, 1996).

Ernulf et al. (1989) reported the first study of the effect of beliefs regarding the cause of homosexuality on attitudes towards "homosexuals" in an international study that included participants from Arizona, Hawaii, the Philippines, and Sweden. Their findings indicate that, in all four samples, the majority of participants believed that "homosexuals" learn or choose to be that way (56-85%) while a minority believe that sexual orientation is preordained at birth. Further, they found that individuals subscribing to the learned/choice belief system were significantly less tolerant of homosexuality than were supporters of the biological hypothesis. In a 1984 study, Aguero et al. included an assessment of the relationship between generalized belief systems regarding the causes of homosexuality (i.e., genetic vs. learned behavior), and attitudes toward "homosexuals." They found that attitudes were slightly more negative in those who endorsed a learned belief than those who endorsed the genetic hypothesis. Ten years later, Gallup poll data collected in the United States (Gallup, 1994) indicated that those who believe that homosexuality is something that develops or is chosen are less supportive of civil rights for lesbians and gay men than those who believe that homosexuality is an inborn characteristic of the individual. Matchinsky and Iverson (1996) found that less negative attitudes toward homosexuality were related to beliefs in biological and natural causes of homosexuality and more negative attitudes were related to beliefs in homosexuality as psychologically caused, changeable or a choice.

Furnham and Taylor (1990) have conducted the most extensive study of the relationship between attitudes towards "homosexuals," and beliefs about the causes of homosexuality. They constructed three multi-item scales for this study. The first scale assessed beliefs about the etiology of homosexuality, which they refer to as "lay theories of homosexuality" (p. 135), with a total of 25 items. The second scale assessed attitudes towards "homosexuals," and beliefs about their characteristics and behaviors (31 items). The third scale, consisting of 24 items, assessed beliefs about the efficacy of various "treatments" for "changing homosexuals into heterosexuals" (p. 138). It is important to note, at this point, that they limited themselves to male homosexuality and did not ask participants about lesbians at any stage of the research.

Furnham and Taylor factor analyzed the responses of 255 British, non-student participants on the three scales separately. They found six factors for the etiology items, which they labeled early relationships (poor early sexual relationships with women), genetics (different genetic configurations), father problems (absent father or traumatic relationship with father), fear of women (finding women aversive or hatred of women), mental illness (being mentally unbalanced), and sexual abuse (history of sexual abuse by a male in childhood). The structure of the attitude items indicated five factors, labeled intolerance (hatred of "homosexuals"), effeminate (possessing stereotyped characteristics such as effeminacy), public face (acceptance of homosexuality as long as it is kept in the private domain and willingness to interact with gay men), identifiability (gay men are readily identified by their behavior and physical characteristics), and promiscuity (gay men are "promiscuous"/unselective about sexual partners). Finally, the "treatment" factors identified were learning (becoming more familiar with heterosexual sexuality), therapies (individual and family therapies), hormonal administration (administration of sex hormones), surgery (psychosurgeries or castration) and exposure to the opposite sex (increased opportunity to meet women and interact with them sexually).

They found that older and less educated persons were more intolerant of gay men, wished to interact with them less (public face), and saw them as more promiscuous than did younger and more educated participants. Participants with higher levels of personal contact with gay men gave lower ratings on all etiology factors except genetics, all attitude factors except effeminate, and, most strongly of all, each "treatment" factor than those with little or no personal contact. The authors note that most individuals did not accept any one theory to the exclusion of all others, but displayed varying levels of acceptance to several, suggesting that, in a manner reminiscent of the academic discourse, the issue of beliefs about etiology was far from clear-cut.

There are a number of limitations to Furnham and Taylor's study. First, they assessed people's beliefs about and attitudes towards gay men only. Second, this study was conducted more than a decade ago, and it is clear that, in the interim, there have been changes in the academic and public discourses about homosexuality. One might expect that this would have an effect on lay theories of etiologies of homosexuality. Indeed, U.S. Gallup poll results indicate an increase from the mid-seventies to the mid-nineties in the belief that homosexuality is an inborn characteristic (Gallup, 1993). Further, there has been some indication that, over time, attitudes towards lesbians and gay men have become less negative (Yang, 1999).

The present research has two purposes. First, it expands the investigation of the beliefs about etiologies of homosexuality to include lesbians as well as gay men. We examine potential differences in beliefs regarding etiology and "treatments" that may underlie greater negativity in attitudes toward gay men versus lesbians that has been reported in previous research (see Kite & Whitley, 1998). The second aim is to examine the effects of level of university education (undergraduate vs. graduate students) on the structure of individuals' beliefs regarding etiology and "treatments," and to assess the impact of these beliefs on attitudes towards lesbians and gay men.

METHOD

Participants

One hundred and forty-one undergraduate students and 94 graduate students at a large metropolitan university in Canada, recruited in late 1996 and early 1997, served as research participants. The undergraduate sample were volunteers recruited from second- and third-year psychology classes at a faculty dedicated to part-time degree studies, while the graduate participants were solicited from a full-time graduate program in psychology via the intercampus mail system.

Procedure

The participants completed a questionnaire package that began with an unsigned informed consent document followed by a 15-item demographic section that asked for information such as age, sex, marital status, religious denomination, frequency of attendance at religious services,[1] major, year of study and the number of lesbians and gay men personally known or met. Two hundred and six respondents were female and 29 were male. They ranged in age from 18 to 61 ($M = 28.70$, $SD = 7.45$). The sample almost universally described themselves as heterosexual (94.4%); the remainder used the terms lesbian (2.6%), gay (.4%) or bisexual (2.6%) to describe their sexual orientation. These latter participants' responses were deleted from analyses as the purpose of this study was to investigate heterosexuals' attitudes. When asked to indicate the number of lesbians or gay men known or met,[2] 44 (20.2%) reported never having met a lesbian, 29 (13.2%) reported never having met a gay male, 75 (34.2%) reported never having personally known a lesbian, and 43 (19.5%) reported never having personally known a gay male.

Following this measure, participants received one of two versions of the questionnaire. One hundred and twenty-one participants (51.5%) were administered Furnham and Taylor's (1990) original 81 questionnaire items assessing etiology beliefs, attitudes towards gay men and beliefs about the efficacy of potential "treatments" for homosexuality. The second version was identical to the first in every respect except that the questions referred to lesbians rather than gay men, with rewording of some items to maintain gender consistency. This version was completed by 114 participants (48.5%).[3] The items were rated on 7-point Likert-type scales. All participants were fully debriefed about the purpose of the study, the nature of the scales they had completed and were provided with several references they could consult if they wished to learn more about the research area. Data analysis was conducted with SPSS 10. Statistical assumptions of all tests were initially explored. Hypotheses were tested using MANOVA and univariate F-tests, followed by post-hoc comparisons of means using Tukey's procedure, as well as bivariate correlations.

RESULTS AND DISCUSSION

Mean scores on the six etiology factors, five attitude factors and five treatment factors originally identified and named by Furnham and Taylor were calculated. [4] The names of the factors are adjusted here to reflect both lesbian and gay male conditions. For example, "fear of women" is reworded as "fear of the opposite sex."

MANOVA with stimulus type (gay male vs. lesbian) and student level (undergraduate vs. graduate students) as factors was conducted on mean scores on all 16 factors. This analysis indicated a significant multivariate effect of stimulus type, $F(16,190) = 4.72$, $p < .001$, and of student level, $F(16,190) = 3.99$, $p < .001$ but no significant interaction of these factors, $F(16,190) = 1.22$, $p = .25$. The main effects of stimulus type and student level accounted for 28.5% and 25.2% of the variance, respectively. Univariate analyses are presented below in separate sections.

Ratings of Etiologies

First, it should be noted that, when comparing ratings from the current study of gay men only, in both Furnham and Taylor's original study and in the current data, genetics was rated as the most likely of the etiological factors to cause homosexuality ($M = 3.78$, in the current study; $M = 4.01$ in Furnham & Taylor),[5] followed by early relationships ($M = 2.63$; $M = 3.58$), fear of opposite sex ($M = 2.41$; $M = 3.36$), sexual abuse ($M = 2.26$; $M = 2.76$), parent problems ($M = 2.27$; $M = 3.07$), and mental illness ($M = 1.78$; $M = 2.28$). It is clear that there are differences between the studies in the perceptions of causes. The smallest difference between the two studies is in ratings of genetics; the more social psychological causes show larger differences, with the current sample rating them as less likely to produce homosexuality in men.

The gay male stimulus elicited significantly higher ratings on genetics, $F(1,205) = 9.56$, $p < .01$ than did the lesbian stimulus. In contrast, the etiological factors of fear of the opposite sex and sexual abuse were rated as more important determinants of homosexuality for lesbians than gay men, $F(1,205) = 16.92$, $p < .001$, and $F(1,205) = 11.31$, $p < .01$ (see Table 1 for means and standard deviations). Participants believe that homosexuality in women is more likely to evolve because of an aversion to or fear of men, while for gay men, homosexuality is perceived to be more likely to be a product of innate, genetic factors. These beliefs are consistent with research exploring the genetics of homosexuality, which has found clearer or stronger effects of genetics for gay men than for lesbians (e.g., Bailey & Bell, 1993; Hamer, Hu, Magnuson, Hu, & Pattatucci, 1993; Hu et al., 1994).

Undergraduate students gave significantly higher ratings to all etiology factors than did graduate students, with the largest difference observed for early relationships and the smallest difference for genetics. It is important to note that, regardless of student level or stimulus type, mean ratings of all etiological factors fall below the midpoint of the 7-point Likert-type scale, indicating that no factor alone is seen as very likely to lead a person to become a lesbian or a gay man.

Ratings of Attitudes

Comparison of the ratings for the five attitude factors to those of Furnham and Taylor indicate that participants gave lower ratings on all five attitudinal factors in this study. With a gay man as a stimulus, this sample rated lower on intolerance ($M = 1.89$; $M = 2.38$ from Furnham & Taylor). They also were less likely to endorse stereotyped characteristics ($M = 3.19$; $M = 3.58$), public face items ($M = 3.13$; $M = 3.49$), and to regard gay men as readily identifiable ($M = 2.74$; $M = 2.99$) or promiscuous ($M = 2.53$; $M = 3.37$).

Univariate analyses indicate that a gay male stimulus was given a significantly higher rating on stereotyped characteristics and was rated as more promiscuous than was a lesbian stimulus (see Table 1). Of particular interest here

TABLE 1. Mean Ratings of Etiology and Attitude Factors as a Function of Stimulus Type and Participant Education Level

	Gay Male Stimulus	Lesbian Stimulus	Undergraduates	Graduates
Etiology Factors				
ER	2.63 a (1.27)	2.74 a (1.11)	3.00 a (1.17)	2.21 b (1.06)
Ge	3.78 a (1.23)	3.30 b (1.14)	3.70 a (1.27)	3.27 b (1.05)
PP	2.27 a (1.01)	2.15 a (0.94)	2.43 a (0.97)	1.87 b (0.88)
OS	2.41 a (1.28)	2.90 b (1.36)	2.93 a (1.28)	2.26 b (1.35)
MI	1.78 a (0.96)	1.59 a (0.87)	1.94 a (1.02)	1.28 b (0.54)
SA	2.26 a (1.52)	2.60 b (1.26)	2.67 a (1.46)	2.09 b (1.22)
Attitude Factors				
Int	2.63 a (1.27)	2.76 a (1.11)	2.29 a (1.10)	1.47 b (0.48)
SC	3.78 a (1.23)	3.30 b (1.14)	3.30 a (1.01)	2.78 a (0.93)
PF	2.27 a (1.01)	2.15 a (0.94)	3.71 a (1.42)	2.46 b (0.97)
Id	2.41 a (1.28)	2.90 a (1.36)	2.79 a (1.28)	2.37 b (1.00)
Pro	1.78 a (0.96)	1.59 b (0.87)	2.33 a (1.36)	1.83 b (0.98)

Note. Standard deviations are in brackets under each mean. Within stimulus type and student level, separately, means with differing subscripts within rows differ significantly at $p < .05$, using Tukey's procedure. For etiology ratings, high scores indicate that this factor is seen as likely to lead a woman (man) to become a lesbian (gay). For attitude ratings, high scores indicate strong agreement with statements. All ratings are on a 7-point Likert-type scale.

ER = Early Relationships, Ge = Genetics, PP = Parent Problems, OS = Problems with the Opposite Sex, MI = Mental Illness, SA = Sexual Abuse, Int = Intolerance, SC = Stereotyped Characteristics, PF = Public Face, Id = Identifiability, Pro = Promiscuity

is the finding that tolerance levels did not differ by stimulus type. This lack of gender of stimulus effect is consistent with some research that finds no such effect. The univariate effect of student level was seen on all attitude factors. Graduate students were significantly more tolerant than were undergraduates, and were much more likely to rate themselves as willing to interact with lesbians and gay men and to accept public homosexuality than were undergraduates. They regarded gay men and lesbians as less identifiable and less promiscuous than did undergraduate students.

Ratings of "Treatments"

As was the case for the other two measures in this study, participants gave lower ratings to all "treatment" factors than did those in Furnham and Taylor (1990). Learning ($M = 1.82$), therapies ($M = 2.02$), hormonal interventions ($M = 2.59$), surgery ($M = 1.42$), and exposure ($M = 2.35$) were all given lower effectiveness ratings than in Furnham and Taylor (M's = 2.90, 3.17, 3.54, 2.07, and 3.58, respectively). It should be noted that, in the current study, hormonal interventions were given the highest rating as a "treatment," while in the original study, exposure was seen as the most effective "treatment." Graduate students rated learning ($M = 1.34$), therapies ($M = 1.52$), hormonal interventions ($M = 2.19$), surgery ($M = 1.17$), and exposure ($M = 1.96$) as significantly less effective "treatments" for homosexuality than did undergraduate students (M's = 2.12, 2.36, 2.63, 1.55, 2.72, respectively). There were no significant univariate effects of stimulus type for "treatment" ratings.

Additional Analyses

In order to examine the relationships between beliefs about etiologies, attitudes, and perceptions of the efficacy of "treatments," correlations between these variables were calculated separately for lesbian and gay male stimulus conditions (see Table 2). First, it is interesting to note that, for both lesbian and gay male stimuli, strength of belief in the social psychological etiologies is more strongly related to attitudes than is strength of beliefs in a biological etiology (genetics). This is particularly the case when participants were rating a gay male. For the lesbian stimulus, belief in sexual abuse as an etiology was related only to agreement with stereotyped characteristics. As well, the social psychological etiology scales are correlated with ratings of all "treatments," while the genetic etiology scale is significantly correlated only with the hormonal interventions and surgery "treatment" scales. The intercorrelations among the etiology factors suggest that, for a gay male, there is a stronger tendency to see ALL types of causation as strongly interrelated, while for a lesbian stimulus, the pattern is not as clear. A similar effect can be observed for "treatments." There is a stronger relationship seen between ratings of the efficacy of all "treatments" when participants rate a gay male stimulus versus a lesbian stimulus. We find it interesting that this does not occur for relationships among the attitude factors; here, gay male and lesbian stimuli evoke similar relationships. The lower correlations between genetic etiology ratings and attitude factors versus the remaining etiologies can be seen to support previous research findings that individuals who endorse biological/genetic etiologies

TABLE 2. Intercorrelations Between Ratings of Etiologies, Attitudes and "Treatments" for Lesbian and Gay Male Stimuli

	ER	GE	PP	OS	MI	SA	Int	SC	PF	Id	Pro	Le	Th	Hor	Sur	Exp
Etiologies																
ER		.26**	.75***	.74***	.67***	.54***	.42***	.18*	.36***	.28**	.41***	.56***	.62***	.21*	.29**	.51***
Ge	.41***		.34***	.21*	.31***	.06	.12	.10	.28**	.22*	.14	.11	.17	.51***	.37***	-.01
PP	.78***	.51***		.68***	.64***	.48***	.24*	.24*	.30**	.30**	.28**	.37***	.47***	.31***	.37***	.34***
OS	.79***	.41***	.80***		.53***	.69***	.29**	.18*	.27*	.22*	.32***	.46***	.53***	.15	.22*	.41***
MI	.70***	.48***	.74***	.64***		.40***	.46***	.11	.50***	.35***	.33***	.58***	.60***	.36***	.48***	.36***
SA	.64***	.35***	.74***	.54***	.62***		.17	.25**	.12	.17	.15	.27**	.35***	.00	.32**	.33***
Attitudes																
Int	.44***	.21*	.35***	.34***	.44***	.44***		.23*	.81***	.57***	.60***	.70***	.63***	.25***	.38***	.54***
SC	.41***	.18*	.50***	.29**	.49***	.43***	.32***		.19*	.56***	.42***	.22*	.51***	.22*	.24*	.29**
PF	.44***	.20*	.33***	.38***	.38***	.38***	.80***	.28**		.56***	.48***	.55***	.52***	.33***	.37***	.44***
Id	.38***	.16	.45***	.35***	.42***	.47***	.62***	.56***	.57***		.52***	.41***	.47***	.30***	.24*	.44***
Pro	.18*	.12	.31***	.18*	.33***	.32***	.48***	.55***	.35***	.53***		.56***	.55***	.22*	.42***	.44***
"Treatments"																
Le	.64***	.16	.46***	.50***	.51***	.51***	.57***	.30***	.56***	.49***	.28**		.92***	.35***	.41***	.74***
Th	.69***	.15	.56***	.58***	.58***	.54***	.50***	.34***	.50***	.46***	.25*	.94***		.36***	.28**	.77***
Hor	.36***	.43***	.40***	.34***	.46***	.37***	.34***	.36***	.35***	.42***	.38***	.55***	.59***		.53***	.28**
Sur	.51***	.41***	.48***	.47***	.67***	.37***	.24*	.44***	.31***	.29**	.29***	.56***	.57***	.59***		.30***
Exp	.69***	.15	.53***	.57***	.49***	.53***	.44***	.40***	.22*	.42***	.19*	.79***	.78***	.45***	.46***	

Note. Correlations for the lesbian stimulus are above the diagonal and for the gay male stimulus are below the diagonal.
*p < .05, ** p < .01, *** p < .001
ER = Early Relationships, Ge = Genetics, PP = Parent Problems, OS = Problems with the Opposite Sex, MI = Mental Illness, SA = Sexual Abuse, Int = Intolerance, SC = Stereotyped Characteristics, PF = Public Face, Id = Identifiability, Pro = Promiscuity, Le = Learning, Th = Therapies, Hor = Hormonal, Sur = Surgery and Exp = Exposure

67

tend to express less negative attitudes towards gay men or lesbians than do those who endorse the learned/choice hypothesis (e.g., Ernulf et al., 1989).

The number of gay men and lesbians that participants reported having met and known was negatively correlated with all etiology factors when rating a gay male stimulus (see Table 3), indicating that all etiological factors were seen as more likely to cause homosexuality in men as participants reported less personal contact with gay men and lesbians. When a lesbian stimulus was rated, there was almost no relationship between amount of contact with gay men and lesbians and ratings of etiologies. When rating a gay male, negative correlations between contact and all attitude factors except promiscuity and stereotyped characteristics were found, indicating that lower contact is associated with less positive attitudes. For the lesbian stimulus, no relationship between contact and stereotyped characteristics was found, but all other attitude factors showed a negative relationship with contact. Greater contact is associated with increased tolerance, lower beliefs in the identifiability of lesbians, greater acceptance of a public presence of lesbians, and a lower likelihood of perceiving lesbians as promiscuous. All "treatments" ratings were negatively correlated with numbers of gay men and lesbians met and known. For both lesbian and gay male stimuli, "treatments" were seen as more effective by those participants with little reported contact with lesbians and gay men than those with greater contact.

The frequency with which participants attended religious services (when controlling for the number of lesbians and gay men met and known) was significantly correlated with ratings of sexual abuse as an etiology, $r(134) = .23, p < .01$; the attitude factors of intolerance, $r(134) = .34, p < .001$; public face, $r(134) = .37, p < .001$; and identifiability, $r(134) = .24, p < .01$; and ratings of learning, $r(134) = .22, p < .05$ and therapies, $r(134) = .17, p < .05$, as "treatments." The relationship between religiosity and attitudes is consistent with previous research (e.g., Herek, 1988; Morrison, Parriag, & Morrison, 1999). The finding that religiosity is related to two of the three social psychological "treatments" and one of the etiology factors suggests that the effect of religiosity is not limited to affective responses to lesbians and gay men.

IMPLICATIONS AND CONCLUSION

The present research provides valuable insight into the structure of beliefs that heterosexuals hold with regards to the etiology and "treatments" of those who are gay male or lesbian. First, we found, as did Furnham and Taylor (1990), that individuals do not subscribe only to innate or chosen etiologies of homosexuality. Rather, their beliefs reflect a mixture of genetic and social psy-

TABLE 3. Correlations Between Ratings of Etiologies, Attitudes and "Treatments" and Numbers of Lesbians and Gay Men Met and Known for Lesbian and Gay Male Stimuli

	ER	GE	PP	OS	MI	SA	Int	SC	PF	Id	Pro	Le	Th	Hor	Sur	Exp
Lesbian Stimulus																
Lesbians met and known	−.23*	.19	−.07	−.05	−.25*	−.09	−.56**	.00	−.54**	−.28**	−.30**	−.38**	−.32**	−.22*	−.20	−.24*
Gay men met and known	−.14	−.05	−.01	−.13	−.12	−.01	−.51**	.03	−.50**	−.23*	−.30**	−.47**	−.43**	−.20	−.20	−.32**
Gay Male Stimulus																
Lesbians met and known	−.39**	−.22*	−.33**	−.35**	−.30**	−.25*	−.23*	−.19	−.35**	−.35**	.03	−.28**	−.34**	−.21*	−.23*	−.31**
Gay men met and known	−.37**	−.25*	−.31**	−.32**	−.28**	−.28**	−.35**	−.14	−.31**	−.32**	−.05	−.30**	−.30**	−.30**	−.26**	−.38**

Note. $*p < .05$ $**p < .01$

ER = Early Relationships, Ge = Genetics, PP = Parent Problems, OS = Problems with the Opposite Sex, MI = Mental Illness, SA = Sexual Abuse, Int = Intolerance, SC = Stereotyped Characteristics, PF = Public Face, Id = Identifiability, Pro = Promiscuity, Le = Learning, Th = Therapies, Hor = Hormonal, Sur = Surgery and Exp = Exposure

chological causes. Second, we demonstrated that heterosexuals' beliefs are structured differently with respect to lesbians and gay men. Not only do participants see etiologies differing for lesbians and gay men, but the relationships between their etiology beliefs and their attitudes towards lesbians and gay men differ. We found that correlations between intolerance and etiology beliefs are stronger when participants rate a gay man versus a lesbian. As well, the interrelationships among etiology beliefs are stronger for a gay male than a lesbian stimulus, as are those among attitude components and among beliefs about "treatment" efficacy. This would suggest that heterosexuals' perceptions of lesbians may be more poorly integrated or organized or more ambivalent than their perceptions of gay men. It would seem prudent, then, that researchers avoid conducting research in which homosexuality is used generically to refer to both lesbians and gay men, as beliefs about lesbians and gay men may well differ (see Simon, 1998 for additional evidence for this position).

The present research also confirms previous findings concerning demographic variables that are strongly correlated with attitudes toward homosexuality. Contact with lesbians and gay men was once again shown to be significantly and negatively correlated with attitudes toward lesbians and gay men, as well as etiology and "treatment" beliefs. It was noted, though, that the correlations vary in strength from factor to factor, and independently, according to sex of stimulus. Again, this suggests that careful attention be paid to the generalizations made regarding homosexuality as a generic in men and women.

Analysis of graduate and undergraduate students' responses indicated significant effects across all areas studied. Graduate students expressed more positive attitudes toward lesbians and gay men, were notably less willing to endorse any etiology, and rejected the efficacy of potential "treatments." This may well suggest that more years of education, at least in psychology, provides a route to the elimination of homophobia, and that education may alter not only the affective component but may also operate on beliefs about etiologies of homosexuality. It is particularly likely that the graduate students in this sample had been exposed to the debate regarding the ethicality of conversion therapies or "treatments" (American Psychiatric Association, 2000) and that this exposure is, at least in part, responsible for their strong rejection of all forms of "treatment" that are to convert gay men and lesbians to heterosexuality.

The results of this study indicate a greater degree of tolerance towards lesbians and gay men than did those of Furnham and Taylor's study. This may well reflect differences in sample types (student versus community based), national differences (Canada vs. the U.K.) and the impact of time of testing (the late 1990s vs. the late 1980s). Despite these differences, these data suggest that "lay theories of homosexuality" are not gender neutral; in this study we found clear evidence for different constructions of homosexuality in lesbians and gay men.

While the study represents a step forward in our understanding of the determinants of responses to gay men and lesbians, it has limitations. First, the sample was restricted to university students and thus the results may not generalize well to the nature of beliefs about and attitudes towards lesbians and gay men in the broader community. Second, comparing undergraduate and graduate students represents a small slice of the range of education, and further research should be conducted across a broader range of education.

Attitudes towards and beliefs about lesbians and gay men are clearly multi-dimensional, and no single approach is likely to provide the key to facilitation of attitude modification. As the evidence is gradually accumulated, it becomes increasingly apparent that, for attitudes and belief structures, there are many variables at work, and that these variables may well operate differently when discussing beliefs about and attitudes towards lesbians and gay men.

NOTES

1. Two questions assessing religious denomination and frequency of attendance of religious services were not included in the questionnaire given to one of the undergraduate classes ($n = 75$).

2. For the contact measure, participants completed four scales, using a 4-point Likert type scale. They indicated how many lesbians and gay men that they had "met" and "personally known," with the following response options: none, one, several or many.

3. An original purpose of this study was to explore additional items on the scales. These longer scale scores were all highly correlated with the mean scores from the original factors (r's = 0.93 to 0.98 across the six etiology factors, r's = 0.97 to 0.98 for the attitude factors, and r's = 0.97 to 0.998 for the treatment factors). Given these strong correlations, analyses are reported only for the original Furnham and Taylor items, which permits a larger overall sample size.

4. To assess the reliability of the subscales, Cronbach's alpha's were calculated separately for the lesbian and gay male versions. The reliability coefficients for all scales for the gay male version are equivalent to those reported by Furnham and Taylor and the reliabilities for the two versions in this study are similar (ranging from 0.53 to 0.93).

5. Furnham and Taylor do not report means of their factored scales, only those of the items themselves. The mean scores reported here were calculated by averaging the item means to obtain a scale mean. Thus, it is impossible to test statistical differences between the means of the two studies as there are no standard deviations available for Furnham and Taylor's results.

REFERENCES

Aguero, J., Bloch, L., & Byrne, D. (1984). The relationships between sexual beliefs, attitudes, experience, and homophobia. *Journal of Homosexuality, 10*, 95-107.

American Psychiatric Association. (2000). *COPP Position Statement on Therapies Focused on Attempts to Change Sexual Orientation (Reparative or Conversion*

Therapies). Retrieved November 12, 2001 from http://www.psych.org/pract_of_psych/copptherapyaddendum83100.cfm

Bailey, J.M., & Bell, A.P. (1993). Familiality of male and female homosexuality. *Behavior Genetics, 23*, 313-322.

Ernulf, K., Innala, S., & Whitham, F. (1989). Biological explanation, psychological explanation, and tolerance of homosexuals: A cross-national analysis of beliefs and attitudes. *Psychological Reports, 65*, 1003-1010.

Furnham, A., & Taylor, L. (1990). Lay theories of homosexuality: Aetiology, behaviour and cures. *British Journal of Social Psychology, 29*, 135-147.

Gallup, G., Jr. (1993). Homosexuality and gay rights. *The Gallup poll: Public opinion 1992* (pp. 101-103). Wilmington, DE: Scholarly Resources.

Gallup, G., Jr. (1994). Homosexuality and gay rights. *The Gallup poll: Public opinion 1993* (pp. 83-89). Wilmington, DE: Scholarly Resources.

Hamer, D.H., Hu, S., Magnuson, V.L., Hu, N., & Pattatucci, A.M.L. (1993). A linkage between DNA markers on the X chromosome and male sexual orientation. *Science, 261*, 321-327.

Herek, G.M. (1988). Heterosexuals' attitudes toward lesbians and gay men: Correlates and gender differences. *Journal of Sex Research, 25*, 451-477.

Hu, S., Pattatucci, A.M.L., Patterson, C., Li, L., Fulker, D.W., Chern,y S.S., Kruglyak, L., & Hamer, D.H. (1994). Linkage between sexual orientation and chromosome Xq28 in males but not in females. *Nature Genetics, 11*, 248-256.

Kite, M.E., & Whitley, B.E., Jr. (1998). Do heterosexual women and men differ in their attitudes towards homosexuality? A conceptual and methodological analysis. In G.M. Herek (Ed.), *Stigma and sexual orientation: Understanding prejudice against lesbians, gay men and bisexuals* (pp. 39-61). Thousand Oaks, CA: Sage.

Matchinsky, D.J., & Iverson, T.G. (1996). Homophobia in heterosexual female undergraduates. *Journal of Homosexuality, 31*, 123-128.

Morrison, T.G., Parriag, A.V., & Morrison, M.A. (1999). The psychometric properties of the homonegativity scale. *Journal of Homosexuality, 37*, 111-126.

Simon, A. (1998). The relationship between stereotypes of and attitudes toward lesbians and gay men. In G.M. Herek (Ed.), *Stigma and sexual orientation: Understanding prejudice against lesbians, gay men and bisexuals* (pp. 62-81). Thousand Oaks, CA: Sage.

Yang, A. (1999). *From wrong to right, 1973 to 1999: Public opinion on gay and lesbian Americans moves toward equality.* New York: Policy Institute of the National Gay and Lesbian Task Force.

A Study of Attitudes
Toward Sexuality Issues
Among Health Care Students in Australia

Mairwen Kathleen Jones
Rosemary Anne Pynor
Gerard Sullivan
Patricia Weerakoon

SUMMARY. This study examined the attitudes of 1132 higher education students enrolled in health profession education degree programs. Students were asked to indicate their anticipated level of comfort in a variety of interactions including working with a lesbian client or a homosexual male, and asking a client about his or her sexual orientation. Students also indicated whether they perceived their degree program had dealt adequately with these issues. High levels of discomfort were identified in our large sample of students. Approximately 30% of the sample

Mairwen Kathleen Jones, PhD, is affiliated with the School of Behavioural and Community Health Sciences, University of Sydney, PO Box 170 Lidcombe, NSW 1825, Australia (E-mail: M.Jones@cchs.usyd.edu.au).

Rosemary Anne Pynor, BBSc (Hons), is a PhD candidate at the The University of Sydney and Associate Lecturer in the School of Behavioural and Community Health Sciences, The University of Sydney.

Gerard Sullivan, PhD, is Associate Dean for undergraduate studies and Head of the School for Policy and Practice in the Faculty of Education at the University of Sydney, NSW 2066, Australia.

Patricia Weerakoon, MBBS (Sri-Lanka), MS (Hawaii), MHPEd (NSW), is a lecturer in the School of Biomedical Sciences of the Faculty of Health Sciences, The University of Sydney, NSW1825, Australia.

[Haworth co-indexing entry note]: "A Study of Attitudes Toward Sexuality Issues Among Health Care Students in Australia." Jones, Mairwen Kathleen et al. Co-published simultaneously in *Journal of Lesbian Studies* (Harrington Park Press, an imprint of The Haworth Press, Inc.) Vol. 6, No. 3/4, 2002, pp. 73-86; and: *Addressing Homophobia and Heterosexism on College Campuses* (ed: Elizabeth P. Cramer) Harrington Park Press, an imprint of The Haworth Press, Inc., 2002, pp. 73-86. Single or multiple copies of this article are available for a fee from The Haworth Document Delivery Service [1-800-HAWORTH, 9:00 a.m. - 5:00 p.m. (EST). E-mail address: getinfo@haworthpressinc.com].

indicated they would be uncomfortable working with a lesbian client and 27% of the sample indicated that they would feel uncomfortable if working with a male homosexual client. There were significant differences for these two items depending on the student's gender. Female students indicated significantly higher levels of comfort in dealing with homosexual male clients than did their male counterparts. Male students indicated significantly greater comfort in dealing with lesbian clients. More than half of our sample indicated that they would not be comfortable asking about a client's sexual orientation. Over 75% of senior-year students believed that their degree program had not adequately dealt with these issues. The impact of homophobia and discomfort on the quality of care health professionals provide for lesbian and gay clients and the role of educational strategies to reduce this are discussed. *[Article copies available for a fee from The Haworth Document Delivery Service: 1-800-HAWORTH. E-mail address: <getinfo@haworthpressinc.com> Website: <http://www. HaworthPress.com> © 2002 by The Haworth Press, Inc. All rights reserved.]*

KEYWORDS. Homosexual, homophobia, health care students, comfort, education

Sexuality is now accepted by educators, health professionals, and the public as an important facet of the total well-being of the individual, and seen to contribute to the bio-psycho-social balance required for health. Sexual health care is thus seen as a significant component of comprehensive health care delivery and an undisputed part of overall health professional training (Payne, Greer, & Corbin, 1988; Weerakoon & Stiernborg, 1996). The recognition of the importance of sexuality and sexual orientation of clients is a significant aspect of holistic care (Hayter, 1996).

While the majority of health care professionals and their clients will be heterosexual, a proportion of the population does not identify as heterosexual (e.g., Laumann, Michael, & Gagnon, 1994). Research has indicated that negative attitudes toward lesbians and gay men are widespread throughout the health and community welfare sector (e.g., Rose, 1994; Smith, 1993; Stevens, 1993; Sullivan & Waite, 1997), and have been identified in a variety of health professional or trainee health professional groups. These include nurses (Jemmott, Freleicher, & Jemmott, 1992; Smith, 1993), social workers (Berkman & Zinberg, 1997; Wisniewski & Toomey, 1987), physical therapy students (Gilchrist, Sullivan, & Heard, 1997), and medical health students (e.g., Klamen, Grossman, & Kopacz, 1999).

The quality of care for lesbian and gay clients may be compromised if health professionals have homophobic or heterosexist attitudes (e.g., D'Augelli, 1989; Hayter, 1996; Morrissey & Rivers, 1998; Stevens & Hall, 1990). Once a client's homosexual orientation is known they may experience social isolation and neglect (e.g., Wilton, 1999). Staff may avoid contact with the client, or refuse to be involved in client care (Jemmott, Freleicher & Jemmott, 1992; Stevens, 1994). Additionally, homosexuals may avoid routine health care because of fear of stigmatization by health care professionals (e.g., Stevens & Hall, 1990), or be reluctant to disclose sensitive issues (Klamen, Grossman, & Kopacz, 1999). Fear of negative reactions from health care providers may even lead gays and lesbians to delay seeking treatment for urgent health problems (Albarran & Salmon, 2000).

Health professionals who are uncomfortable in sexual situations are argued to be at high risk of neglecting their patients' specific health care concerns (Coyle & Young, 1998). Gallop, McCoy, Cote, Garley, Harris, and Vermilyea (1993) suggest that the term *comfort* is a multidimensional construct. The term *uncomfortable* is said to be synonymous with embarrassment, or nervousness (Kirkpatrick, 1994), unease, or disquiet (Pollard & Liebeck, 1994). The experience of discomfort when interacting with a homosexual client may not necessarily indicate that the health professional is homophobic. For example, they may not be confident working with clients whose background is different from their own and consequently may worry that they will not provide effective care. This does not necessarily mean the client will receive less than optimal care as the carer may seek out information and advice from more experienced peers.

However, it is suggested that if discomfort does lead to negative feelings, thoughts and behaviours toward homosexual clients then, by definition, the health professional is exhibiting homophobia. Additionally, homophobic individuals are said to display a range of affective responses, one of which is discomfort (Hudson and Ricketts, 1980).

Several researchers have examined comfort in clinical interactions that involve homosexual clients. Vollmer and Wells (1988) examined the anticipated level of comfort in first-year medical students when taking sexual histories from four types of clients. These included heterosexual women, heterosexual men, homosexuals (female and male combined), and clients with AIDS. Students anticipated being significantly more comfortable with heterosexual patients. More recently, Stokes and Mears (2000) found that nurses were more comfortable discussing sexual health issues with female patients and teenagers than with male patients and those of different sexual orientations.

THE STUDY

This study further investigated the attitudes of students enrolled in a number of health professional educational degree programs. These include physical therapy, occupational therapy, medical radiation sciences, rehabilitation counselling, leisure and health and behavioural health sciences. The study used a questionnaire that enabled the collection of information about the level of comfort for 19 items that have sexual implications, including anticipated comfort when working with female and male homosexual clients, and asking a client about his/her sexual orientation. We hypothesized that high levels of discomfort for these three items would be found in our large sample of students enrolled across these health professional education degree programs.

It is frequently argued that health professionals will be able to deliver appropriate health care if they are adequately prepared for a range of clinical interactions that have sexual implications (e.g., Giddings & Wood, 1998). Adamson, Harris and Hunt (1997) found that a variety of health professionals, including physical therapists and occupational therapists, reported being underprepared by their university education for interacting with clients whose backgrounds and cultures were different from their own. This study assessed the degree to which trainee health professionals considered their degree program to have effectively dealt with a number of sexually-themed items. These include asking a client about his/her sexual orientation, and working with a range of clients, including those who are homosexual. The relationship between education and levels of comfort for the homosexual items was also examined.

Sample

The sample consisted of 1132 students from a large metropolitan university in Sydney, Australia. Data collection occurred in 2000. Students were enrolled in undergraduate degrees in occupational therapy (n = 340), medical radiation sciences (n = 336), physical therapy (n = 333), rehabilitation counselling (n = 63), leisure and health sciences (n = 39), and behavioural health science (n = 19). Two students did not indicate the professional program in which they were enrolled. The mean age of the participants was 20.62 years (SD 3.64, Range 17-48). Approximately 84% were aged between 18 and 22 years and 78% of the participants were female. This gender distribution accurately reflects the largely female enrolment in health science degree programs. Twelve students did not indicate whether they were male or female. Approximately 39% of the students were in their first year of study, 25% were in their second year, 26% were in their third year and 11% were completing a fourth year of study. The seemingly low representation of students in their fourth year of study reflects the fact that occupational therapy and physical therapy were the only degree programs to have a fourth year at the time this study was conducted and half of fourth year physical therapy students were on clinical placement during the data collection period. Two students did not indicate their current year of study. Demographic characteristics are presented in Table 1.

Instrument

The instrument used for this study was based on the Comfort Scale Questionnaire developed by Cohen, Byrne, Hay, and Schmuck (1996). Results were analysed using SPSS version 10. Cronbach's alpha coefficient was calculated in order to determine the internal consistency reliability. The coefficient obtained was 0.8947 which indicates a high level of internal consistency in students' responses to the items in the questionnaire. The instrument consists of 19 items assessing anticipated levels of comfort in clinical interactions that have sexual implications. The items either involved how comfortable participants would feel dealing with a particular client group (such as a lesbian or male homosexual) or a particular situation (such as asking a client about his/her sexual orientation). Students were instructed to indicate how comfortable they felt for each item using a 5-point Likert-type scale ranging from 1

TABLE 1. Summary of Demographic Characteristics

Variable	N	%
Age		
Mean (Yr)	20.6	
SD	3.64	
Range	17 - 48	
Sex		
Male	245	21.9
Female	875	78.1
Degree		
Occupational Therapy	340	30.1
Medical Radiation Sciences	336	29.7
Physical Therapy	333	29.7
Rehabilitation Counselling	63	5.6
Leisure and Health Sciences	39	3.5
Behavioural Health Science	19	1.7
Year		
First	438	38.8
Second	277	24.5
Third	293	25.9
Fourth	122	10.8

(uncomfortable) to 5 (comfortable). Permission was obtained to adapt the questionnaire by asking students to indicate (yes/no) for each of the 19 items whether they believed their degree program had adequately dealt with the issue listed. First- and second-year students were considered not to have had sufficient educational training to provide a meaningful answer and their responses for the "dealt with" question were not included in the analyses.

Procedure

At the beginning of classes, students were invited by one of the researchers to participate in the study by completing the comfort questionnaire anonymously. Students completed the questionnaire during class time. A detailed subject information sheet was given to each participant and the project was approved by the University's human ethics committee.

RESULTS

Table 2 presents the percentage of all students who indicated that they would feel uncomfortable in dealing with particular types of clients or situations as well as the mean response and standard deviation. The items are arranged in order from highest to lowest level of discomfort. The percentages for each item represent the percentage frequency scores of students who endorsed numbers 1-3 (indicating discomfort) on the Likert-type scale. As can be seen from this table, the three items that students indicated as most uncomfortable were "Walking in on a patient/client who is masturbating" (92.7%), "Dealing with a patient/client who makes an overt sexual remark" (78.8%), and "Dealing with a patient/client who makes a covert sexual remark" (74.7%). The three items for which the least percentage of students indicated they would feel uncomfortable were "Homosexual male" (27.2%), "14-year-old female seeking contraception" (28.9%), and "Lesbian" (30.3%). Approximately 55% of the sample indicated they would feel uncomfortable when asking a client about his/her sexual orientation.

Table 3 presents the percentage of discomfort and mean scores and SD's for the three items for which students reported they would have the highest and lowest level of discomfort. Data for male and female students are presented separately. Fifty percent of male students and 20.6% of female students reported that they would feel uncomfortable working with a male homosexual client. For the item "lesbian" client, 26.3% of males and 31.5% of females expressed anticipated discomfort. These gender differences were analysed using t-tests to determine if the differences in anticipated comfort were significant.

TABLE 2. Percentages, Means and Standard Deviations of Students Reporting a Lack of Comfort When Dealing with Client/Situation

Question	%	M	SD
Walking in on a patient/client who is masturbating.	92.7	1.71	.99
Dealing with a patient/client who makes an overt sexual remark.	78.8	2.56	1.16
Dealing with a patient/client who makes a covert sexual remark.	74.7	2.75	1.13
Asking a patient/client about his/her sexual practice.	65.1	3.04	1.16
Asking a patient/client about his/her sexual experience.	63.8	3.06	1.20
Conducting a physical examination that involves exposure of the breasts or genitalia.	59.3	3.13	1.19
Asking a patient/client about his/her sexual orientation.	55.2	3.28	1.16
Male prostitute.	54.6	3.25	1.17
Answering patient/client questions on matters relating to sexuality.	51.2	3.44	.98
30-year-old married man identified as having gonorrhoea.	49.4	3.50	1.05
Person confirmed of having AIDS.	48.2	3.42	1.13
Person suspected of having AIDS.	47.3	3.47	1.07
Female prostitute.	45.0	3.53	1.08
70-year-old widow who is inquiring about sexual options.	44.3	3.55	1.13
21-year-old unmarried female seeking a second abortion.	42.1	3.62	1.12
Handicapped individual who is inquiring about sexual options.	34.7	3.82	1.04
Lesbian.	30.3	3.93	1.13
14-year-old female seeking contraception.	28.9	3.97	1.04
Homosexual male.	27.2	4.00	1.11

Female students indicated significantly higher levels of comfort in dealing with homosexual male clients than did their male counterparts (t = −8.878, df 323.791, p = .000). This result was reversed for the item concerning working with lesbian clients. Male students indicated significantly greater comfort in dealing with a lesbian client than did their female counterparts (t = 2.122, df 1102, p = .034).

Table 4 shows the percentage of third- and fourth-year students who believed their current degree program had not adequately dealt with the issues involved in each of the 19 items. Three quarters of these students believed that their degree program had not adequately dealt with a potential clinical interaction with a homosexual male. Almost 80% of students believed that their degree program had not adequately dealt with a potential clinical interaction with a lesbian client. The items involving working with a lesbian or a male homosexual client were ranked 10th and 12th of the 19 items with regard to being

TABLE 3. Percent Discomfort, Mean Scores and Standard Deviations by Gender for the Highest and Lowest Three Items on the Questionnaire

	Males			Females		
Question	%	M	SD	%	M	SD
Walking in on a patient/client who is masturbating.	86.3	2.01	1.28	94.5	1.62	.92
Dealing with a patient/client who makes an overt sexual remark.	78.8	3.21	1.14	84.1	2.38	1.09
Dealing with a patient/client who makes a covert sexual remark.	74.7	3.39	1.11	80.6	2.57	1.07
Lesbian.	26.3	4.06	1.05	31.5	3.89	1.14
14-year-old female seeking contraception.	35.3	3.78	1.11	27.0	4.02	1.02
Homosexual male.	50.0	3.39	1.28	20.6	4.18	.98

perceived by students as being the least dealt with in their degree program. Additionally, approximately 83% of participants believed that their degree program had not adequately dealt with the issue "asking a client about their sexual orientation." The item that the highest percentage of students indicated had been most adequately dealt with in their degree program was "a covert sexual remark" (55.2%). Interestingly, students endorsed the third lowest level of comfort for this item. The item that the lowest percentage of students endorsed as being adequately dealt with in their degree program was "working with a male prostitute." Ninety-five percent of students claimed their degree program has not adequately dealt with this issue. Yet interestingly, students endorsed more comfort with this item than for seven of the other items. Overall, more than 85% of students claimed that their degree program had not dealt adequately with the issue/client group entailed in seven of the 19 sexually themed items.

For the items "homosexual male" and "lesbian," the relationship between students' degree of comfort and whether these students believed their degree program had adequately dealt with these issues was analysed using Pearson Chi-Square analyses. For the item "male homosexual," there was no relationship between comfort level and dealt with, $[X^2(4, 1132) = 7.833, p = .98]$. Similarly, for the item "lesbian" there was no relationship between comfort level and dealt with, $[X^2 (4, 1132) = 6.533, p = .163]$. That is, comfort level was independent of whether students believed their degree program had adequately dealt with these issues.

TABLE 4. Percentage of Third- and Fourth-Year Students Who Believe Their Degree Program Did Not Deal Adequately with the Issue/Client Group

Item	%
Male prostitute.	95.3
Female prostitute.	92.2
Walking in on a patient/client who is masturbating.	89.2
14-year-old female seeking contraception.	88.0
21-year-old unmarried female seeking a second abortion.	87.8
30-year-old married man identified as having gonorrhoea.	86.7
Asking a patient/client about his/her sexual experience.	85.9
Asking a patient/client about his/her sexual practice.	83.5
Asking a patient/client about his/her sexual orientation.	82.5
Lesbian.	79.4
70-year-old widow who is inquiring about sexual options.	76.0
Homosexual male.	74.4
Answering patient/client questions on matters relating to sexuality.	70.5
Person suspected of having AIDS.	68.9
Person confirmed of having AIDS.	65.4
Handicapped individual who is inquiring about sexual options.	60.9
Conducting a physical examination that involves exposure of the breasts or genitalia.	60.6
Dealing with a patient/client who makes an overt sexual remark.	57.0
Dealing with a patient/client who makes a covert sexual remark.	55.2

DISCUSSION

The results of this study suggest that students anticipate least comfort when encountering explicit sexual behavior or discussion thereof. Nevertheless, as predicted, high levels of discomfort in addressing sexual orientation and/or working directly with gays and lesbians were identified in our large sample of students enrolled across a number of health profession education programs. While the items "working with a homosexual male" and "working with a lesbian" were two of three items with which students indicated they would anticipate having the most comfort, it is important to note that almost a third (30 percent) of the sample indicated they would be uncomfortable working with a lesbian client. Similarly, more than a quarter (27 percent) of the sample indicated that they would feel uncomfortable if working with a male homosexual client.

Health care delivery often requires direct and intimate contact with clients. Occupational therapists are often engaged in intimate activities including assessing clients while they are bathing and toileting (Couldrick, 1998; Schneider, Weerakoon, & Heard, 1999). Physical therapy usually involves direct contact with a patient's body. Tasks other health professionals in our sample may undertake include positioning patients for investigation and treatment procedures (radiographers) and detailed personal history taking (rehabilitation counsellors, leisure and health consultants and behavioral scientists). Therefore, it is expected that a degree of comfort is required when involved in such interactions. High student levels of anticipated discomfort towards interactions with homosexuals may translate as less than optimal client care when these students graduate and are working in their chosen occupations.

More than half of our sample indicated that they would not be comfortable asking about a client's sexual orientation. By avoiding asking about sexual orientation, the unique health needs of lesbian and gay clients may be overlooked and inaccurate assumptions may be made about a client's sexuality. For example, lesbian clients may feel embarrassed or alienated if a health provider assumes they are heterosexual and asks about contraceptive use. Clients may be hesitant to disclose their sexuality at a later point or ask questions if they believe that their sexuality has been placed outside the "norm."

We find it interesting that there were significant gender differences in anticipated comfort levels. These findings should be noted, as educational strategies to reduce discomfort may need to take into account the gender differences we observed. In regard to explicit sexual behavior or suggestive remarks, more women than men were uncomfortable and to a greater degree. In regard to sexual minority groups and teenage sex, more women than men were uncomfortable (except in regard to lesbians). Nevertheless, while five percent more women than men were uncomfortable with lesbians, approximately thirty percent more men than women reported that they would be uncomfortable treating a gay man. This is consistent with other findings on attitudes toward lesbians and gay men. Males consistently have more negative attitudes toward gay men than females toward gay men (Herek, 1984; Sullivan, 1998).

In this study we investigated whether the education of our trainee health professionals was perceived to satisfactorily cover sexuality issues like homosexuality. We found that at least three quarters of senior students believed that their degree program had not adequately dealt with issues concerning working with lesbians and gay male clients and asking a client about their sexual orientation. When looked at in light of the low levels of comfort for all items on the Comfort Scale Questionnaire (Cohen et al., 1996), it seems that students feel unprepared to deal with a range of future clinical interactions that have sexual implications.

However, the relationship between level of comfort and extent to which students perceived their degree program to have dealt with sexual issues was not a straightforward one. Our findings did not endorse the view that students will anticipate feeling more comfortable working with lesbians or gay men if they have a strong belief that their degree program had adequately dealt with these topics. Comfort level did not appear to be related to a student's perception of adequate coverage of these issues in their degree program. This appears consistent with the research of Berkman and Zinberg (1997) who found no relationship between amount of education about homosexuality-related topics and levels of homophobia and heterosexism. Similarly, Gilchrist et al. (1997) found that a series of lectures on HIV disease actually raised the level of anxiety and discrimination against people living with AIDS.

Other researchers have suggested that educational strategies *are* important in decreasing homophobia (e.g., Cramer, Oles, & Black, 1997; Eichstedt, 1996; Herek, 1984). While there is a paucity of research investigating the effectiveness of these interventions in health professional student samples, some authors have presented findings in support of this proposition (see further, Ben-Ari, 1998; Cramer, Oles, & Black, 1997; Serdahely & Ziemba, 1984). The findings from these studies indicate that attitude change is possible.

Low levels of comfort across a range of sexually themed items, including those related to homosexuality, were found in our large sample of health professional students. It is suggested that this is potentially detrimental for both students and clients. Future research that clarifies the utility of different educational interventions may increase our understanding of how to reduce this phenomenon. Clearly, there is a need for further investigation of the origin and nature of discomfort and the ways in which it can be decreased.

Finally, a limitation of this study is that measures of homophobia commonly utilized such as the Index of Homophobia (Hudson & Ricketts, 1980) were not employed. While we have argued that discomfort and homophobia are related terms, future exploration of the relationship between the two needs to be conducted. Specifically, both the Comfort Scale Questionnaire (Cohen et al., 1996) and homophobic measures should be used in the same sample.

AUTHOR NOTES

Dr. Jones is a senior lecturer in the School of Behavioural and Community Health Sciences, The University of Sydney and a registered psychologist. Her main areas of research include human sexuality and the nature, origin and treatment of anxiety. She has been the Acting Director of the University of Sydney's Anxiety Disorders Clinic and is currently Co-Director of the Australian Centre for Gay and Lesbian Research.

Rosemary Anne Pynor is a community psychologist and is completing a PhD investigating the role of voluntary support groups for people with genetic disorders. She lectures in the psychosocial aspects of physical disability including sexuality as well as conflict management and negotiation, and she is a committee member of the Australian Psychological Society's Women and Psychology Interest Group (E-mail: R.Pynor@cchs.usyd.edu.au).

Dr. Sullivan's recent publications include *Gay and Lesbian Asia: Culture, Identity and Community* and *Multicultural Queer: Australian Narratives*, both published by The Haworth Press, Inc. He is on the editorial boards of *Journal of Homosexuality* and *Journal Gay & Lesbian Social Services* (E-mail: g.sullivan@edfac.usyd.edu.au).

Patricia Weerakoon's primary research interest is in the area of sexuality and client-health professional interactions. She is also involved in the development and implementation of sexuality education for health professionals (E-mail: P.Weerakoon@cchs.usyd. edu.au).

REFERENCES

Adamson, B. J., Harris, L. M., & Hunt A. (1997). Health science graduates: Preparation for the workplace. *Journal of Allied Health, 26,* 187-199.

Albarran, J. W., & Salmon, D. (2000). Lesbian, gay and bisexual experiences within critical care nursing, 1988-1998: A survey of the literature. *International Journal of Nursing Studies, 37,* 445-455.

Ben-Ari, A. T. (1998). An experiential attitude change: Social work students and homosexuality. *Journal of Homosexuality, 36,* 59-72.

Berkman, C. S., & Zinberg, G. (1997). Homophobia and heterosexism in social workers. *Social Work, 42,* 319-332.

Cohen, G. S., Byrne, C., Hay, J., & Schmuck, M. L. (1996). An 18-month follow-up on the effectiveness of a sexuality workshop: Some methodological pitfalls. *Journal of Sex & Marital Therapy, 22,* 3-8.

Couldrick, L. (1998). Sexual issues: An area of concern for occupational therapists. *British Journal of Occupational Therapy, 61,* 493-496.

Coyle, C. L., & Young, E. W. (1998). Affective sexuality education in graduate nurse practitioner programs in the United States. *Journal of Sex Education and Therapy, 23,* 62-69.

Cramer, E., Oles, T. P., & Black, B. M. (1997). Reducing social work students' homophobia. *Arete, 21,* 36-49.

D'Augelli, A. R. (1989). Fears and homophobia among rural nursing personnel. *AIDS Education and Prevention, 1,* 277-284.

Eichstedt, J. L. (1996). Heterosexism and gay/lesbian/bisexual experiences: Teaching strategies and exercise. *Teaching Sociology, 24,* 384-388.

Gallop, R., McCoy, E., Cote, F. H., Garley, D., Harris, J., & Vermilyea, D. (1993). A scale to measure nurses' comfort working with clients who have been sexually abused. *The International Journal of Psychiatric Nursing Research, 1,* 15-20.

Giddings, L. S., & Wood, P. J. (1998). Revealing sexuality: Have nurses' knowledge and attitudes changed? *Nursing Praxis in New Zealand, 13,* 11-25.

Gilchrist, H., Sullivan, G., & Heard, R. (1997). Attitudes of Australian physiotherapy students towards AIDS. *Physiotherapy Theory and Practice, 13,* 265-278.

Hayter, P. (1996). Is non-judgmental care possible in the context of nurses' attitudes to patients' sexuality? *Journal of Advanced Nursing, 24,* 662-666.

Herek, G. M. (1984). Beyond "homophobia": A social psychological perspective on attitudes toward lesbians and gay men. *Journal of Homosexuality, 10,* 1-21.

Hudson, W. W., & Ricketts, W. A. (1980). A strategy for the measurement of homophobia. *Journal of Homosexuality, 5*, 357-372.

Jemmott, J. B., Freleicher, J., & Jemmott, L. S. (1992). Perceived risk of infection and attitudes toward risk groups: Determinants of nurses' behavioral intentions regarding AIDS patients. *Research in Nursing & Health, 15*, 295-301.

Kirkpatrick, B. (1994). *The Oxford Paperback Thesaurus.* London: Oxford University Press.

Klamen, D. L., Grossman, L. S., & Kopacz, D. R. (1999). Medical student homophobia. *Journal of Homosexuality, 37*, 53-63.

Laumann, E. O., Michael, R. T., & Gagnon, J. H. (1994). A political history of the national sex survey of adults. *Family Planning Perspectives, 26*, 34-38.

Morrissey, M., & Rivers, I. (1998). Applying the Mims-Swenson sexual health model to nurse education: Offering an alternative focus on sexuality and health care. *Nurse Education Today, 18*, 488-495.

Payne, M. J., Greer, D. L., & Corbin, D. E. (1988). Sexual functioning as a topic in occupational therapy training: A survey of programs. *American Journal of Occupational Therapy, 42*, 227-230.

Pollard, E., & Liebeck, H. (1994). *The Oxford Paperback Dictionary.* London: Oxford University Press.

Rose, L. (1994). Homophobia among doctors. *British Medical Journal, 308*, 585-587.

Schneider, J., Weerakoon, P., & Heard, R. (1999). Inappropriate client sexual behaviour in occupational therapy. *Occupational Therapy International, 6*, 176-194.

Serdahely, W., & Ziemba, G. (1984). Changing homophobic attitudes through college sexuality education. *Journal of Homosexuality, 10*, 109-116.

Smith, G. B. (1993). Homophobia and attitudes toward gay men and lesbians by psychiatric nurses. *Archives of Psychiatric Nursing, 7*, 377-384.

Stevens, P. E. (1993). Lesbian health care research: A review of the literature from 1970 to 1990. *Health Care for Women International, 13*, No. 2. Reprinted in P. N. Stern (Ed.), *Lesbian Health: What are the issues?* (pp.158-169). Washington DC: Taylor & Francis.

Stevens, P. E. (1994). Lesbians' health-related experiences of care and non-care. *Western Journal of Nursing Research, 16*, 639-659.

Stevens, P. E., & Hall, J. M. (1990). Abusive health care interactions experienced by lesbians: A case of institutional violence in the treatment of women. *Response to the Victimisation of Women and Children, 13*, 23-27.

Stokes T., & Mears, J. (2000). Sexual health and the practice nurse: A survey of reported practice and attitudes. *British Journal of Family Planning, 26*, 89-92.

Sullivan, G. (1998 October 28-29). *Health professionals' attitudes toward lesbian and gay clients.* Paper presented at the Health Sciences Research Conference, held in Leura, Australia.

Sullivan, G., & Waite, H. (1997). Fact or fantasy: Educating health professionals about lesbian and gay clients In J. Richters, I. R. Duffin, J. Gilmour, J. Irwin, R. Roberts, & A. Smith (Eds.), *Health In Difference: Proceedings of the first national lesbian, gay, transgender and bisexual health conference.* Sydney: Australian Centre for Lesbian and Gay Research, University of Sydney. (pp. 165-171).

Vollmer, S. A., & Wells, K. B. (1988). How comfortable do first year medical students expect to be when taking sexual histories. *Medical Education, 22,* 418-425.

Weerakoon, P., & Stiernborg, M. (1996). Sexuality education for health care professionals: A critical review of the literature. *Annual Review of Sex Research, 7,* 181-217.

Wilton, T. (1999). Towards an understanding of the cultural roots of homophobia in order to provide a better midwifery service for lesbian clients. *Midwifery, 15,* 165-176.

Wisniewski, J., & Toomey, B. G. (1987). Are social workers homophobic? *Social Work, 32,* 454-455.

Lesbians, Gays and Religion:
Strategies for Challenging Belief Systems

Bernie Sue Newman

SUMMARY. This study measured the effects of religious affiliation and gender on attitudes about lesbians and gay men among 2,846 college graduates who were beginning graduate study in social work or counseling. Males were more negative than females in their attitudes toward both lesbians and gay men. Conservative Protestants were the most negative in their attitudes toward lesbians and gay men, while those who were Atheist, Agnostic, Jewish or claimed no religion were most positive. Beliefs that the Bible forbids homosexuality are discussed and readings and arguments challenging this belief that can be used as class content are presented. *[Article copies available for a fee from The Haworth Document Delivery Service: 1-800-HAWORTH. E-mail address: <getinfo@haworthpressinc.com> Website: <http://www.HaworthPress.com> © 2002 by The Haworth Press, Inc. All rights reserved.]*

KEYWORDS. Religion and attitudes toward lesbians and gay men, social work and counseling students' attitudes

Bernie Sue Newman, MSW, PhD, is Associate Professor, Temple University, School of Social Administration, 13th and Cecil B. Moore Avenue, 505 Ritter Hall Annex, Philadelphia, PA 19122 (E-mail: bernie.newman@temple.edu).

[Haworth co-indexing entry note]: "Lesbians, Gays and Religion: Strategies for Challenging Belief Systems." Newman, Bernie Sue. Co-published simultaneously in *Journal of Lesbian Studies* (Harrington Park Press, an imprint of The Haworth Press, Inc.) Vol. 6, No. 3/4, 2002, pp. 87-98; and: *Addressing Homophobia and Heterosexism on College Campuses* (ed: Elizabeth P. Cramer) Harrington Park Press, an imprint of The Haworth Press, Inc., 2002, pp. 87-98. Single or multiple copies of this article are available for a fee from The Haworth Document Delivery Service [1-800-HAWORTH, 9:00 a.m. - 5:00 p.m. (EST). E-mail address: getinfo@haworthpressinc.com].

Those who identify with conservative religions or who express a high degree of religiosity have consistently been found to hold negative attitudes toward homosexuals and homosexuality (Herek, 1988; Larsen, Cate & Reed, 1983; Levitt & Klassen, 1974; Schope & Eliason, 2000). Those who do not identify with an organized religion and those who are non-orthodox Jews, Unitarian, Presbyterian, Congregational or Episcopalian have been found to hold relatively more accepting attitudes (Alston, 1974; Herek, 1988; Irwin & Thompson, 1977; Nyberg & Aston, 1977).

The empirical data reported in this study reflect the influence that gender and religious affiliation have on a large sample of college graduates entering a masters degree program in social work or counseling. It is particularly desirable that social workers and counselors accept lesbians and gay men since they have a professional responsibility to work effectively with members of this group. The level of acceptance when entering graduate counseling and social work degree programs reflects a useful baseline for teaching about professional work with lesbians and gay men. In addition, an understanding of the influence of student attributes associated with homophobia is necessary to address the issues with which students may struggle in the process of attitude change.

RELIGION

Members of Conservative Christian religions have consistently been found to express negative attitudes toward homosexuality. Herek (1984) concluded that those with less favorable attitudes toward lesbians and gay men are more likely to subscribe to a conservative religious ideology. In 1974, Alston reported that between 76% and 88% of his sample of Baptists, Methodists, and Lutherans believed that homosexuality is always wrong. In the same study, between 27% and 41% of Jews, Episcopalians, or those with no religious affiliation responded that homosexuality is not wrong at all. Nyberg and Alston (1977) and Irwin and Thompson (1977) found that Conservative Protestants and Catholics reported less tolerance than either Jews, Episcopalians and those with no religious affiliation. Herek's (1987a) study of 205 undergraduates found that negative attitudes toward gays and lesbians were related to a "self-expressive function," meaning those attributes that reinforce self-conception and identity, one of which might include religious affiliation. Respondents with these negative attitudes were more likely than those expressing positive attitudes to attend religious services at least once monthly, to belong to a conservative religious denomination[1] and to endorse an orthodox religious ideology. Schope and Eliason (2000) found that their respondents were more likely to participate in homophobic behaviors when they reported fundamentalist or conservative religious beliefs. Even as homosexuality becomes increasingly accepted in American society, those who identify with a conservative religion continue to be among those who espouse negative attitudes toward lesbians and gay men.

GENDER

Males have been found to express more negative attitudes toward lesbians and gay men than females in many recent studies (Ben-Ari, 2001; Hogan & Rentz, 1996; Kite & Whitley, 1998; Simoni, 1996). Herek (1988) showed a consistent tendency for heterosexual males to express more hostile attitudes than heterosexual females, especially toward gay men. Lieblich and Friedman (1985) found that both Israeli and American men were more homophobic than their female counterparts. Schope and Eliason (2000) reported that males in their study tended to participate in homophobic behaviors more than females did.

Two studies were found that reported no relationship between gender and attitudes toward lesbian and gay persons. Black, Oles and Moore (1998) found no gender differences in homophobia among their 331 social work students. Wells and Daly (1992) reported no gender effects among their sample of 177 undergraduate students at a midwestern university.

An additional issue regarding gender and attitudes toward homosexuals is the relationship between gender of subject and gender of attitude object. A number of studies have found that males express more negative attitudes toward gay men than they do toward lesbians (Herek, 1988; Kerns & Fine, 1994; Kite & Whitley, 1998; Kyes & Tumbelaka, 1994; Simoni, 1996; Weinberger & Milham, 1979). However, these same studies have reported mixed results on female attitudes toward lesbians. In some studies, females report more negative attitudes toward lesbians than toward gay men (Herek, 1988; Kyes & Tumbelaka, 1994; Weinberger & Milham, 1979), while other studies demonstrate no difference between female attitudes toward lesbians compared to their attitudes toward gay men (Kerns & Fine, 1994; Kite & Whitley, 1998; Simoni, 1996).

Previous research on attitudes toward lesbians and gay men among social workers and counselors suggests that a notable percentage of those entering either profession express negative attitudes. Bieschke, McClanahan, Tozer, Grzegorek, and Park (1999) provide an historical review of counseling professionals' attitudes toward gay men, lesbians, and bisexuals. In many of these earlier studies, counselors tended to pathologize gay men and lesbians

(Garfinckel & Morin, 1978). DeCrescenzo (1984) compared the levels of homophobia among 140 mental health practitioners and found that social workers scored at the highest level of homophobia, while psychologists were found to be the least homophobic. Wisnewski and Toomey (1987) provided an early survey of 71 social workers in which a third expressed homophobic attitudes. Weiner (1989) found that her sample of 125 senior social work students from five universities was more homophobic than sexist or racist. Berkman and Zinberg (1997) report that approximately 10% of the 187 practicing social workers responding to their study could be considered homophobic and that a majority of their respondents expressed some heterosexist attitudes.

Acceptance of diversity and its correlates are of special concern to counseling and social work graduate programs. Preparing those entering the fields of social work and counseling for work with lesbian and gay clients is a necessary part of education for professional competence and effectiveness. It was the purpose of this study to identify the types of attitudes expressed by a cohort of college graduates upon entry into a master-level program in social work or counseling and to determine the influence of gender and religious affiliation on these attitudes. It is important to understand the present influence of these two attributes of students because they have consistently been found to correlate with levels of homophobia and attitudes toward lesbians and gay men. Some additional knowledge about the strength of association between these attributes and attitudes could be useful in developing curriculum to address factors that may affect professional social work and counseling practice.

METHODS

Participants and Recruitment Procedures

Participants for the investigation consisted of college graduates who had been accepted into an accredited master-level social work or counseling program in the United States. A list of accredited M.S.W. programs ($N = 127$) was obtained from the Council on Social Work Education (C.S.W.E.) Web site in January, 1999. A list of Council for Accreditation of Counseling and Related Education Programs accredited counseling programs ($N = 129$) was obtained from the Spring 1999 issue of *The Journal of Counseling and Development*. Students were eligible to participate in the study if they were newly admitted to their respective program.

Faculty members or administrators responsible for admissions were contacted by telephone prior to the onset of the 1999-2000 academic year. Fifty-three social work and 29 counseling programs arranged for the administration and return of the questionnaires. The informed consent form was attached to the questionnaire and distributed during the orientation or first class meeting. The purpose of the study was explained as the first stage of a pre-test post-test investigation of attitudes toward lesbians and gay men among beginning graduate students in social work and counseling with the post-test administered upon completion of their degrees. Participating students then completed the survey. The surveys were returned to the faculty member who then sealed a return-postage-paid envelope, which was mailed to the principal investigator. Approximately 5,622 questionnaires were sent out to the 82 schools that participated in the study; 2,846 questionnaires were returned producing a response rate of 50.6%.

The age range of the sample was 20 to 63; average age was 30.23 (*s.d..* = 8.96). Racial distribution for the sample was 77.5% Caucasian (*n* = 2,332); 10% African-American (*n* = 302); 7.5% Latino (n = 210); and 5.5% Asian American (*n* = 164). Those respondents who categorized themselves as bi-racial (*n* = 27), American Indian (*n* = 19) and West Indian (*n* = 8) were not included because of the small sample size for each. The gender distribution over-represented women with 84% female, 16% male. There were 2,585 of the completed questionnaires in which the respondent reported a sexual orientation of heterosexual. The 261 responses (9.17%) in which a lesbian, gay, or bisexual orientation was reported were not used since the population of interest is heterosexual students.

Measures

The survey packet consisted of an informed consent form, demographic items, and the 20-item scale of attitudes toward lesbians and gay men.

Demographic Form. Participants completed a demographic form comprising items pertaining to their master's degree of study, gender, age, religion, undergraduate major, race, and sexual orientation. With the exception of degree of study, all demographic choices were open-ended. The respondents named over 200 religious preferences. Based on the suggestions of Roof and McKinney (1987) and the classifications Herek (1987b) used, the religions were collapsed into six categories: (1) Catholic; (2) Jewish; (3) no religion; (4) Liberal Protestant; (5) Moderate Protestant; (6) Conservative Protestant. Religions that did not fit into these categories were not included in the analysis.

Attitudes Toward Lesbians and Gay Men. The Attitudes Toward Lesbians and Gay Men Scale (ATLG) (Herek, 1988) served as the measure of affective response to lesbians and gay men in this study. The ATLG is a 20-item self-report measure originally administered as a nine-point Likert-type scale. The first ten items comprise a subscale that measures respondents' attitudes toward lesbians and the last ten items can be viewed as a subscale which assesses respondents' attitudes toward gay men. Participants in this study were asked to respond to the 20-items using a 7-point Likert-type scale (1 = strongly agree; 7 = strongly disagree). Seven items were reverse-coded so that higher scores are indicative of more positive attitudes toward lesbians and gay men.

The ATLG has excellent reliability. Coefficient *alpha* estimates range from .80 to .94 for the full scale (Berkman & Zinberg, 1997; Herek, 1987a, 1987b, 1988; 1994; Herek & Glunt, 1991). Test-retest reliability has been shown to be .90 (Herek, 1988; 1994). Herek (1988) also found support for the discriminant validity of the ATLG in that it differentiated between individuals who supported and who did not support a local gay rights initiative. Despite the change to the Likert-type range, sample reliability for the 20-item scale in this study was good (*Alpha* coefficient = .95).

RESULTS

The mean score on the seven-point Attitudes Toward Lesbian and Gay Men Scale for the 2,585 heterosexual respondents was 5.62 (*s.d.* = 1.34). This reflects an average score in the low- to mid-positive range. Individual mean scores ranged from the most negative (all 1.00s) to the most positive (all 7.00s), with 7.00 being the modal or most frequent score. All of this suggests a relatively positive set of attitudes toward lesbians and gay men among these college graduates entering a helping profession. Nearly seven percent (6.7%; n = 173) of the sample, however, expressed negative attitudes. These respondents received a score of 3.0 or less; that is, below the midpoint of neutral.

Male respondents' scores were significantly lower and therefore more negative than female respondents' scores on the two subscales. The male *mean* on the attitudes toward lesbians sub-scale was 5.54; *s.d.* = 1.42 and the female *mean* on attitudes toward lesbians was 5.84; *s.d.* = 1.21 ($t = -3.85$; $df = 510$; $p < .001$). Similarly, the male *mean* on attitudes toward gay men was 4.98; *s.d.* = 1.73 while the female *mean* was significantly more positive at 5.53; *s.d.* = 1.45 ($t = -6.08$; $df = 518$; $p < .001$).

A general linear model ANOVA was computed with religious affiliation and gender as the fixed factors and attitudes toward lesbians and gay men as the dependent variable (see Table 1). The two factors, religious affiliation and gender, accounted for close to 20% of the variance in attitudes toward lesbians and gay men (*Adjusted R^2* = .197). Religious affiliation played the strongest role, accounting alone for almost 14% of the variance in attitudes toward lesbians and gay men (*eta^2* = .139). There was no significant interaction between religious affiliation and gender.

TABLE 1. Analysis of Variance on Attitudes Toward Lesbians and Gay Men

	Sum of Squares	df	F*	Significance	Eta²
Religion	557.76	5	75.76	.000	.139
Gender	31.52	2	1.41	.000	.009
Religion × Gender	15.09	5	2.05	ns	.004

Adjusted R² = .197

*Error variance of the dependent variable was found to be significantly different according to Levene's Test of Equality of Variances ($F = 46.39$; $df1 = 11$; $df2 = 2354$, $p < .001$). Therefore, for post-hoc tests, Dunnet's *C*, in which equality of variances are not assumed, was used.

Males were more negative in their attitudes toward lesbians and gay men than were females (male *mean* = 5.31, *S.E.* = .12; female *mean* = 5.73; *S.E.* = .05; *p* < .05). Conservative Protestants were the most negative in their attitudes toward lesbians and gay men, while those who were Atheist, Agnostic, Jewish or claimed no religion were most positive. Liberal Protestants and Catholic respondents were more accepting than moderate or conservative Protestants (*p* < .05) (see Table 2).

DISCUSSION AND IMPLICATIONS

On average, this sample of college graduates entering a master-level program in social work or counseling expresses relative acceptance of lesbians and gay men. Individual scores range from most negative to most positive, but cluster in the positive range. A minority of respondents expresses attitudes that were mostly negative. Overall, however, almost 86% of the sample scored on the positive side of the seven-point continuum. Thus, most students seeking graduate degrees in social work and counseling in this study reflect the national tendency to be accepting reported by Yang (1999). Only 6.7% express mostly negative beliefs about lesbians and gay men.

In addition, gender differences were found in both expressions of attitudes and attitude object. Attitudes toward gay men in the overall sample were significantly more negative than attitudes toward lesbians. Males expressed more negative attitudes toward gay men than lesbians did; while female respondents expressed more positive attitudes toward both lesbians and gay men when compared to males. It is not surprising that men expressed more negative atti-

TABLE 2. Religion and Attitudes Toward Lesbians and Gay Men

Religion	Mean Score	Std. Deviation	n
Conservative Protestant	4.19*	1.54	97
Moderate Protestant	5.04**	1.53	916
Liberal Protestant	5.86	1.19	190
Catholic	5.89	0.98	691
None, Atheist or Agnostic	6.32***	0.78	349
Jewish	6.30***	0.14	123

*statistically more negative at $p < .05$ from all other groups.
**statistically more negative at $p < .05$ from Liberal Protestant or Catholic.
***statistically more positive at $p < .05$ from all other groups.

tudes toward gay men than lesbians since this has been a relatively consistent finding in past studies. Females in this sample, however, had more positive attitudes than males about both lesbians and gay men. Perhaps, this reflects gender differences such as more liberal gender role attitudes usually expressed by women than by men. Previous studies have found that gender role attitudes or sexism can be an important correlate of attitudes toward gays and lesbians, especially for men who hold restrictive gender role attitudes (Harry, 1995; Kite & Whitley, 1996; Newman, 1989a).

Religious affiliation was also found to be influential in this sample's degree of acceptance. Those who identified with Conservative Protestant religions scored significantly more negatively in their attitudes toward lesbians and gay men. What are conservative religious beliefs that promote the development of negative attitudes toward lesbians and gay men? Appleby (1995) points out that several possible references to the disapproval of homosexuality have been identified from Judeo-Christian scripture. Boswell (1980) provides a scholarly rebuttal of each one of these that could be used in a classroom.

Boswell asserts that the only place in the Old Testament where homosexual acts are mentioned is Leviticus. He argues that the Hebrew word translated as *abomination,* to describe "a man [who] lie[s] with mankind as he lieth with a woman," usually refers to "an infringement of ritual purity," that which distinguishes Jewish believers from other people, such as not keeping traditional dietary laws or not being circumcised (1989, pp. 100-101).

Boswell (1980) identifies the passages in the New Testament that are often used as prohibitions against homosexuality or arguments that homosexuals will not "enter the kingdom of heaven." He argues that the passages in Corinthians and Timothy in the writing of Paul could refer as readily to heterosexual persons or activities as to homosexual ones. He asserts that the point of the passage written by Paul in Romans is to censure infidelity, not homosexuality.

McNeil (1993) calls for a reappraisal of the traditional moral position of the Catholic Church and asserts that the limitations on pastoral practice imposed will be destructive of the majority of Catholic homosexuals who attempt to live according to the directives of the Catholic church. His book provides a key resource for examining the validity of religious beliefs to justify prejudice. He reviews many scholars' treatment of the passages in the Old and New Testaments often cited as dealing with homosexuality.

Appleby (1995) summarizes arguments made that counter many Biblical references used to castigate homosexuality. Van Wormer, Wells and Boes (2000) provide an inset called "What the Bible Says About Homosexuality" that in short form dispels many of the arguments often used from the Bible. These readings could be used to examine beliefs that students may have been socialized to express, although perhaps not carefully investigated.

Although this approach might be helpful with some students, others may not reconsider their interpretation of the morality of homosexual behavior. Another way to reach students could be to provide information, personal contact, and knowledge about the group. Cramer, Oles and Black (1997) found that religion and religiosity became less important correlates of attitudes about lesbians and gay men following all four versions of providing information, speakers, and readings about lesbian and gay issues. This suggests that relevant information, experiences and knowledge may also challenge belief systems.

The limitations of this study should be considered, which include a nonrandom sample with a low response rate. Since only religious affiliation was measured, it is not discernible if degree of religiosity played a role. Relationships between attitudes and professional social work or counseling behavior were not assessed. Known correlates such as personal contact with lesbians and gay men were not controlled for in the sample. The large sample size, while helpful in avoiding Type II errors, makes it likely that between group differences would be statistically significant even if effect sizes were moderate or low. The group of college graduates was selected based on their entering graduate programs in social work and counseling and therefore are not representative of college graduates in general.

Nevertheless, the study shows that the majority of college graduates entering a master program in social work or counseling hold positive attitudes toward lesbians and gay men. However, a minority of these students holds negative attitudes about a group with whom they will need to work. Curricula designed to prepare students to work in any helping profession must include content that educates graduates on working with sexual minorities. Strategies for effectively teaching about lesbian and gay issues, in social work and counseling, already exist in the literature (for examples see Buhrke, 1989; Cramer et al., 1997; Murphy, 1992; Newman, 1989b).

Curriculum development in other fields may also need to include content that challenges prejudicial thinking and stereotypes. Educational experiences cannot and should not dictate attitudes or beliefs. Education at the college level can build abilities to critically examine beliefs to uncover their underlying assumptions. It is our responsibility as educators to offer accurate information, alternative interpretations and a scholarly dialogue that challenges beliefs founded upon hate and intolerance of any population.

NOTE

1. Herek (1987b) classified these denominations as conservative: Latter Day Saints (Mormons), Seventh Day Adventist, Catholic, Baptist, Lutheran, Orthodox and Conservative Jewish, Methodist, and Christian fundamentalist sects.

REFERENCES

Alston, J. (1974). Attitudes toward extra-marital and homosexual relations. *Journal for the Scientific Study of Religion, 13*, 479-481.

Appleby, G. A. (1995). AIDS and homophobia/heterosexism. *Journal of Gay & Lesbian Social Services, 2*(3/4), 1-23.

Ben-Ari, A. T. (2001). Homosexuality and heterosexism: Views from academics in the helping professions. *British Journal of Social Work, 31*, 119-130.

Berkman, C.S., & Zinberg, G. (1997). Homophobia and heterosexism in social workers. *Social Work, 42*, 4, 319-335.

Bieschke, K. J., McClanahan, M. Tozer, E., Grzegorek, J. L., & Park, J. (2000). Programmatic research on the treatment of lesbian, gay, and bisexual clients. In R. M. Perez, K. A. Debord, & K. J. Bieschke (Eds.) *Handbook of counseling and therapy with lesbian, gay, and bisexual clients* (pp. 309-336). Washington, D.C.: American Psychological Association.

Black, B., Oles, T. P., & Moore, L. (1998). The relationship between attitudes: Homophobia and sexism among social work students. *Affilia, 13*(2), 166-189.

Boswell, J. (1980). *Christianity, social tolerance, and homosexuality.* Chicago: The University of Chicago Press.

Buhrke, R. A. (1989). Incorporating lesbian and gay issues into counselor training: A resource guide. *Journal of Counseling and Development, 68*, 77-80.

Cramer, E., Oles, T., & Black, B. N. (1997). Reducing social work students' homophobia: An evaluation of teaching strategies. *Arete, 21*, 36-49.

DeCrescenzo, T. (1984). Homophobia: A study of the attitudes of mental health professionals toward homosexuality. *Journal of Social Work and Human Sexuality, 2*, 115-136.

Garfinckel, E. M., & Morin, S. F. (1978). Psychologists' attitudes toward homosexual psychotherapy clients. *Journal of Social Issues, 34,* 101-112.

Harry, J. (1995). Sports ideology, attitudes toward women and anti-homosexual attitudes. *Sex Roles, 32*(1-2), 109-116.

Herek, G. M. (1984). Beyond "homophobia": A social psychological perspective on attitudes toward lesbians and gay men. *Journal of Homosexuality, 10,* 1-21.

Herek, G. M. (1987a). Can functions be measured? A new perspective on the functional approach to attitudes. *Social Psychology Quarterly, 50,* 285-303.

Herek, G. M. (1987b). Religion and prejudice: A comparison of racial and sexual attitudes. *Personal and Social Psychology Bulletin, 13,* 56-65.

Herek, G. M. (1988). Heterosexuals' attitudes toward lesbians and gay men: Correlates and gender differences. *The Journal of Sex Research, 25*(4), 451-477.

Herek, G. M. (1994). Assessing attitudes toward lesbians and gay men: A review of empirical research with the ATLG Scale. In B. Greene & G. M. Herek (Eds.). *Lesbian and gay psychology: Theory, research and clinical applications* (pp. 206 228). Thousand Oaks, CA: Sage Publications.

Herek, G. M., & Glunt, E. K. (1991). AIDS-related attitudes in the United States: A preliminary conceptualization. *The Journal of Sex Research, 28,* 99-123.

Hogan, T. L., & Rentz, A. L. (1996). Homophobia in the academy. *College Student Development, 37,* 309-314.

Irwin, P., & Thompson, N. (1977). Acceptance of the rights of homosexuals. *Journal of Homosexuality, 3*(2), 107-121.

Kerns, J. G., & Fine, M. A. (1994). The relation between gender and negative attitudes toward gay men and lesbians: Do gender role attitudes mediate this relation? *Sex Roles, 31,* 297-307.

Kite, M. E., & Whitley, B. E. (1996). Sex differences in attitudes toward homosexual persons, behavior and civil rights: A meta-analysis. *Personality and Social Psychology Bulletin, 22,* 336-353.

Kite, M. E., & Whitley, B. E. (1998). Do heterosexual women and men differ in their attitudes toward homosexuality? A conceptual and methodological analysis. In G. M. Herek (Ed.). *Stigma and sexual orientation: Understanding prejudice against lesbians, gay men and bisexuals* (pp. 39-51). Thousand Oaks, CA: Sage Publications.

Kyes, K. B., & Tumbelaka, L. (1994). Comparison of Indonesians and American college students' attitudes toward homosexuality. *Psychological Reports, 74,* 227-237.

Larsen, K. S., Cate, R., & Reed, M. (1983). Anti-black attitudes, religious orthodoxy, permissiveness and sexual information: A study of the attitudes of heterosexuals toward homosexuals. *Journal of Sex Research, 19*(2), 105-118.

Levitt, E., & Klassen, A. (1974). Public attitudes toward homosexuality: Part of the national survey by the Institute for Sex Research. *Journal of Homosexuality, 1,* 29-43.

Lieblich, A., & Friedman, G. (1985). Attitudes toward male and female homosexuality and sex-role stereotypes in Israeli and American students. *Sex Roles, 12,* 561-571.

McNeil, J. J. (1993). *The Church and the homosexual* (4th edition). Boston: Beacon Press.

Murphy, B. C. (1992). Educating mental health professionals about gay and lesbian issues. *Journal of Homosexuality, 25*, 229-246.

Newman, B. (1989a). The relative importance of gender role attitudes to attitudes toward lesbians. *Sex Roles, 21*(7/8), 447-461.

Newman, B. (1989b). Including curriculum content on lesbian and gay issues in the social work curriculum. *Journal of Social Work Education, 25*, 202-211.

Nyberg K., & Alston, J. P. (1977). Analysis of public attitudes toward homosexual behavior. *Journal of Homosexuality, 2*(2), 99-107.

Roof, W. C., & McKinney, W. (1987). *American mainline religions: Its changing shape and future*. New Brunswick, NJ: Rutgers University Press.

Schope, R. D., & Eliason, M. J. (2000). Thinking versus acting: Assessing the relationship between heterosexual attitudes and behaviors toward homosexuals. *Journal of Gay & Lesbian Social Services, 11*, 69-92.

Simoni, J. M. (1996). Pathways to prejudice: Predicting students' heterosexist attitudes with demographics, self-esteem and contact with lesbians and gay men. *Journal of College Student Development, 37*, 68-78.

van Wormer, K., Wells, J., & Boes, M. (2000). *Social work with lesbians, gays and bisexuals: A strengths perspective*. Boston: Allyn and Bacon.

Weinberger, L. E., & Millham, J. (1979). Attitudinal homophobia and support of traditional sex roles. *Journal of Homosexuality, 4*(3), 237-247.

Weiner, A. (1989). Racists, sexist and homophobic attitudes among social work students and the effects on assessment of client vignettes. *Dissertation Abstracts International, 50*, 3741.

Wells, J., & Daly, A. (1992). University students' felt alienation and their attitudes toward African-Americans, women and homosexuals. *Psychological Reports, 70*(2), 623-626.

Wisniewski, J. J., & Toomey, B. G. (1987). Are social workers homophobic? *Social Work, 32*, 454-455.

Yang, A. (1999). *From wrongs to rights: Public opinion on gay and lesbian Americans moves toward equality*. Washington, DC: Policy Institutes of the National Gay and Lesbian Task Force.

A Lesbian/Straight Team Approach to Changing Attitudes Toward Lesbian, Gay, Bisexual, and Transgendered People

Becky J. Liddle
Angela M. Stowe

SUMMARY. Advantages of a lesbian/heterosexual team approach to education on lesbian, gay, bisexual and transgender issues are examined and a case study is analyzed. A lesbian guest lecturer provided a contact experience, personal anecdotes, passion, and expertise. Facilitation of later class discussion by the heterosexual instructor allowed for frank discussion among students, processing of presentation content, and modeling of gay-affirmative attitudes by the instructor and other students. Summaries of the guest lecture (fantasy exercise and informational lecture) and later discussion are provided. Student comments during discussion demonstrated evidence of deep challenge, attitude change, and heightened understanding. *[Article copies available for a fee from The Haworth Document Delivery Service: 1-800-HAWORTH. E-mail address: <getinfo@haworthpressinc.com> Website: <http://www.HaworthPress.com> © 2002 by The Haworth Press, Inc. All rights reserved.]*

Becky J. Liddle, PhD, is Associate Professor, Department of Counseling and Counseling Psychology, Auburn University, Auburn, AL 36849-5222 (E-mail: liddlbj@auburn.edu).

Angela M. Stowe, PhD, was a doctoral candidate, Counseling and Counseling Psychology, Auburn University, when this article was written. She is now a counselor at the Counseling and Wellness Center at the University of Alabama at Birmingham, Birmingham, AL 35294-2100 (E-mail: amstowe@uab.edu).

[Haworth co-indexing entry note]: "A Lesbian/Straight Team Approach to Changing Attitudes Toward Lesbian, Gay, Bisexual, and Transgendered People." Liddle, Becky J., and Angela M. Stowe. Co-published simultaneously in *Journal of Lesbian Studies* (Harrington Park Press, an imprint of The Haworth Press, Inc.) Vol. 6, No. 3/4, 2002, pp. 99-108; and: *Addressing Homophobia and Heterosexism on College Campuses* (ed: Elizabeth P. Cramer) Harrington Park Press, an imprint of The Haworth Press, Inc., 2002, pp. 99-108. Single or multiple copies of this article are available for a fee from The Haworth Document Delivery Service [1-800-HAWORTH, 9:00 a.m. - 5:00 p.m. (EST). E-mail address: getinfo@haworthpressinc.com].

KEYWORDS. Homosexuality (attitudes toward), attitude change, sexual orientation, homophobia, college students

Early in the twentieth century we already knew that processing of information was important for learning (Dewey, 1938). Recent theories of attitude change such as dual processing theories and the cognitive miser metatheory all theorize the centrality of processing in attitude change (Chaiken, 1980, Petty & Cacioppo, 1981, and Fiske & Taylor, 1984, as cited in Johnston & Coolen, 1995). Despite this, many attempts at improving attitudes toward lesbian, gay, bisexual, and transgendered (LGBT) people have been one-shot informational interventions, with no opportunity for processing. It is perhaps no surprise, then, that results of these interventions have been mixed. For example, two articles report LGBT panels that produced significant attitude change (Green, Dixon, & Gold-Neil, 1993; Lance, 1987), whereas a third was found to be ineffective (Cotten-Huston & Waite, 2000). The successful LGBT panels involved extended processing–either a three-hour question and answer period (Lance) or informal conversation in addition to the formal presentation (Green, Dixon, & Gold-Neil). Cotten-Huston and Waite, whose panel was found to be ineffective in changing attitudes, speculated afterward that "perhaps an intervention time period that allowed for more discussion and greater exploration of issues would have a greater chance of producing effective change" (p. 126).

The sexual orientation of the presenter may also be important. Cramer (1997) found more attitude change when an educational unit was presented by an out lesbian than when presented by an out heterosexual woman. Contact with LGBT people has been shown to be linked to positive attitudes (e.g., Cotten-Huston & Waite, 2000) and to have positive effects on attitudes (Case & B. Liddle, 2001).

This article describes an approach that included both ingredients: a lesbian presenter and opportunities for processing of information and reactions. A lesbian counseling psychology professor experienced in doing education about LGBT issues provided a guest lecture in an undergraduate Counseling and Human Services course attended by students in pharmacy, nutrition and dietetics, family development, and psychology. The following week the heterosexual instructor conducted a class discussion, inviting the students to process their reactions to the presentation. Anecdotal comments during that discussion indicated that the combination of the presentation and the follow-up discussion were remarkably effective in changing some students' attitudes.

Inviting an LGBT panel or guest lecturer to an undergraduate course is commonplace. What seemed uniquely powerful in this case study was the combination of the presentation with a follow-up discussion led by the heterosexual course instructor the following week. This team approach has a number of advantages. First, the heterosexual instructor need not have tremendous LGBT expertise. Second, homophobic students often see LGBT presenters as being self-serving or biased. Because credibility of presenter is an important factor in attitude change (Johnson & Coolen, 1995), having the discussion led by a heterosexual may provide more credibility with some students. The facilitator also serves as a gay-affirmative role model. Having a discussion with the lesbian presenter absent allows students to speak more freely, allowing homophobic students an opportunity to process their reactions, which is an important part of the attitude change process. Finally, holding this frank discussion in the absence of the presenter is merciful for her. Doing anti-homophobia education in conservative environments is exhausting work, and no matter how strong one's self-esteem, it is insulting and tiring to hear contempt for oneself and one's people. A heterosexual ally can facilitate the discussion without taking (as much) personal offense at negative attitudes expressed.

GUEST LECTURE
(NARRATOR: BECKY LIDDLE)

Having a gay or lesbian presenter offers several advantages. In this case, I am not only an expert in the area (as LGBT research is my area of research) but I also provide the class with a visible example of a professionally successful lesbian. This is important in combating the stereotypes of homophobic students and also in providing role models for LGBT students. Having a lesbian presenter also allows access to a level of passion as well as personal anecdotes that might not be available to many heterosexual lecturers.

To engage students actively in my presentation I begin with a fantasy and values clarification exercise in which students find themselves on a planet where nearly everyone is gay, and straight people are oppressed. (See Appendix for full text.) After the fantasy is read, the students must stand beneath one of four signs indicating how they would live their lives in this situation. All four options have serious drawbacks. If students want to offer a fifth option I let them, but I insist that all students make some choice. When they begin to grumble, I say "You're right. They all suck." This both gets a laugh and also makes the point that there are no good options for coping with stigma. When explaining their choices, students invariably refer back to their values, personalities, and/or their life situations. I point out that, because values and circumstances vary from person to person, decisions about stigma management will also vary.

After students return to their seats I begin my lecture by stating that every major professional mental health organization has come out officially as gay-affirmative and I read a statement from at least one. This helps combat the view that I have no official sanction for my gay-affirmative views, which are seen as radical on this conservative Alabama campus. I cover use of gay-affirmative language, then give a brief overview of the typical coming out process. I explicitly come out as a lesbian at this point, using my own coming out process as an example. I believe that being open about my sexual orientation is an important part of the intervention, both because contact with LGBT people can have positive effects on attitudes (Case & B. Liddle, 2001), and also because being able to use personal experiences brings the lecture alive.

Next I summarize the research on the causes of sexual orientation, stating that there is no credible evidence for social/parenting theories (e.g., any correlation between rejecting fathers and gay sons is more parsimoniously explained by fathers rejecting non-traditional sons than by sons somehow becoming gay because of a distant father), and that research shows some biological basis (e.g., identical twin research showing high concordance). Covering the biological evidence is important because belief that sexual orientation is a choice is correlated with negative attitudes (e.g., K. Liddle, 2000).

After ten years of giving these presentations, I have come to believe that (at least at this university, where 44% of undergraduates believe that *the Bible is the actual word of God and it should be taken literally, word for word*; K. Liddle, 2000), no lecture on LGBT issues can hope to be effective without addressing certain Bible verses. In this lecture I referred to 1 Peter 2:18: "Slaves, submit yourselves to your masters with all respect, not only to those who are good and considerate, but also to those who are harsh" and discussed how it was used for hundreds of years to justify slavery. I said I was sure that no one now sees any Bible quote as a justification for slavery, but that, taken out of context, certain Bible verses are very convenient for people who are looking to justify their behavior. I then mention various oft-cited passages from the Bible and explain how misinterpretation or mistranslation has led to the impression that they condemn gay and lesbian people. This content is taken from Helminiak (1994). I say repeatedly that my goal in talking about the Bible is to let them know that there is no conflict between being a good Christian and being a gay-affirmative teacher, counselor, social worker, etc. I refer interested (and skeptical) students to Helminiak's book, which our university library purchased at my request. Reinterpreting Bible verses allows fundamentalist Christians to maintain their literal interpretation of the Bible while questioning the view that the Bible clearly condemns homosexuality.

I come prepared to talk about additional topics: legal issues including discrimination and marriage, medical issues, parenting, community resources, etc. However, I encourage students to ask questions, and allow them to guide the remainder of my lecture. In my responses I try to be both informative and

personal–not only outlining the abstract issues but also saying how these issues have affected my own life and those of my friends.

FOLLOW-UP DISCUSSION FACILITATED
BY HETEROSEXUAL ALLY
(NARRATOR: ANGELA STOWE)

At the beginning of the discussion, students expressed very negative reactions to the LGBT lecture. Many said that they believed the presenter was trying to "shove her opinion down their throats" and trying to "force them to
believe what she believed." One student said she was so upset that after class
she went home and called her mother and cried for an hour because she could-
n't believe that she "had to listen to that in a class." Another said "I wasn't even
going to participate in the exercise. I didn't want to get out of my seat. I could-
n't believe she was having us think about such things. I don't agree with it and I
didn't want to participate in it." Students also said they did not like how she
challenged their religious beliefs when she discussed the Bible. Throughout
this portion of the discussion, I let them vent their feelings without challenging
them. I empathized (without agreeing with their assessments) by saying repeatedly that I understood that this was a difficult topic and was very upsetting
to them. I would say that I could see they were shaken by it, or that they had
very strong feelings. I refrained from challenging their opinions to allow for
the discharge of the negative emotion. This restraint was difficult, but I knew
that until they felt heard they would be unable to move on to a new understanding of the experience.

After extensive venting of feelings, I moved the discussion on, asking what
they found helpful about the presentation, and what new insights they had
gained. Students admitted that the presentation challenged them to think about
issues they had not considered before. I acted primarily as a facilitator, inviting
other students to contribute their opinions when some view needed to be challenged. For example, when a student said, "if someone came to me and told me
that she thought she was a lesbian, it is my job as a believer to witness to her–I
would have to tell her that it is a sin," I asked what other students thought. Two
students, identifying as fellow Christians, said that telling someone that they
are sinning will not help the person and might turn that individual away. When
a student began monopolizing the discussion I would say something like, "So
you believe that homosexuality is a sin because of your strong religious background. Who can respond in light of what Dr. Liddle shared last week?"

Most of the time, I did not offer my personal opinions. However, occasionally I felt I had to intervene. At one point I reminded the class that they were

choosing human services professions where it would be their job to help the individuals who come to them in need. I stated, "As a human service professional, it is not your job, responsibility, or right to judge clients or patients. It is unethical to impose personal values on anyone. If you encounter clients with whom you have value conflicts which will impede your ability to serve them effectively, it is your responsibility to refer them to someone who can help them."

By the end of class, each student in the class had participated at least once, most students more than once. By the end of the discussion, some students seemed to show dramatic attitude change. The student who at first said he had almost refused to participate in the fantasy exercise stated, "I changed my mind. I've thought about it and if I had to do what she [the presenter] did, I wouldn't do it any differently. I wouldn't hold back anything. I would tell it how it is. I would do exactly what she did." In response, another student, who had also initially disagreed with the presentation said, "Yeah, that really takes guts to talk about it the way she did." Another student said, "I bet she wanted us to feel intense emotions. Maybe she was trying to provoke a response out of us." Other students reported that the presentation helped them understand how the lives of LGBT people are affected by prejudice and discrimination. These comments came from the same students who, at the beginning of the discussion, had emphatically stated that they were offended by the presentation.

Some students showed evidence of greater understanding of LGBT issues. For example, close to the end of the discussion, one student said that she had a gay friend who was not publicly out and she "now would understand if he decided to never come out." Another student demonstrated new understanding by admitting that she had not thought about how saying something like "so tell me, are you dating anyone . . . what's *he* like?" could send a message that she was not open to a lesbian relationship. A student who works in a daycare setting said in the past she had asked children about their "mom and dad." She now realized that she needed to be aware of how she asked children about their parents. Students also said that they had not thought about the issues raised in the presentation such as health care, questions about marital status on forms, insurance, and marriage issues. Several students also reported how beneficial the presentation was in helping them understand the daily issues faced by LGBT people. The progression of the discussion from anger to discussion to learning and attitude change was exciting to watch, and convinced us of the efficacy of this team approach. It is possible that some positive student statements were the result of trying to please the instructor, who was clearly gay-affirmative. However, the fact that students felt free to express their homophobic attitudes early in the discussion suggests that the stated changes in their views were likely legitimate.

CONCLUSION AND DIRECTIONS FOR FUTURE RESEARCH

This article discusses a team approach to changing students' attitudes concerning LGBT people: the combination of a guest lecture by a lesbian professor and a follow-up discussion facilitated by a heterosexual instructor. Although no formal attitude assessment was conducted, student comments during the discussion seemed to indicate that this combination resulted in attitude change and greater understanding of LGBT issues among some students. We believe that scientific advances can emerge from serendipitous events. We hope that the anecdotal evidence of the effectiveness of this team approach will result in more formal research assessing its impact. To be of greatest use to future educators such research should have a qualitative component (examining students' beliefs about the impact of various components on their attitudes) as well as the more typical quantitative (pre-test/post-test) component. While quantitative studies can be useful in demonstrating effectiveness, without qualitative components determining *which parts* of the interventions were and were not effective, other presenters have little guidance in formulating their own programs. We have presented details of our program to aid those readers who might be interested in approximate replication of various parts. However, we have no illusions that the exact content of this presentation and discussion form some magical whole that is more effective than many other programs. We believe (based on student comments during the discussion) that the important aspects of this program were the presence of a lesbian presenter, a frank and engaging presentation that maintained student interest and challenged their existing views, and the opportunity to process their reactions with a trusted heterosexual facilitator. We hope that our positive experience with this formula will induce others to try this approach and to research its impact on student attitudes.

REFERENCES

Case, A. B., & Liddle, B. J. (2001, August). Factors integral to valuing diversity among majority group members. Paper presented at the annual convention of the American Psychological Association, San Francisco, CA.

Cotten-Huston, A. L., & Waite, B. M. (2000). Anti-homosexual attitudes in college students: Predictors and classroom interventions. *Journal of Homosexuality, 38,* 117-133.

Cramer, E. P. (1997). Effects of an educational unit about lesbian identity development and disclosure in a social work methods course. *Journal of Social Work Education, 33,* 461-472.

Dewey, J. (1938). *Experience and education.* New York: Collier Books.

Green, S., Dixon P., & Gold-Neil, V. (1993). The effects of a gay/lesbian panel discussion on college student attitudes toward gay men, lesbians, and persons with AIDS (PWAs). *Journal of Sex Education and Therapy, 19,* 47-63.

Helminiak, D. A. (1994). *What the Bible* really *says about homosexuality.* San Francisco: Alamo Square.

Johnston, L., & Coolen, P. (1995). A dual processing approach to stereotype change. *Personality & Social Psychology Bulletin, 21,* 660-674.

Lance, L. M. (1987). The effects of interaction with gay persons on attitudes toward homosexuality. *Human Relations, 40,* 329-336.

Liddle, K. (2000). *Close encounters: Visibility and acceptance of gays and lesbians.* Unpublished master's thesis, Auburn University, Auburn, AL.

McNaught, B. (1993). *Gay issues in the workplace.* New York: St. Martin's Press.

APPENDIX:
Fantasy Exercise

(Adapted from a fantasy by Brian McNaught, 1993, pp. 18-23)

"I'm going to walk you through a fantasy. It'll take about 10 minutes. At the end I'll ask you to make some decisions about how you would live your life. I'll ask you to share those decisions and why you made them. (For this exercise we need to assume you are heterosexual. If you are gay, lesbian, or bisexual, please pretend for the duration of this exercise that you are heterosexual.) . . . Relax. As I read, try to imagine what this situation would really feel like.

"Tomorrow you wake up, stretch, look around, get your bearings, and realize that *your entire life, as you now experience it, has been a dream.* Your heart sinks as you remember that on *your* planet, nearly everyone is gay or lesbian. You're still heterosexual, but everyone you know is gay or lesbian. Virtually all public figures are either gay or pretend to be. Your parents (both are male if you're male; both are female if you're female) are gay or lesbian, as are your siblings. All children on your planet are created through cloning, and only same-sex couples are allowed to reproduce. (If you find a clinic that *will* clone known heterosexuals, and you manage to have a baby, the government may take your child away if they find out you're heterosexual. After all, how could anyone be a fit parent to a child of a *different gender?* Anyone in their right mind could see *that's* not natural!) You've *heard* there are other heterosexual people, but they are despised. You don't know any other heterosexuals yourself and don't know where to find them.

"You realize that the life you dreamed on earth was just wishful thinking–you just wanted to be yourself, and belong. So you created this happy dream world where everyone else was like you. But in fact, *you are alone*. You are, sadly, a heterosexual, and (although you've tried to convince yourself otherwise) you know you cannot change that.

"You know your parents assume you're gay and would be terribly hurt and worried if they knew you were attracted to members of the other gender. Your religious leaders tell you attraction between different genders is unnatural and sick . . . yet you *know* it feels right to you. You only get romantic feelings toward members of the other sex, and the idea of making love to someone of your own gender sounds disgusting to you.

"Up until now you've tried to fake it to please your parents and friends and society. You've tried dating others of your gender, and you like them OK, but you never fall in love. You've even tried to have sex, but the idea of sex with someone of your gender turns your stomach. You nearly always bail out before you get far. You did follow through and have gay sex once, and it was awful. Afterwards you felt dirty and shameful and shaky.

"You went to a counselor and confessed you are attracted to members of the other gender. The counselor was supportive and told you that's OK–that heterosexuality is natural for many people, but that life as a heterosexual is hard–you'll face ostracism and discrimination in housing and work, and some occupations will be completely closed to you. You realize you have some difficult choices to make:

"You could find someone of your own gender that you like OK, and marry, and hope they won't want sex very often. But the idea of that kind of sex makes you queasy, and the idea of sharing your life with someone you're not in love with makes you sad.

"You could stay single forever. Resign yourself to having no one to be your companion through life, and to having no children, though you long for them.

"You think perhaps you'd better live true to yourself as a heterosexual. But you know if you live openly, you will lose many of your friends and possibly be rejected by your family. You cannot be a teacher or minister or serve in the military. In most other fields you can find a job eventually, but many employers will not hire you if they know you're heterosexual, and if you don't tell them up front, and they find out later, you may lose your job. Most landlords won't rent to known heterosexuals, so if you can't afford to buy, it may be hard to find an apartment to rent. You may find your true love, but life will be hard. You'll get threatening phone calls, you'll be called perverts, your children (if you manage to have any) will be harassed at school, or may be taken away entirely.

"You're not sure you're up for all that, so you think maybe you'll live a heterosexual life, but secretly. That would be easier on your family and friends and career. But then you realize how lonely that would be. You'd be unlikely to find a lover–they wouldn't know you were heterosexual and vice versa, and so you might never find each other. You could settle for going to sleazy heterosexual bars and picking up partners, but you're unlikely to find your true love. You could go into any career you like, but you'd have to stay on guard–if you have a life partner or someone you're dating, you cannot mention them at work. When people ask what you did over the weekend or on vacation you'll have to be very vague, or lie. If you ever are discovered, your career may be ruined. Your parents will constantly ask if you're dating, and will worry about you. Your friends will constantly try to fix you up with people–always people of your own gender of course. No one–not even your closest friends–will know you very well, because you have to screen everything you say, to keep up the pretense of being normal.

"You've looked at all your options and none looks very appealing: Be open about your heterosexuality and face contempt and discrimination; be secret about your heterosexuality and be lonely and scared; or fake it to fit in: either by marrying someone of your own gender, or by staying single forever. These are tough choices. I'm very sorry you had the misfortune to be born heterosexual, but you were. Which option will *you* choose?

"Please look at the four signs in the four corners of the room. These are your options. Choose one of these options and go to that corner of the room. Then I'd like you to share why you made the decision that you did." [As I tape up the four signs I read them aloud:] [1] "I would stay closeted but would try to find a (hidden) community of heterosexuals, probably mostly in sleazy heterosexual bars. I would be lonely, but I could have a successful career, as long as I'm very careful." [2] "I would stay closeted and marry a gay person of my gender and have gay sex and a family. This might not be fair to my partner (who will be hurt that I hate sex so much and will always love me more than I love them), but this is the only way I know to have a family and I really want kids." [3] "I would come out as a heterosexual and work to end discrimination against people like me. I would be discriminated against in housing and work and church, and I may be rejected by my family, but I have to be true to myself." [4] "I would stay closeted and stay single and celibate forever. I would give up my chance of ever having a spouse or children."

PART III
PRACTITIONER TRAINING PROGRAMS

Practitioner Training
for Counseling Lesbian, Gay,
and Bisexual Clients

Melissa A. Lidderdale

SUMMARY. The combined effects of heterosexual bias and lack of formal training on lesbian, gay, and bisexual (LGB) issues are hypothesized to manifest inappropriate mental health practitioner behaviors. Research on graduate therapist training and student attitudes has found heterosexual bias and inadequacies in preparation to serve LGB clients. The need for graduate level training of mental health practitioners is apparent. This article reviews recommended training methods for providing training in LGB issues. A psychoeducational model developed to concurrently increase trainee awareness, knowledge, and skills in counseling LGB people is presented. Suggestions for implementation of curricula and strategies for use in addressing heterosexism in the training environment are also provided. *[Article copies available for a fee from The Haworth Document Delivery Service: 1-800-HAWORTH. E-mail address: <getinfo@ haworthpressinc.com> Website: <http://www.HaworthPress.com> © 2002 by The Haworth Press, Inc. All rights reserved.]*

Melissa A. Lidderdale, MA, is a doctoral student in the Department of Counselor Education and Counseling Psychology at Western Michigan University. She gratefully acknowledges the support of Joy Whitman in the development of this article.

Address correspondence to: Melissa A. Lidderdale, 3102 Sangren Hall, Western Michigan University, Kalamazoo, MI 49008 (E-mail: melissa.lidderdale@wmich. edu).

[Haworth co-indexing entry note]: "Practitioner Training for Counseling Lesbian, Gay, and Bisexual Clients." Lidderdale, Melissa A. Co-published simultaneously in *Journal of Lesbian Studies* (Harrington Park Press, an imprint of The Haworth Press, Inc.) Vol. 6, No. 3/4, 2002, pp. 111-120; and: *Addressing Homophobia and Heterosexism on College Campuses* (ed: Elizabeth P. Cramer) Harrington Park Press, an imprint of The Haworth Press, Inc., 2002, pp. 111-120. Single or multiple copies of this article are available for a fee from The Haworth Document Delivery Service [1-800-HAWORTH, 9:00 a.m. - 5:00 p.m. (EST). E-mail address: getinfo@haworthpressinc.com].

KEYWORDS. Gay, lesbian, bisexual, counselor, training

When considering barriers to professional therapy services, a special focus has been on the obstacles faced by minority and oppressed people including increased interest in issues regarding barriers to appropriate psychotherapeutic services for lesbian female, gay male, and bisexual female and male (LGB) individuals. Research has suggested that LGB clients have experienced a range of inappropriate counselor practices that reveal homophobia or heterosexism (Garnets, Hancock, Cochran, Goodshilds, & Peplau, 1991; Liddle, 1996, 1997; Moss, 1995). Studies focused on graduate training of students in mental health professions have found evidence of heterosexual bias and inadequate training for therapists in dealing with sexual minorities (e.g., Liddle, 1995; Phillips & Fischer, 1998; Pilkington & Cantor, 1996). The combined effects of heterosexual bias and lack of formal training on LGB issues have been hypothesized to manifest in inappropriate practitioner behaviors in addressing the needs of LGB clients.

Inappropriate and discriminatory practitioner behaviors when working with LGB clients are in violation of the codes of ethics and practice guidelines of mental health organizations (e.g., American Counseling Association, 1995; American Psychological Association, 1992; National Association of Social Workers, 1996). Thus, specific graduate level training of mental health practitioners to address the concerns of LGB people in an unbiased manner is warranted. Several different formats for providing training in LGB issues have been suggested for mental health professional trainees. Incorporation of LGB issues into every course in a training program, focused practicum and group experiences, and a total class devoted to the topic are the formats discussed in the literature (Buhrke & Douce, 1991; Phillips, 2000; Whitman, 1995). Beyond incorporation across the training curricula, programs need to focus in-depth on LGB issues to further develop student competency and preparedness for working with LGB clients.

A course specific to mental health concerns of LGB people that utilizes didactic and experiential instructional methods offers an effective way to focus more in-depth on the experiences of LGB people, challenge participants to explore their own attitudes regarding sexual orientation, and raise awareness of societal oppression. Research on attitudes and bias toward LGB people suggests that student self-exploration is an integral part of effective training for counselors (Iasenza, 1989; Murphy, 1991; Phillips, 2000). This article presents a psychoeducational model developed to concurrently increase trainee awareness, knowledge, and skills in counseling LGB people. This article also provides suggestions for implementing the described model in academic programs so future mental health professionals are more prepared to meet the needs of LGB clients.

PROPOSED PSYCHOEDUCATIONAL COURSE DESIGN

The exploration of internal beliefs and values is crucial even for LGB iden-tified students since all students are influenced by social forces including ho-mophobia and heterosexism. If one-time exposure workshops and groups are effective with creating student sensitivity (Rudolph, 1989; Whitman, 1995), then utilizing and expanding on these formats would be beneficial due to more in-depth content coverage within a course structure. I designed this course to utilize a variety of teaching modalities–didactic, multi-media, speaker panels, role playing, and other experiential activities–to increase graduate student awareness of the history and current issues facing LGB people. The models presented by Murphy (1991) and Whitman (1995) shaped the development of the model presented in this article.

Murphy (1991) proposed the use of three components of training: informa-tion, interplay, and interaction. The *interplay* component of training involves increasing student awareness to the link between the individual, sexuality, and society. The *interaction* component involves experiential student exploration of attitudes and comfort level concerning sexual orientation. Whitman (1995) incorporated experiential methods in her course model to intentionally create affectional reactions to the new information. Both Murphy and Whitman sug-gest using a variety of teaching methods such as fictional readings, music, lec-tures, films, role-plays, experiential activities, and field research.

The model of training proposed in this article builds upon the work of previ-ous authors and adds an intentional focus on systematic facilitation of group discussion and processing of the information and experiences. I have adapted activities and strategies from the curricula proposed by Whitman (1995) and from experience in co-facilitation of LGB programming presented in counsel-ing practicum courses. The uniqueness of the design is the intentional combin-ing of group, relational, nurturance, and change theories together with a focus on experiential learning and traditional LGB curricula. Discussions about the information presented and "in the moment" experiences of the students are the major components of this course. The class structure is similar to a psychoeducational group, in which the instructor is responsible for facilitating student participation and group development while also teaching. The nature of the course design requires a small class size and caution on the role of the in-structor to maintain a psychoeducational focus versus a therapeutic focus.

The relational component of the course structure is based on feminist and social learning ideals regarding the power and influence of relationships. Relational influence can contribute encouragement and accountability toward the development of LGB affirmative attitudes, beliefs, and skills. A major premise is that professionals and students can acquire and strengthen these LGB affirmative qualities through socialization. In accordance with Iasenza's observation that "education is a socialization process that imparts values of the dominant culture" (p. 73, 1989), it would seem advantageous to create a culture within the profession, or even specific institution, to socialize students and impart LGB affirmative values. The group structure functions to facilitate relationships between students and to create an environment of respect and safety for students to explore their beliefs regarding sexual orientation. Schreier and Werden (2000) discuss nurturance theory and the importance of creating an environment in which the beliefs of each student are treated with respect and challenged in a manner that preserves the dignity of the student as a person.

Each student in the course will have somewhat different needs in regard to increasing her or his awareness regarding LGB issues. Tyler, Jackman-Wheitner, Strader, and Lenox (1997) describe how to apply the Transtheoretical Model of Change as a framework for assessing student readiness to change heterosexist beliefs and/or attitudes. The proposed course model utilizes this framework to assess stage of change for students in order to make adjustments to better meet student needs. An initial assessment of student stage of change begins in the first session with gathering information from each student regarding their personal goals for participating in the course, current knowledge and attitudes about LGB issues, and willingness to take risks. Students in the pre-contemplation stage are unaware or confused regarding the need to change their behavior or attitudes toward LGB people. Students in the contemplation stage are aware of the negative impact of heterosexism and oppression on LGB people. Students in the action stage are ready to learn and practice new LGB-affirmative behaviors and attitudes. Students in the maintenance stage continue to change and seek support from other people for the change that has occurred.

The course design is structured to expose students to activities that could facilitate their movement through the stages of change. Activities early in the course focus on addressing the needs of students in pre-contemplation and contemplation stages. Activities later in the course focus on the needs of students in the action and maintenance stages. However, the overall focus of the course could be adjusted to account for the unique needs of the students. For example, if a majority of the students have limited exposure to LGB people and issues, then these students could benefit from more course time focused on experiential and basic information aimed at facilitating student movement from pre-contemplation to contemplation.

General Structure

The course is designed to be an elective graduate level course for pre-internship graduate students in a mental health professional training program (e.g., counseling, psychology, social work). The course instructor must be a trained mental health professional who possesses expertise in group practice and LGB issues. The major educational objective for the course is to increase awareness of attitudes toward LGB people, knowledge of LGB people and unique concerns, and skills in counseling LGB clients across the lifespan. Recommended prerequisite qualifications for students include multicultural and counseling technique courses. These prerequisites are important because they provide the student with basic counseling skills and a multicultural context to further their understandings of more complex LGB issues (e.g., identity development, multiple oppression).

A psychoeducational course design has the potential for ethical dilemmas. The student members must be educated at the start of the course on the format, risks of participation, and expectations. Potential risks of participating in the course should be discussed in the first session (e.g., there is no guarantee of confidentiality; change in beliefs and attitudes may influence relationships outside of the course). Student evaluation in the course is based on participation and completion of written assignments, such as reaction papers and a final "Coming-Out" paper. The reaction papers include student reaction to material and activities across the physical, intellectual, and emotional experiential domains. The "Coming-Out" paper is the student's identity development story as an LGB person or ally.

Education Sessions

The format of each session contains the following elements: opening, information presentation, experiential activities, and discussion. The sessions focus on interaction with the didactic information and become less structured as the course progresses. Session topics and activities are outlined in the Appendix. Descriptions of experiential activities are available from the author and additional experiential activities are available from a variety of sources (e.g., Schreier & Werden, 2000). The beginning four sessions of the course focus on basic information and exploration of student attitudes that are designed to meet needs of students falling in the late pre-contemplation to early contemplation stages of change.

The first session of the course is extremely important in developing the tone and expectations. The instructor explains the course guidelines to the students and facilitates an introduction activity where the students share their names, programs of study, and reasons for taking the course. Prior to the information presentation, the students are requested to participate in a values clarification exercise that allows students to express their beliefs and attitudes before being exposed to course material. Information from both activities informs the assessment of student readiness for change. Session two begins with the experiential activity called "One Degree of Separation" and then addresses a historical perspective of sexual orientation. Session three focuses on sexual identity development and management with a focus on bisexual identity development (see Firestein, 1996; Klein, 1993). Through challenging students to question dichotomous views of sexual orientation, the complexity of sexual orientation is highlighted. Session four emphasizes the normal developmental themes for LGB people in relationships and family.

Sessions five and six are designed to meet the needs of students in the contemplation stage of change through more detailed information and contact with LGB people. Session six addresses diversity within the LGB population and provides opportunity for personal interaction with LGB people. Sessions seven and eight are designed to meet the needs of students in the early action to maintenance stages of change. Session seven focuses on mental health issues and learning LGB affirmative counseling techniques. Using sample LGB client cases, students apply LGB affirmative skills to case conceptualization and role-play in small groups. Session eight is devoted to closure activities for the course. Students are encouraged to share from their "Coming-Out" papers and/or what they have gained from taking the course. The "Coming-Out" paper incorporates learning from the course and contains the student's identity development story (as LGB or ally) with regard to the physical, mental, social, sexual, emotional, and spiritual aspects of coming out. The final student activity is writing a final reaction and commitment to one activity they will do in the next three months to continue learning about LGB concerns. The song "Everything Possible" (Small, 1993) is played as students write.

IMPLEMENTATION AND DISCUSSION

I was leader of an instructional team that taught a modified version of the described course design. Some of the content and activities were altered from the above general model in order to accommodate time constraints and student needs. The university where this course model was implemented was located in an urban area that had an active LGB student group and LGB community, thus indicating some degree of supportive attitudes toward LGB people. The implementation of this course was pursued by graduate students who recognized the deficits in their training programs in regard to LGB concerns. The following are highlights from the three-session seminar as observed by students and instructors.

The first course session proved extremely important in setting the tone for the educational experience. Time in the first session was devoted to creating an affirmative environment for the students by decorating the room with symbols from the LGB community, sharing instructor backgrounds, and engaging in other introductory activities. I disclosed my lesbian sexual orientation and the other instructors disclosed their identities as LGB allies. As facilitator of the discussion during the values clarification activity, I intentionally encouraged students to share views that were not held by the majority of students. The purpose of illustrating the unpopular views was to acknowledge that those values exist and to communicate a sense of safety for anyone who may have secretly held those values. Reaction papers from the first session of the seminar reflected that students appreciated the values clarification activity, felt comfortable with each other and the instructors, and had concerns regarding their lack of knowledge about LGB people. Based on the fact that students had elected to take the course and the information shared by the students during the first session, the students were assessed to be in the late pre-contemplation or contemplation stages of change in regard to LGB issues.

Student feedback suggested that the second and third sessions elicited emotional responses and in-depth examination of student attitudes. The second education session was conducted at the local LGB community center where LGB members shared stories of success in the face of oppression and ways that counselors and psychologists could contribute to the strengths of LGB and transgender (LGBT) people. This session was designed to function as the interaction component as described by Murphy (1991). After the panel members left, students were provided an opportunity to interact with each other as they explored their reactions to contact with LGBT people. Students indicated that this event was the most valuable of the seminar because, for many, it was the first interaction with LGBT people. This time spent discussing reactions at the end of the session allowed the students to share on a more personal level with each other, thus strengthening the relational component of the course.

During the last session, students discussed affectional reactions to the video segment and shared feedback for the course experience. They shared feelings of uncertainty about their competency to counsel LGB people. Student writings revealed that they did not feel competent to participate in the counseling role-plays due to all they had learned but had not processed yet. Overall, the students in this seminar reported a lack of coverage of LGB issues in their core courses and indicated that they would have benefited from a longer LGB-focused course. Many students suggested a full three-credit course. Students indicated strengths of the course as the experiential activities, structure, and efforts of the instructors to create a "safe" environment to explore the information. The creation of this safe environment through application of relational and nurturance notions resulted in the students feeling comfortable discussing LGB issues. Course discussions and student writings became more personal and revealing as the course progressed, suggesting that students were not as likely to withhold negative views at the end of the course. The only negative feedback received was that the course was not long enough.

The general psychoeducational course model presented in this article provided the basis for this successful seminar. During the seminar implementation process, assessing the level of LGB affirmative support within the department, university, and community was of major importance as suggested by Phillips (2000). Student learning experiences were enhanced by the use of the university student LGBT group and LGB community center. Instructor flexibility to balance content with experiential knowledge was critical. This article provides a course structure that could be intentionally implemented by mental health training programs to bridge the gap between students with differing attitudes, levels of skill, and levels of knowledge.

REFERENCES

American Counseling Association. (1995). *Code of ethics and standards of practice.* Alexandria, VA: Author.

American Psychological Association. (1992). Ethical principles of psychologists and code of conduct. *American Psychologist, 47*, 1597-1611.

Buhrke, R. A. & Douce, L.A. (1991). Training issues for counseling psychologists in working with lesbians and gay men. *The Counseling Psychologist, 19*, 216-234.

Firestein, B. A. (Ed.). (1996). *Bisexuality: The psychology and politics of an invisible minority.* Thousand Oaks, CA: Sage.

Garnets, L., Hancock, K. A., Cochran, S. D., Goodchilds, J., & Peplau, L. A. (1991). Issues in psychotherapy with lesbians and gay men. *American Psychologist, 46*, 964-972.

Iasenza, S. (1989). Some challenges of integrating sexual orientations into counselor training and research. *Journal of Counseling & Development, 68*, 73-76.

Klein, F. (1993). *The bisexual option* (2nd ed.). New York: Harrington Park Press.

Liddle, B. J. (1995). Sexual orientation bias among advanced graduate students of counseling and counseling psychology. *Counselor Education & Supervision, 34*, 321-331.

Liddle, B. J. (1996). Therapist sexual orientation, gender, and counseling practices as they relate to ratings on helpfulness by gay and lesbian clients. *Journal of Counseling Psychology, 43*, 394-401.

Liddle, B. J. (1997, Spring). Gay and lesbian clients' selection of therapists and utilization of therapy. *Psychotherapy, 34*, 11-18.

Moss, J. F. (1995, August). *Gay, lesbian, and bisexual clients' perceptions of bias in psychotherapy*. Paper presented at the 103rd Annual Convention of the American Psychological Association, New York.

Murphy, B. C. (1991). Educating mental health professionals about gay and lesbian issues. *Journal of Homosexuality, 22*, 229-246.

National Association of Social Workers. (1996). *Code of ethics*. Washington, DC: Author.

Phillips, J. C. (2000). Training issues and considerations. In R. M. Perez, K. A. DeBord, & K. J. Bieschke (Eds.), *Handbook of counseling and psychotherapy with lesbian, gay, and bisexual clients* (pp. 337-358). Washington, DC: American Psychological Association.

Phillips, J. C., & Fischer, A. R. (1998). Graduate students' training experiences with lesbian, gay, and bisexual issues. *The Counseling Psychologist, 26*, 712-734.

Pilkington, N. W., & Cantor, J. M. (1996). Perceptions of heterosexual bias in professional psychology programs: A survey of graduate students. *Professional Psychology: Research & Practice, 27*, 604-612.

Rudolph, J. (1989). Effects of a workshop on mental health practitioners' attitudes toward homosexuality and counseling effectiveness. *Journal of Counseling & Development, 68*, 81-85.

Schreier, B. A., & Werden, D. L. (2000). Psychoeducational programming: Creating a context of mental health for people who are lesbian, gay, or bisexual. In R. M. Perez, K. A. DeBord, & K. J. Bieschke (Eds.), *Handbook of counseling and psychotherapy with lesbian, gay, and bisexual clients* (pp. 359-382). Washington, DC: American Psychological Association.

Small, F. (1993). *Everything Possible–Fred Small in Concert*. Cambridge, MA: Rounder Records.

Tyler, J. M., Jackman-Wheitner, L., Strader, S., & Lenox, R. (1997). A change-model approach to raising awareness of gay, lesbian, and bisexual issues among graduate students in counseling. *Journal of Sex Education, 22*, 37-43.

Whitman, J. S. (1995). Providing training about sexual orientation in counselor education. *Counselor Education and Supervision, 35*, 168-176.

APPENDIX

Overview of Session Content

Session	Stage of Change	Major Focus	Experiential Activities
One	Pre-contemplation	Creating Affirmative Environment	Values clarification
		Creating a common vocabulary Heterosexism/Homophobia	Stereotypes
Two	Pre-contemplation Contemplation	Historical Perspective	"One Degree of Separation"
Three	Pre-contemplation Contemplation	Identity Development & Management Bisexuality Coming Out	Mask activity
Four	Pre-contemplation Contemplation	Relationships and Family	LGB speaker panel Visualization activity Video: "If These Walls Could Talk –2" (HBO)
Five	Contemplation	LGB Health & Wellness Spirituality/Religion Conversion therapy	Elimination activity Relationship visualization Religion speaker panel
Six	Contemplation	Diversity within LGB population Ethnic/Racial Gender/Transgender Disability	LGBT community speaker panel One Degree of Separation Activity–revisited
Seven	Contemplation Action Maintenance	Mental Health Issues Bias in assessment Diagnostic issues Affirmative counseling techniques	Case conceptualizations Role plays
Eight	Contemplation Action Maintenance	Group Closure Coming Out papers Resources Future learning experiences	Song "Everything Possible" (Small, 1992)

Note: Experiential activities and learning objectives are available from the author.

Policy and Practice:
A Holistic Approach to Addressing Homophobia and Heterosexism Among Social Work Students

Lori Messinger

SUMMARY. This article outlines a variety of structural approaches that together work to interrupt heterosexism and homophobia in social work programs. The approaches offered include policy development, recruitment and hiring practices, and the development of innovative student support services. Program evaluation is suggested as a way to assess program performance and target areas for change. While these strategies are targeted at social work programs, the recommendations in this article are appropriate to most academic disciplines. *[Article copies available for a fee from The Haworth Document Delivery Service: 1-800-HAWORTH. E-mail address: <getinfo@haworthpressinc.com> Website: <http://www.HaworthPress.com> © 2002 by The Haworth Press, Inc. All rights reserved.]*

KEYWORDS. Social work education, educational policy, homophobia, organizational climate

---

Lori Messinger, MA, MSW, PhD, is Assistant Professor in the School of Social Work, University of Alabama, Box 870 314, Tuscaloosa, AL 35487 (E-mail: Lori_Messinger@mindspring.com).

[Haworth co-indexing entry note]: "Policy and Practice: A Holistic Approach to Addressing Homophobia and Heterosexism Among Social Work Students." Messinger, Lori. Co-published simultaneously in *Journal of Lesbian Studies* (Harrington Park Press, an imprint of The Haworth Press, Inc.) Vol. 6, No. 3/4, 2002, pp. 121-132; and: *Addressing Homophobia and Heterosexism on College Campuses* (ed: Elizabeth P. Cramer) Harrington Park Press, an imprint of The Haworth Press, Inc., 2002, pp. 121-132. Single or multiple copies of this article are available for a fee from The Haworth Document Delivery Service [1-800-HAWORTH, 9:00 a.m. - 5:00 p.m. (EST). E-mail address: getinfo@haworthpressinc.com].

Compared to many academic disciplines, social work appears especially progressive on gay and lesbian issues. The Council on Social Work Education (CSWE), the national accrediting body for academic social work programs, requires that graduates from social work undergraduate and graduate programs be able to engage in respectful, knowledgeable, and skilled practice with gay men and lesbians. The National Association of Social Workers (NASW), the largest professional social work organization, has taken positions supporting civil rights for gay and lesbian people, acceptance of gay and lesbian identities as normal sexual orientations, and the empowerment of gay and lesbian clients. Yet, these policies and positions do not guarantee a welcoming environment for gay and lesbian social work students and faculty and staff members.

Qualitative studies with gay and lesbian students reveal the depth of these problems in academe: students report homophobic and heterosexist comments, attitudes, and acts by heterosexual peers and program staff and faculty members. Although few studies have discussed the affect of this homophobia specifically on gay and lesbian social work students (e.g., Messinger & Topal, 1997), researchers have studied the impact of hostile contexts on gay men and lesbians in other academic arenas, including as undergraduates (DeSurra & Church, 1994; Waldo, 1998), medical students (Oriel, Madlon-Kay, Govaker, & Mersy, 1996; Risdon, Cook, & Willms, 2000), and law students (Austin, Cain, Mack, Strader, & Vaseleck, 1998). Gay and lesbian students in these studies describe feeling invisible, being mocked, having their opinions and/or personal relationships devalued, having property destroyed, and being physically attacked. Effects of these actions can be overwhelming for students, including psychological stress, academic failure, attrition, and suicide (DeSurra & Church,1994; Harbeck, 1992).

Even if gay and lesbian students did not face a demeaning academic climate, they may find that the coming out process inhibits their learning. Fassinger (1995) and Prince (1995) found that gay and lesbian students who are coming out are often "intensely pre-occupied with exploring sexuality, intimate relationships, social (and for some, political) networks, and changing family relationships, and may have little residual energy or motivation for dealing with career concerns" (Fassinger, p. 157). It is imperative, therefore, that social work programs find ways to support gay and lesbian students, particularly those who are dealing with coming out concerns, while addressing issues of homophobia and heterosexism in academic contexts.

Social work educators use a variety of different instructional strategies to address students' homophobia and heterosexism in the university classroom. Oles, Black, and Cramer (1999) provide a comprehensive review of techniques including readings, role-plays, ethnographic research assignments, instructor disclosure of sexual orientation, discussion of sexual orientation, and panels of gay and/or lesbian speakers. Materials related to gay men and lesbians can and should be integrated throughout the curriculum (Morrow, 1996). Yet, many studies have found that, despite these interventions, homophobia and heterosexism persist among social work students (e.g., Black, Oles, & Moore, 1996; Oles et al., 1999; Weiner, 1989).

Mackelprang, Ray, and Hernandez-Peck (1996), Morrow (1996), and Logan et al. (1996) suggest that students' homophobia and heterosexism find additional supports in the structure and practices of social work programs. This article builds on their work to outline an array of structural interventions that address homophobia and heterosexism within social work programs, while supporting gay and lesbian students and faculty and staff members.

The suggestions offered herein are based on the professional literature, my research with gay and lesbian social work students,[1] and my own experiences as a lesbian social work student and instructor. The adoption of inclusive policies is recommended as a first step in this process. Other strategies address areas such as student recruitment, hiring practices, field placement, extracurricular activities, student mentoring and career placement, and program evaluation.

It should be noted that faculty and administrators have many interests and concerns to balance as they try to create and maintain the best learning environment for students. This article does not imply that gay men and lesbians are more important than any other identity group; nor is it my intention that special attention should be paid to gay men and lesbians at the expense of members of other historically disadvantaged populations. I believe, however, that members of different identity groups have distinct needs that we need to recognize and be prepared to address. It is in that spirit, then, that these recommendations are offered.

POLICIES

Faculty members, who may have limited control over the policies of their larger institutions, have relatively more power on the program or department level. Traditional nondiscrimination policies–at the university, college, school, or program level–should be enhanced by the program's mission statement and other program policies insuring the creation of an open, supportive atmosphere in the program. These policies, described in more detail below, can have a strong positive influence on the experiences of gay and lesbian students and faculty and staff members. All such policies should be posted prominently and included in all written materials about the program, such as employee and student handbooks.

Nondiscrimination Policies

Gay and lesbian advocates have been very vocal in recent years about the need for businesses and other organizations to implement nondiscrimination policies. Some educational institutions have such policies on the university or college level, while others have these policies only within their own social work schools, departments, or programs. Although most nondiscrimination policies insure employment security, they do not guarantee equal benefits for sexual minority employees, such as partner health benefits. Similarly, additional policies are needed that articulate support for research on and teaching about sexual minority populations or issues of heterosexism and homophobia. Clearly, while nondiscrimination policies are a good start, they are not enough to insure a safe and supportive atmosphere for gay and lesbian students and faculty and staff members.

Mission Statement

The mission statement is a representation of a program's values: It defines what faculty and staff members think is important and, by omission, suggests what is unimportant. If a declaration of support for diverse populations is not included in the program mission statement, the maintenance of separate nondiscrimination policies or procedures becomes untenable. This diversity statement should be strengthened by a clear delineation of included groups, one that identifies gay men and lesbians.

Additional Supportive Policies

In addition to employment policies and the mission statement, social work programs often develop policies for academic procedures, such as grading, teaching, student rights and responsibilities, and grievance processes. Each of these areas can include policies to support gay and lesbian students and faculty and staff members.

Social work programs can set "an agreed definition of what constitutes anti-discrimination/anti-oppressive practice for staff, students, and teachers" and use this definition in creating "consistent [grading] criteria for the students to [be] measured against" (Logan et al., 1996, p. 44). By including staff and faculty members in the policy on anti-oppressive practice, the students would see these criteria as standards that apply to the social work profession as a whole.

The North Carolina State University Department of Sociology and Anthropology (1999) recognizes specific issues facing gay and lesbian graduate student instructors. The department has a policy stating that these instructors "are free, at their own discretion, to reveal their sexual orientation in the conduct of their teaching responsibilities. The departmental administration supports all instructors' freedom to use personal life experiences, as appropriate, in support of pedagogical goals" (p. 1). This policy normalizes the use of gay and lesbian instructors' perspectives and experiences in the classroom, while reassuring those who choose to disclose that the department will support them in this decision, even in the face of student hostility. This kind of support would likely increase gay and lesbian instructors' comfort in the classroom.

Policies can be developed that give gay and lesbian students' control over deciding if and when to disclose to faculty and staff members and other students. The program can adopt a policy supporting gay and lesbian students' right to a faculty advisor who is knowledgeable concerning issues facing these students. Grievance procedures can also include protections for gay and lesbian students and faculty members, securing the right to unbiased persons to serve on the hearings committees.

RECRUITMENT AND HIRING

Gay, Lesbian, Bisexual, and Questioning Students

One way to insure the diversity of the student population is through thoughtful student recruitment efforts. Austin et al. (1998) suggest:

> Nondiscrimination policies . . . should be featured in recruitment materials. Those materials also should identify the [gay and lesbian] organization, if any, and should include among the profiles of faculty, students, or alumni people who are actively working in [gay and lesbian]-related fields. Admissions personnel should be prepared quickly to provide names and contact information for at least one openly gay student, faculty member, or alumnus should an applicant ask. . . . Finally, recruiters should be aware of the actual climate at their schools for [gay and lesbian] students and be prepared to discuss it openly and honestly. (p. 163)

The design of application materials also indicates the gay-friendliness of the social work program. "The adoption of common procedures in the design and completing of forms and records to avoid categories such as 'marital status' or terms such as 'single,' 'divorced,' etc. would minimize the tendency to exclude lesbians and gay men" (Logan et al., 1996, p. 53). Offering the choice of "partner," for example, would express to potential applicants the openness and awareness of the program staff.

Gay and Lesbian Faculty and Staff Members

In recruiting faculty and staff members, programs should advertise an interest in hiring openly gay men and lesbians. There are many benefits to having openly gay and lesbian faculty and staff members. First, we are visible and approachable sources of information for heterosexual students, many of whom have not knowingly interacted with gay and lesbian individuals before. Second, schools that employ gay and lesbian faculty and staff members teach students how to engage others in environments where the expression of homophobic and heterosexist attitudes is neither welcomed nor encouraged. Students' heterosexist speech and thinking are challenged by our presence; they quickly learn to become more sensitive in this area.

Gay and lesbian students also gain role models in these openly gay and lesbian faculty and staff members. "These role models should be representative of the gay and lesbian community as a whole"–i.e., not all white or all male, so students can find mentors with whom they can connect (DeVito, 1979, p. 4). Openly gay and lesbian social work faculty and staff members can provide insights into practice and research that might assist gay and lesbian students.

While it should not be left to the gay and lesbian faculty and staff members to raise these issues (Logan et al., 1996), we do bring unique perspectives that can inform program discussions. In one study, for example, a student reported that his program has "several out gay/lesbian faculty, which helps us, if for no other reason than to keep issues visible at the faculty level" (Austin et al., 1998, p. 173).

Gay and lesbian faculty and staff members who conduct research on gay and lesbian populations could potentially offer even more opportunities for student learning. We can discuss this research in our courses, reflecting on ways that it illuminates the course materials. We can also involve students in our research through research assistantships and independent studies.

Heterosexual Faculty and Staff Members

It is not enough to hire openly gay and lesbian faculty and staff members; it is also important to hire heterosexual faculty and staff members who are supportive and educated about gay and lesbian issues. There are three reasons to consider this issue in hiring. First, heterosexual faculty and staff allies can support the mission and policies of the program in addressing homophobia and heterosexism, discussing heterosexual privilege, and creating a welcoming and safe learning environment. In doing this, the heterosexual faculty and staff members model for heterosexual students openness and acceptance towards homosexuality.

Second, heterosexual allies will be prepared to integrate materials on gay and lesbian populations into their courses, support gay and lesbian students, and work well with openly gay and lesbian colleagues. Third, these allies will be willing and ready to support their openly gay and lesbian colleagues as they face the promotion and tenure processes (DeVito, 1979). When a program has hired openly gay and lesbian faculty members, it is important to make sure that we can stay and prosper in our programs.

FIELD PLACEMENT

The field placement is the time when students apply what they are learning in the classroom to interactions with clients. It is imperative, therefore, that field placement agencies be in locations where students can be trained to work with gay and lesbian clients in a manner that exemplifies the values and ethics of social work practice. To that end, field education programs need to assess potential agencies and field instructors regarding their training, values, policies, and practices with gay and lesbian clients. Further, agency settings should also be assessed for their ability to provide gay and lesbian students with safe and supportive learning environments (Logan et al., 1996).

The creation of practica with gay and lesbian organizations would assure all students the opportunity to learn about practice with these populations. Examples of appropriate placements include: agencies serving people with AIDS; health centers for lesbians; counseling services programs; leadership programs and resource centers for gay, lesbian, bisexual, transgendered, and questioning youth; political action organizations; agencies offering coming out groups; university anti-homophobia training programs; and domestic violence programs that serve lesbians and gay males in battering relationships.

It is also important that gay and lesbian students in field placement get appropriate supervision. While sexual orientation issues should be discussed in supervision with all students (Murphy, 1992), it is important to create possibilities for gay and lesbian social work students to discuss issues arising for them in practice. If an openly gay or lesbian person is not available or comfortable serving in this role in the placement agency, one should be located within the students' local area. Some social work programs and agencies might not have sufficient resources to address these needs; moderated Internet chatrooms and email listservs offer an alternative way for gay and lesbian students from different programs and agencies to find needed fellowship and support.

EXTRACURRICULAR ACTIVITIES

With all that is required of the social work curriculum, not all topics get the coverage they deserve. Courses may present the basic concepts of sexual orientation and the ways in which discrimination and bias limit opportunities for gay men and lesbians. Yet, there is much more that can be discussed, investigated, and read about these populations. That is why extra-curricular events make such wonderful opportunities for student learning.

At North Carolina State University, the Social Work Program hosted a one-day Diversity Institute for social work undergraduate students from across the state. This institute outlined concerns for working with diverse populations, including gay and lesbian parents and youth, in child welfare settings. Students had the chance to interact with one another, ask questions of an openly lesbian faculty member, and reflect on the similarities and differences of different identity groups in a more sustained fashion than would be offered in a classroom. They reported great learning and increased interest after attending the institute. These interventions are not only a resource for students, but also offer opportunities for continuing education for faculty and staff members, and local social work practitioners.

Another option for extracurricular learning is to offer guided fieldtrips to gay and lesbian agencies and businesses. In my multicultural social work course, I take students to visit the local gay and lesbian bookstore. Since this is one of the primary referrals that students are encouraged to give to gay, lesbian, and questioning clients, students are required to learn about this resource firsthand. This notion could also be extended to the creation of summer travel courses that would offer more sustained investigation of regional gay and lesbian communities.

Students can also learn about gay and lesbian issues by attending meetings and events hosted by campus sexual minority student associations. These support groups, advocacy organizations, and religious groups for sexual minority students usually welcome participation by heterosexual student allies.

INTERACTIONS WITH GAY AND LESBIAN STUDENTS

Issues in the Classroom

Instructors' interactions with gay and lesbian students are sometimes fraught with tensions. Instructors need to value and affirm gay and lesbian students, but are not always able to identify them as such. Instructors should support openly gay and lesbian students who contribute to class discussions, but should not single them out to "speak for" all gay and lesbian people. These tensions may be confusing to instructors. However, the professional literature provides some basic standards for all teachers.

First, allow gay and lesbian students to control disclosure of their sexual orientations. No one should ever have his or her sexual orientation disclosed by the instructor. Second, never assume, no matter what the evidence, that your students are of any particular sexual orientation. Just because someone is married does not mean that they define themselves as heterosexual.

Third, recognize that students, both gay and straight, are likely to spend time trying to figure out their instructor's sexual orientation. Some instructors choose to be vague about their sexual orientation through "strategic nonnaming," in an effort to "more effectively challenge students' expectations or assumptions" (Logan et al., 1996, p. 25). In my opinion, this strategy distances instructors from students and keeps the students preoccupied about something other than the course material. While I have experienced the fear and concern that causes many gay and lesbian instructors to maintain secrecy regarding their orientations, I have received support for my decision to be open about my identity as a lesbian. Moreover, I have found that my relationships to students were enhanced by my candidness, and my personal examples helped students relate to the material.

Finally, instructors should be self-aware of our own feelings as we interact with students around issues of sexuality. Students, especially undergraduates, often articulate opinions and ideas that we may find upsetting. The challenge for faculty is to manage our own feelings of vulnerability, embarrassment, ignorance, and anger, while encouraging students to think critically about their own ideas and opinions, as well as the ideas and opinions of others. While we must speak out to support the perspectives of oppressed populations, we must not silence students as they learn.

Administrative Issues

Social work faculty and staff members should be prepared to advocate for gay and lesbian students in the classroom and in the field. We must enforce all supportive policies related to sexual orientation, oversee grievances regarding violations of these policies, and address conflicts that these students might encounter. Administrators should rely on the university attorney's office for advice around these issues.

Faculty and staff members should also provide emotional support to gay and lesbian students regarding the special issues that arise for them. In my research, gay and lesbian students identified many issues that arose during their time in the social work program: coming out; disclosure; physical safety; acts of heterosexism and homophobia in the school and/or the agency setting; relationship issues; and internalized homophobia. It is important that faculty and staff members are comfortable and knowledgeable about these issues and have a list of referral resources available for students (Schoenberg, 1989).

Career Placement

Social work programs need to consider the needs and interests of gay and lesbian students when helping them find jobs. While not all gay and lesbian students want to work exclusively for gay and lesbian organizations, some may be interested in these organizations. Therefore, organizing and direct practice positions with gay- and lesbian-identified organizations should be among the program's job postings, and these organizations should be asked to participate in job fairs. This task will be easier if these organizations serve as field placement sites for students, as the program will already have established relationships with these organizations.

Alumni

Social work programs rely heavily on their alumni to provide feedback to the program, to offer financial support and help with fundraising, to assist with recruiting, and to serve as future field instructors. In each of these areas, having active and supportive gay and lesbian alumni is essential.

Gay and lesbian alumni can provide a unique perspective on the strengths and weaknesses of the program. These alumni can be loyal financial contributors and can tap into gay and lesbian networks that are inaccessible to many heterosexual alumni. Recent gay and lesbian graduates can also serve as resources for gay and lesbian potential students, giving them the inside perspective on life in the program. Finally, gay and lesbian alumni can serve as field instructors and unofficial advisors to students engaged in fieldwork. For all of these reasons, social work programs should make special efforts to reach out to gay and lesbian graduates and recruit them for leadership positions in alumni organizations.

PROGRAM ASSESSMENT

The Council on Social Work Education requires that all social work programs engage in ongoing self-evaluation. If a program chooses to adopt the changes outlined in this article, they should also adopt new related objectives. Possible objectives include: appropriate inclusion of materials on gay and lesbian clients as well as social workers; successful recruitment of gay and lesbian students, faculty and staff members; successful completion of the program by openly gay and lesbian students; high rates of retention and promotion of gay and lesbian faculty and staff members; functional mechanisms for supporting gay and lesbian students, faculty and staff members; low rates of grievances filed by gay and lesbian faculty and staff members and students; and effective enforcement of current policies and programs related to gay and lesbian persons in the program.

CONCLUSION

No program is perfect. We must all continually work to make our programs better for students, faculty and staff members, and alumni. I hope that faculty members and administrators can use this article as a guide to improve their policies and practices in regard to gay and lesbian issues. Perhaps this article can also be a springboard to help us to think about how members of other identity groups encounter similar and distinct problems, and to creatively consider what policies and practices would be helpful to them as well.

NOTE

1. Data collection from this research project, *Gay and lesbian students in field placement: An exploratory study*, is ongoing; further information about this study can be obtained by contacting the author.

REFERENCES

Austin, J.L., Cain, P.A., Mack, A., Strader, J.K., & Vaseleck, J. (1998). Results from a survey: Gay, lesbian, and bisexual students' attitudes about law school. *Journal of Legal Education*, 48 (2), 157-175.

Black, B., Oles, T.P., & Moore, L. (1996). Homophobia among students in social work programs. *Journal of Baccalaureate Social Work*, 2, 23-41.

Cain, R. (1996). Heterosexism and self-discosure in the social work classroom. *Journal of Social Work Education*, 22, 52-72.

DeSurra, C.J., & Church, K.A. (1994, November). *Unlocking the classroom closet: Privileging the marginalized voices of gay/lesbian college students*. Paper presented at the Annual Meeting of the Speech Communication Association, New Orleans, LA (ERIC Document Reproduction Service No. ED 379697).

Devito, J.A. (1979). *Educational responsibilities to the gay and lesbian student*. Paper presented at the 65th Annual Meeting of the Speech Communication Association, San Antonio, TX (ERIC Document Reproduction Service No. ED 184 167).

Fassinger, R.E. (1995). From invisibility to integration: Lesbian identity in the workplace. *The Career Development Quarterly, 44,* 148-167.

Harbeck, K.M. (Ed.) (1992). *Coming out of the classroom closet: Gay and lesbian students, teachers, and curricula.* New York: Harrington Park Press.

Logan, J., Kershaw, S., Karban, K., Mills, S., Trotter, J., & Sinclair, M. (1996). *Confronting prejudice: Lesbian and gay issues in social work education.* Aldershot, England: Arena/Ashgate Publishing Limited.

Mackelprang, R.W., Ray, J.A., & Hernandez-Peck, M. (1996). Social work education and sexual orientation: Faculty, student, and curriculum issues. *Journal of Gay & Lesbian Social Services, 5* (4), 17-31.

Messinger, L. & Topal, M. (1997). "Are you married?" Two sexual-minority students' perspectives on field placements. *Affilia: Journal of Women and Social Work, 12* (1), 106-113.

Morrow, D.F. (1996). Heterosexism: Hidden discrimination in social work education. *Journal of Gay & Lesbian Social Services, 5* (4), 1-16.

Murphy, B.C. (1992). Educating mental health professionals about gay and lesbian issues. In K.M. Harbeck (Ed.)., *Coming out of the classroom closet: Gay and lesbian students, teachers, and curricula* (pp. 229-246). Binghamton, NY: Haworth Press.

North Carolina State University Department of Sociology and Anthropology (1999). *Commitment to diversity.* [Online]. Available: http://server.sasw.ncsu.edu/S&A/grad/dversity.htm

Oles, T.P., Black, B.M., & Cramer, E.P. (1999). From attitude change to effective practice: Exploring the relationship. *Journal of Social Work Education, 35* (1), 87-99.

Oriel, K.A., Madlon-Kay, D.J., Govaker, D., & Mersy, D.J. (1996). Gay and lesbian physicians in training: Family practice program directors' attitudes and students' perceptions of bias. *Journal of Family Medicine, 28* (10), 720-725.

Prince, J.P. (1995). Influences on the career development of gay men. *The Career Development Quarterly, 44,* 168-177.

Risdon, C., Cook, D., & Willms, D. (2000). Gay and lesbian physicians in training: A qualitative study. *CMAJ, 162* (3), 331-334.

Rust, P.C. (1993). "Coming out" in an age of social constructionism. *Gender and Society, 7,* 50-77.

Schoenberg, R. (1989). *Unlocking closets in the ivory tower: Lesbian and gay identity formation and management in college.* Paper presented at the meeting of the American College Personnel Association, Washington, DC.

Waldo, C.R. (1998). Out on campus: Sexual orientation and academic climate in a university context. *American Journal of Community Psychology, 26* (5), 745-774.

Weiner, A.P. (1989). *Racist, sexist, and homophobic attitudes among undergraduate social work students and the effects on assessments of client vignette.* Unpublished doctoral dissertation, University of Wisconsin, Madison.

Addressing Homophobia and Heterosexism in the Mental Health Classroom: An Intersubjective Frame for Learning

Susanne Bennett

SUMMARY. Homophobia and heterosexism among mental health students is addressed through recognizing the intersubjective nature of the instructor-student relationships in the classroom. Theories about human behavior and clinical practice often present heterosexist views that go unchallenged. Unexamined views and prejudices can impact group dynamics and stir internalized homophobia within the sexual minority instructor or student. This article applies an intersubjective perspective to classroom vignettes, and it invites the educator to examine his or her theories and unconscious views as a precursor to providing an open learning environment for discussion and critique. *[Article copies available for a fee from The Haworth Document Delivery Service: 1-800-HAWORTH. E-mail address: <getinfo@haworthpressinc.com> Website: <http://www.HaworthPress.com> © 2002 by The Haworth Press, Inc. All rights reserved.]*

KEYWORDS. Intersubjectivity, homophobia, heterosexism, mental health education

Susanne Bennett, MSW, PhD, is a psychotherapist in private practice in Falls Church, VA. Recent research has focused on the attachment relationships between lesbian co-parents and their internationally adopted children. She is also Adjunct Faculty, School of Social Work, Northern Virginia Program, Virginia Commonwealth University, 6295 Edsall Rd., Suite 240, Alexandria, VA 22314 (E-mail: Subenn@aol.com).

[Haworth co-indexing entry note]: "Addressing Homophobia and Heterosexism in the Mental Health Classroom: An Intersubjective Frame for Learning." Bennett, Susanne. Co-published simultaneously in *Journal of Lesbian Studies* (Harrington Park Press, an imprint of The Haworth Press, Inc.) Vol. 6, No. 3/4, 2002, pp. 133-143; and: *Addressing Homophobia and Heterosexism on College Campuses* (ed: Elizabeth P. Cramer) Harrington Park Press, an imprint of The Haworth Press, Inc., 2002, pp. 133-143. Single or multiple copies of this article are available for a fee from The Haworth Document Delivery Service [1-800-HAWORTH, 9:00 a.m. - 5:00 p.m. (EST). E-mail address: getinfo@haworthpressinc.com].

133

The education of students in the mental health professions is an interactive process, encompassing far more than didactic teaching of biopsychosocial theories of human development, clinical practice, and psychopathology. The learning process for students at both the college and graduate levels involves self-exploration because future clinicians are encouraged to think critically and stretch beyond their commonly held assumptions about human behavior. Consequently, beliefs and feelings about controversial topics–such as sexual orientation–can become particularly charged discussions for mental health students (Cain, 1996). In order to facilitate the learning process, it is vital for educators to provide a classroom environment that can contain emotions aroused in students when their worldviews are shaken.

Intersubjectivity theory provides a framework for understanding group dynamics when topics for class discussion challenge personal values and evoke intense affects for both instructor and students (Harwood & Pines, 1998). This theory, which evolved out of early phenomenological philosophy, proposes that there are contributions from all parties in the exchange of knowledge, including unconscious views that may become triggered within and among individuals. An intersubjective perspective underscores the influence of context, defined in this paper as the interrelated conditions that exist in any environment. In terms of the classroom environment, for example, it is the context of the class discussion and the relationships within the room that both shape and inform the content that is taught. The emotionally laden issues of homophobia and heterosexism may be understood through examining the context of the learning environment and the contributions of *both* the instructor and the students, including the meaning that is created between the parties in the communication about these topics.

Some of the concepts salient to intersubjectivity theory are apparent in contemporary educational approaches to teaching about difference. Gitterman (1991) has given recognition to the importance of mutual influence in dealing with issues of racial diversity within the classroom, and Cain (1996) and Cramer (1997) have examined the influence of instructor self-disclosure regarding sexual minority status. Merdinger (1991) recognizes the influence of gender, and he emphasizes the special needs of women students in shaping the relationships in the classroom. The current article examines the benefits of considering the interrelationship of the subjective contributions of *both* the instructor and the students, a stance that is central to intersubjectivity theory. The following discussion explores the group dynamics in the mental health classroom through an intersubjective theoretical lens, and it suggests an approach for addressing the heterosexism and homophobia that often emerges when personal differences are expressed.

THEORETICAL FRAMEWORK

Intersubjectivity theory is based on assumptions about the nature of human relating, and its basic tenets developed out of European philosophy over two hundred years ago (Frie & Reis, 2001). Phenomenologists originally proposed that all experience is subjective, and human beings constantly recreate themselves through an ongoing, never static process. This philosophy challenged positivistic paradigm assumptions about the objectivity and infallibility of science by recognizing that knowledge is a created process, shaped by the interplay of multiple forces and subjectivities. Concepts central to this philosophy played a role in shifting psychological paradigms that originally maintained that psychopathology was rooted within the patient rather than through the influence of situation and culture (Stolorow, Atwood, & Brandchaft, 1994). As these viewpoints shifted, a theory of intersubjectivity emerged, influencing both the social sciences and the humanities in the twentieth century. It has had a considerable effect on the discourse among contemporary psychoanalysts, psychologists, and social workers.

As a theory of intersubjectivity began to alter beliefs about human behavior and clinical practice, a dialogue emerged regarding the impact of mutual influence on the organization of an individual's subjective experience (Aron, 1996; Benjamin, 1999). The works of child developmentalists and infant researchers (Beebe, Lachmann, & Jaffe, 1997; Stern, 1985) supported emerging relational theories about the importance of mutual connections with early caregivers in organizing the emotional life of the child and, ultimately, the adult individual (Orange, Atwood, & Stolorow, 1997). This viewpoint served as a foundation for the stance that the therapist and the patient both bring their subjective experiences and organized emotional histories to the therapeutic relationship.

Expanding on the influence of intersubjectivity in clinical practice, Aron (1996) points out that the therapeutic relationship is asymmetrical and continually emerging through an ongoing communication that is mutual, though not equal, in its influence. In a desire to know and connect with the therapist, the patient makes assumptions and probes the therapist to self-disclose, and despite the therapist's attempts at maintaining "neutrality," the therapist inevitably is self-revealing. Aron (1996) says: "We can never be aware in advance of just what it is that we are revealing about ourselves, and, when we think we are deliberately revealing something about ourselves, we may very well be communicating something else altogether" (p. 84). Benjamin (1999) enriches this discussion by viewing the therapeutic relationship as a developmental progression where a need for recognition depends paradoxically on the will of one party to be recognized by the second party, while the second has a capacity for negating or destroying the former. She (1999) proposes that an intersubjective stance shifts the power struggle from a need for authority over the other "to an understanding of the meaning of the struggle (what feeling or aim is at stake in this difference between us)" (p. 204).

While Benjamin views intersubjectivity as a process and developmental achievement, Stolorow and his colleagues (Orange, Atwood, & Stolorow, 1997; Stolorow, Atwood, & Brandchaft, 1994) stress that intersubjectivity can exist between *any* two people. Stolorow et al. have been at the forefront of the development of an intersubjectivity theory, and they have played a significant role in bringing these views to the attention of the mental health community. Their views are set apart from the perspectives of other authors because they place such a "thorough-going emphasis on contextualism" (Frie & Reis, 2001, p. 320). As a result of this emphasis on context in human relating, intersubjectivity often serves as a theoretical frame for studies about gender and difference, and it informs clinical understanding of the psychotherapy experience with sexual minority patients (Drescher, 1998; O'Dell, 2000).

APPLICATIONS OF INTERSUBJECTIVITY TO THE CLASSROOM

The concepts of intersubjectivity theory have also been applied to group situations, with emphasis placed on the power of bonding between individuals who recognize their similarities of experience (Harwood & Pines, 1998). Although the mental health classroom is not a psychotherapy group, a bonding can occur when the instructor elicits similarities among the students and enables them to have empathic connections with each other as human beings and mutual learners. Furthermore, dynamics within instructor-student relationships resonate with the dynamics of the clinical exchange because these are asymmetrical relationships. In addressing heterosexism and homophobia, the instructor may have the power to support or diminish student prejudices. The following is an examination of possible contributions of the instructor and the students regarding these issues.

Contributions from the Instructor

Referring to the psychotherapist, Orange, Atwood, and Stolorow (1997) state: "What we inquire about or interpret or leave alone depends upon who we are" (p. 9). Likewise, what the instructor chooses to teach, chooses to ignore, and how he or she addresses and interprets what the students say depends upon that instructor. Like the clinician, the instructor who harbors homophobic or heterosexist views shapes the classroom discussion, regardless of sexual orientation or conscious intent. If one is a sexual minority, for example, the instructor may have experienced prejudice in the past and may recoil at the uninformed and, perhaps, prejudiced views of students. Or, if one is a new instructor, he or she may lack the confidence and skill to manage debate or open criticism, whether or not one is a minority. In both situations, the classroom conversation may stimulate unresolved personal feelings within the instructor who may respond too quickly and in a critical manner. Finally, the inexperienced instructor may inhibit discussion in an effort to hide vulnerability and uncertainty. In this situation, the instructor may silence the students and shut down the learning process, rather than engage the students in an exploration of new viewpoints.

In addition to the personal contributions, the instructor's professional history contributes to an ability to address issues pertaining to sexual minorities (Mackelprang, Ray, & Hernandez-Peck, 1996). Many mental health professors were educated prior to the 1986 removal of homosexuality from the Diagnostic and Statistical Manual of Mental Disorders (DSM-III-R) or prior to revised policy stands taken by the social work, psychology, and psychiatry professions regarding homosexuality (Krajeski, 1996). Many were not educated regarding treatment with sexually diverse populations and may have learned developmental and family theories without sufficient critical examination, leading to their support of heterosexist views embedded in the unexamined but familiar theories they teach.

Contributions from the Student

Mental health students bring a variety of motivations and life experiences to the educational process and, consequently, some students of psychology, social work, nursing, or other clinical professions may be unresolved in their relational and interpersonal lives and may be in conflict with professional values and standards about homosexuality (Van Soest, 1996). As an added complication, some college- and young master's-level students are in the process of differentiating from their parents as authority figures, which may lead them to view the professor as an authority worthy of a transferred power struggle. Still other students may be hiding their feelings of shame and experiences with oppression. In other words, like the instructor, the student's personal history and subjective experiences shape how he or she interprets what is read, hears what is discussed, and responds to classmates and professor.

With this prelude in mind, it is important to note that discussions about sexual orientation may be profoundly uncomfortable for the sexual minority student or the student with unexamined or unresolved views about sexuality. The lesbian student who is anxious about exposure or defensive about orientation may experience homophobia from classmates or heterosexism in the course textbooks because of a heightened sense of difference and society's oppression. The student may experience the invitation to critically analyze heterosexist readings as the professor's own heterosexism or insensitivity, when in actuality that may not be the intent. The student with personal or religious views that run counter to acceptance of homosexuality may also feel defensive and misunderstood in a value system that sometimes collides with professional standards regarding discrimination of sexual minorities (Cramer, 1997; Van Soest, 1996). Undisclosed assumptions about the instructor may be made, a situation reflective of Aron's (1996) comments regarding the patient's observation of the therapist. Unexplored verbal exchanges or silent withdrawal of students in any of these classroom examples can shape the group dynamics, affecting the learning process of the whole.

Classroom Vignettes

The following classroom vignettes explore the contributions from an instructor and her students to a classroom environment. Drawn from my experiences teaching two sections of the same graduate-level course, these situations exemplify the creation of an intersubjective space that allowed heterosexism and homophobia to be addressed. Although these introductory social work classes in human behavior used the same texts and syllabus, the classes had separate challenges. For the first assignment, students in both classes were asked to choose three of the cultural variables that the social work code of ethics lists as important to consider; a list that includes sexual orientation as well as race, ethnicity, class, gender, ability, and religion. They were asked to discuss in a brief introductory essay how these variables influenced their personal identity development. I chose not to disclose my sexual orientation as part of my introduction to the two classes.

Class One. Class One was composed of eighteen part-time students, two-thirds of whom were female. Four of the students in this class wrote about the impact of sexual orientation on their development. As faculty sponsor of the Gay-Straight Student Alliance, I wrote a special invitation on the papers of the four students to participate in the student group, and I felt comfortable inviting the whole class to join the alliance if interested. Perhaps affirmed by my personal invitations, these four students apparently felt safe in becoming outspoken in the classroom discussions. I presented the content of the course in a manner and format that included an infusion of material about all forms of diversity and oppression. The class was alive with stimulating discussion, including respectful debate. The students in Class One were glowing in their mid-term evaluations of the class, without suggestions for change.

Issues around homophobia and heterosexism emerged during the second semester. When we were discussing family diversity and nontraditional family structures, one of the male heterosexual students made a blatantly heterosexist comment that it was unnatural for lesbians to have children and unhealthy for the child to be fatherless. I encouraged him to explore the origin and meaning of his views, and he backed up his opinions with "research" by a well-known religious radio talk show host. I could see the startled reactions on the faces of a number of students. Rather than criticize this student, I opened the conversation to a dialogue, encouraging a wide range of viewpoints. He was able to express his views and questions and receive responses from his fellow students. For example, the lesbian student felt free to talk about her experiences as a mother and what it was like to have a nontraditional family. Her personal testimony meant far more than anything I could have said in response to his misinformation and genuine curiosity.

Class Two. A slightly larger group, Class Two had only one male and was composed of twenty-four full-time students. No one in this class discussed sexual orientation in the initial autobiography. In contrast to my subjective experience of Class One, I felt awkward in this class when I issued the same invitation to the Gay-Straight Alliance. Although the content of the class was presented in a similar manner, the climate in Class Two felt tense and the discussion was sometimes stilted. Responses from the mid-term evaluations included a small group of students who were critical of the class format and my teaching style. I particularly noted the anonymous comment: "You talk about the gays too much!"

I found myself wondering about the meaning of the different evaluations. I wondered what was behind the complaints about the class format and if they were a smoke screen for other issues. Although I had not disclosed my sexual orientation to the class, I wondered how the students perceived me, and if their perceptions of my orientation were affecting critiques of the course. I felt concerned about the "gays" comment and wondered if the student's criticism was widespread in this class. I began to question how my sexual orientation impacted my acceptance by the students and my effectiveness as a professor. Privately acknowledging my subjective impressions and talking with colleagues freed me to explore the meaning of the dissatisfaction.

I did not want to back down on presenting content about diverse populations, yet I wanted to understand the context of the comments, that is, the underlying and interrelated conditions that contributed to the evaluations. I took the time to summarize the evaluations and wonder with the class about their meaning, and the discussion unfolded into a much-needed conversation about the fears and difficulties these full-time students experienced in managing the volume of their work. When the students felt heard, we were able to explore together the class process and make some changes in the format, such as providing outlines of my presentations and increasing opportunities for collaborative learning and class involvement. Without being strong-handed, I gave recognition to the discomfort some students felt about the diversity content while underscoring the value of this topic for their professional education. Addressing the context of the evaluations allowed the content to be better received, and the class developed a more open and lively learning environment.

Discussion. An intersubjective perspective recognizes the contributions of all the participants in the learning process, and these classroom vignettes suggest the importance of that concept. Professionally, I was fresh out of a doctoral program that prepared me well as a scholar of contemporary theories about human behavior, but I was less experienced in the methods of classroom teaching. I relied instead on my abilities as a psychotherapist and group leader. My clinical training led me to value neutrality as a starting point in relationships, which influenced my decision not to disclose private information about my sexual orientation to the classes. Personally, I continued to be aware of the internalization of the homophobia and heterosexism that was pervasive in my cultural experience and my theoretical training. In other words, my professional and personal subjectivity created my unique capacity to respond to my students. In addition, the context of the learning environment was influenced by contributions from the students. One class had openly gay and lesbian students, while the other did not, which inevitably contributed to the subjective experiences for instructor and students alike. The classes were different sizes, and the full-time students were more bonded as a group because they were taking all their classes together. These characteristics—and others that are unknown—contributed to the different classroom environments.

An intersubjective perspective also gives credence to mutual influence within relationships, as demonstrated by these vignettes. The class responses to the initial assignment and one student's complaints about "the gays" influenced my subjective sense of heterosexism or homophobia within Class Two. I wondered about the assumptions—and perhaps critical judgments—made about me due to my faculty sponsorship of the Gay-Straight Alliance and my open inclusion of sexual orientation in the discussions about human behavior. My uncertainty resonates with Aron's (1996) observation that we do not always know what we are communicating about ourselves to others. The turning point in this class seemed to occur when the group risked exploring the underlying meaning of the evaluations. This dialogue contributed to my personal understanding that it is unfair to generalize to an entire class a comment made by one student. In Class One, my comfort level was influenced by the awareness of the presence of gay and lesbian students in the classroom. The support I gave them by inviting them to the alliance possibly signaled that this class was a place where they could disclose their identity. Their openness in turn cued the group that they could explore questions about sexual diversity content, though others may have hidden unfavorable views to avoid offending the gay students.

Finally, these vignettes lend support to Benjamin's (1999) view of intersubjectivity as a process in which there is a constant tension between "recognition and destruction." In response to the male student's prejudiced remark, I could have increased his defensiveness and his homophobia with a critical reply, risking his humiliation. Instead, an intersubjective space for learning for this student and his classmates was created out of a stance of mutual curiosity and empathy. Through focusing on "what feeling or aim is at stake in this difference between us" (Benjamin, 1999, p. 204), understanding could emerge within the group. In addition, the process provided these future mental health professionals with an example of how to address differences, prejudices, and conflicting opinions.

CONCLUSION

The instructor with an intersubjective perspective incorporates concepts from the theory into a teaching approach and a frame for learning. Such a frame leads the instructor first to think critically about the implication of what is taught and then to be open to both questions and challenges from students. Students are invited to wonder about the cultural biases embedded in their readings and the lectures. Second, the instructor presents as a mutual learner, rather than an all-knowing expert. Such a stance frees the individual student to ask questions and frees the group members to question each other. The risk for the instructor, however, is that a feeling of personal vulnerability may emerge if the instructor is not in the position of "expert." Third, the instructor must be self-aware and use that personal knowledge in the teaching process. That is, the instructor must wonder why he or she is feeling insecure, uncertain, or even threatened. What is the meaning of what is taking place within the room that is stimulating these personal feelings, and how can this be used to deepen and enhance the learning process?

From the instructor's vantage point, the benefit of an intersubjective frame is that the professor becomes a facilitator for learning, rather than an authority solely responsible for didactic teaching. The instructor affirms the knowledge and experience of the students, noting their nonverbal cues and monitoring the group dynamics. The instructor encourages a sense of curiosity and wonder about the meaning of what is read, spoken, and unspoken. For the mental health student, this frame facilitates critical thinking skills and provides a method of relating that can be both clinically useful and intellectually stimulating. As Gitterman (1991) says, "the instructor models what he/she is trying to teach about helping processes" when the instructor undergoes a "full and undefensive exploration" of personal contributions to the class (p. 70). When homophobia or heterosexism emerge, as they predictably will, all can openly examine these views because an environment of mutual learning has been established.

Ultimately, it is the instructor's responsibility to examine his or her theories and consider personal unconscious views as a precursor for providing this open learning environment. Because the instructor-student relationship is asymmetrical, the instructor must assume the role of providing a safe climate for learning. The goal is to facilitate a mutual exchange of all ideas, rather than a silencing of debate, so that a variety of viewpoints can be critiqued. Attention to the intersubjective relationship between the instructor and the students can create such an environment, one that allows heterosexism and homophobia to be addressed and all voices–even if they are painful–to be heard.

REFERENCES

Aron, L. (1996). *A meeting of minds: Mutuality in psychoanalysis.* Hillsdale, NJ: The Analytic Press.

Beebe, B., Lachmann, F., & Jaffe, J. (1997). Mother-infant interaction structures and presymbolic self- and object representations. *Psychoanalytic Dialogues, 7*(2), 133-182.

Benjamin, J. (1999). Recognition and destruction: An outline of intersubjectivity. In S. Mitchell & L. Aron (Eds.), *Relational psychoanalysis: The emergence of a tradition* (pp. 181-210). Hillsdale, NJ: The Analytic Press.

Cain, R. (1996). Heterosexism and self-disclosure in the social work classroom. *Journal of Social Work Education, 32*(1), 65-76.

Cramer, E. (1997). Effects of an educational unit about lesbian identity development and disclosure in a social work methods course. *Journal of Social Work Education, 33*(3), 461-472.

Drescher, J. (1998). *Psychoanalytic therapy & the gay man.* Hillsdale, NJ: The Analytic Press.

Frie, R., & Reis, B. (2001). Understanding intersubjectivity: Psychoanalytic formulations and their philosophical underpinnings. *Contemporary Psychoanalysis, 37,* 297-327.

Gitterman, A. (1991). Working with difference: White instructor and African-American students. In R. Middleman & G. Wood (Eds.), *Teaching secrets: The technology in social work education* (pp. 65-79). New York: The Haworth Press, Inc.

Harwood, I., & Pines, M. (Eds.). (1998). *Self experiences in group: Intersubjective and self psychological pathways to human understanding.* London: Jessica Kingsley Publishers.

Krajeski, J. (1996). Homosexuality and the mental health professions: A contemporary history. In R. Cabaj & T. Stein (Eds.), *Textbook of homosexuality and mental health* (pp. 17-31). Washington: The American Psychiatric Press.

Mackelprang, R., Ray, J, & Hernandez-Peck, M. (1996). Social work education and sexual orientation: Faculty, student, and curriculum issues. *Journal of Gay & Lesbian Social Services*, 5(4), 17-31.

Merdinger, J. (1991). Reaching women students: Their ways of knowing. In R. Middleman & G. Wood (Eds.), *Teaching secrets: The technology in social work education* (pp. 41-51). New York: The Haworth Press, Inc.

O'Dell, S. (2000). Psychotherapy with gay and lesbian families: Opportunities for cultural inclusion and clinical challenge. *Clinical Social Work Journal*, 28(2), 171-182.

Orange, D., Atwood, G., & Stolorow, R. (1997). *Working intersubjectively: Contextualism in psychoanalytic practice*. Hillsdale, NJ: The Analytic Press.

Stern, D. (1985). *The interpersonal world of the infant*. New York: Basic Books.

Stolorow, R., Atwood, G., & Brandchaft (Eds.). (1994). *The intersubjective perspective*. Northvale, NJ: Jason Aronson.

Van Soest, D. (1996). The influence of competing ideologies about homosexuality on nondiscrimination policy: Implications for social work education. *Journal of Social Work Education*, 32(1), 53-63.

PART IV
PEDAGOGY AND CLASSROOM INTERVENTIONS

Homophobia and Academic Freedom

David Moshman

SUMMARY. Addressing homophobia and heterosexism as a teacher raises issues of respect for the intellectual freedom of your students. The central thesis of this article is that these issues are best addressed on the basis of general principles of academic freedom–that is, intellectual freedom in educational and research contexts. Three cases are analyzed on the basis of principles developed by the Academic Freedom Coalition of Nebraska (AFCON). These principles permit advocacy, rather than requiring neutrality, but do not permit indoctrination. That is, instructors may express and justify their own ideas relevant to the curriculum and try to convince students to adopt those ideas and/or abandon alternatives, but must not coerce or require belief, censor or punish students who remain unconvinced, or restrict access to alternative views. *[Article copies available for a fee from The Haworth Document Delivery Service: 1-800-HAWORTH. E-mail address: <getinfo@ haworthpressinc.com> Website: <http://www.HaworthPress.com> © 2002 by The Haworth Press, Inc. All rights reserved.]*

KEYWORDS. Homophobia, academic freedom, intellectual freedom, censorship, indoctrination

---

David Moshman, PhD, is Professor of Educational Psychology at the University of Nebraska-Lincoln, and Policy Coordinator of the Academic Freedom Coalition of Nebraska.

[Haworth co-indexing entry note]: "Homophobia and Academic Freedom." Moshman, David. Co-published simultaneously in *Journal of Lesbian Studies* (Harrington Park Press, an imprint of The Haworth Press, Inc.) Vol. 6, No. 3/4, 2002, pp. 147-161; and: *Addressing Homophobia and Heterosexism on College Campuses* (ed: Elizabeth P. Cramer) Harrington Park Press, an imprint of The Haworth Press, Inc., 2002, pp. 147-161. Single or multiple copies of this article are available for a fee from The Haworth Document Delivery Service [1-800-HAWORTH, 9:00 a.m. - 5:00 p.m. (EST). E-mail address: getinfo@haworthpressinc.com].

Addressing homophobia and heterosexism as a teacher immediately raises issues of respect for the intellectual freedom of your students. How free should you be to raise issues of sexual orientation in your classes? How free should you be to express and argue for your own views on these issues? How free should students be to express views that you deem homophobic or heterosexist?

The central thesis of this article is that issues of this sort are best addressed on the basis of principles of academic freedom. By academic freedom, I mean intellectual freedom in educational and research contexts, the definition used by the Academic Freedom Coalition of Nebraska (AFCON) since its founding in 1988. Thus academic freedom fully encompasses students and faculty at all levels of education. Some aspects of academic freedom may be legally protected in some contexts, but academic freedom is not a set of legal rights. Rather, it is a social context of liberty justified by the role of intellectual freedom in education and by the various moral and professional rights and responsibilities associated with this.

On the basis of this conception AFCON has developed a set of Principles of Academic Freedom (see appendix a) and a subsequent Statement applying these principles to matters of sexuality. In the next section I briefly describe the history leading to the adoption of these documents. The rest of the article illustrates the application of academic freedom principles to three cases.

PRINCIPLES OF ACADEMIC FREEDOM

AFCON was founded in 1988 as a coalition of Nebraska organizations concerned with intellectual freedom in the educational institutions of Nebraska. Current members of the coalition include the Nebraska State Education Association, the Lincoln Education Association, the Nebraska Educational Media Association, the Lincoln Public School Media, the Nebraska English/Language Arts Council, the Nebraska High School Press Association, the Nebraska State Reading Association, the University of Nebraska–Lincoln (UNL) Academic Senate, the UNL Chapter of the American Association of University Professors, the Nebraska Chapter of the National Association of Scholars, ACLU Nebraska, the Nebraska Library Association, the Nebraska Press Association, the Nebraska Center for the Book, Journal Writers of Nebraska, the Story Monkey, and the Nebraska Writers Guild. Members of the coalition select representatives to serve on the AFCON Board of Directors.

Since its beginning AFCON has construed academic freedom as intellectual freedom in educational and research contexts. Such freedom can sometimes be protected in U.S. public education by invoking the First Amendment rights of individual students or faculty (Kors & Silverglate, 1999; O'Neil,

1997). AFCON has consistently maintained, however, along with the American Association of University Professors (1940/2001), that academic freedom is fundamentally a condition for education and research, not just a set of legal rights. That is, adherence to principles of academic freedom fosters excellence in education and research while simultaneously respecting the autonomy of individual students and faculty. This emphasis on the intellectual and moral, as opposed to legal, basis for academic freedom has become increasingly important since *Hazelwood v. Kuhlmeier* (1988), in which the U.S. Supreme Court greatly restricted the application of the First Amendment in curricular contexts.

Throughout its history, many of the cases coming to AFCON's attention have involved issues of sexual orientation. Given that this experience was fully consistent with national trends and showed no sign of abating, the AFCON Board decided in 1998 to develop a policy statement concerning issues of academic freedom related to sexual orientation. Although drafts of such a policy received positive feedback from a variety of sources, an unexpected problem arose. Some people thought it odd that AFCON was singling out sexual orientation for special attention and wondered whether the policy was providing special protection for the topic of sexual orientation and/or special rights for sexual minority faculty and/or students.

Within AFCON it was obvious to everyone that there was no question of special protections or special rights. The principles central to the draft policy were the principles AFCON had consistently applied throughout its history in addressing all sorts of academic freedom issues and controversies. We realized, however, that our most fundamental principles had for the most part been implicit in our analyses and positions rather than explicit objects of systematic attention. Outside our organizational context, our proposed policy on sexual orientation did indeed seem to be creating special protections and rights for certain topics and persons.

With these considerations in mind we decided that, rather than approve a special document concerning sexual orientation, it would be better to step back, formulate and approve an explicit version of our general principles of academic freedom, and then return to the topic of sexual orientation as part of a more general treatment of sexuality that was itself based directly on AFCON's general principles. The result of this process was a set of Principles of Academic Freedom adopted by the AFCON Board in September 1999 (see appendix a) and a longer statement entitled "Sexuality and Academic Freedom," based on these principles, that was approved by the AFCON Board in April 2000 (available at http://www.NebrWesleyan.edu/offices/library/Afcon).

AFCON's statement on sexuality begins by noting AFCON's concern that "the dozens of cases involving human sexuality that AFCON has addressed in recent years are just the tip of the iceberg that chills education about sexuality throughout

Nebraska" (p. 1). Far from receiving special protection, the topic of sexuality is routinely treated as one requiring especially stringent restrictions on expression:

> Implicit in most efforts to restrict discussion of sexuality is a widely-shared assumption that human sexuality is special in ways that render standard principles of academic freedom irrelevant. We see no justification for this view. In this statement we apply general principles of academic freedom to seven overlapping areas of concern with regard to sexuality and academic freedom. (p. 1)

The statement then goes on the address (a) sexuality within the curriculum, (b) teaching sexual responsibility, (c) student freedom of belief and expression, (d) freedom of inquiry, (e) sexual harassment, (f) equal opportunity, and (g) sexual orientation. With regard to the latter it notes that

> [s]everal of the examples used in this policy statement involve sexual orientation. This reflects the reality that a large proportion of the complaints and concerns that come to our attention involve sexual orientation. The fact that issues of sexual orientation are controversial in our society does not justify censorship. On the contrary, recognizing that the urge to restrict intellectual freedom is always strongest with regard to controversial matters, school authorities should be especially vigilant in protecting intellectual freedom with regard to matters of sexual orientation. (p. 3)

In the remainder of this article, I analyze three illustrative cases involving matters of sexual orientation. The first, involving the use of an epithet to express an offensive point of view, is hypothetical. The second, involving an offended Christian, is adapted from my own experiences teaching about the development of sexual orientation and sexual identity in a course on adolescent psychology. The third, in which a graduate assistant teaches about alleged cures for homosexuality, is an actual case that arose in the counseling psychology program of my department. Beyond whatever specific insights these analyses may yield, I hope to demonstrate that AFCON's general principles of academic freedom provide a useful framework for generating consistent and justifiable responses to educational issues and circumstances concerning matters of sexual orientation.

CASE STUDIES

Case One. In a class discussion of what is encompassed in the concept of fundamental rights, a student argues that fundamental rights include the right not to be discriminated against because of your sexual orientation. Another student says this sort of absurd claim shows the problem with vague notions of human rights. A third student agrees with the second, noting how vagueness leads to overly broad conceptions of rights that protect immoral behavior and evil people. A fourth student adds that human rights can't protect everyone and everything. The first student replies that human rights, by definition, are rights that protect all people. "Yeah, people," murmurs a fifth student, "not faggots." You're the teacher.

It is readily understandable that a teacher in this situation might feel increasingly disappointed and frustrated by the successive comments of the second, third, and fourth students. Even if you recognize the right of these three students to express their views you may be tempted, especially given this context, to penalize the fifth student for using the term "faggot" or at least to warn students that they will be punished for using that word. This temptation, I will argue, should be resisted, not only out of respect for the rights of your students but also because, from an educational point of view, there are better ways to handle this situation.

A central theme of AFCON's Principles is that academic freedom applies not only to faculty but to students as well. Your students, no less than you, have "a right to believe whatever they believe" (Principle 2) and "a right to express their views" (Principle 3). These principles can be justified on both moral and educational grounds. Morally, respect for persons entails respect for their intellectual autonomy, even if you justifiably believe them to be less developed and/or less educated than yourself (Kors & Silverglate, 1999). Educationally, moreover, there is substantial evidence that learning and development are fostered by contexts of intellectual freedom (Moshman, 1998, 1999).

It might be argued that freedom of expression is not absolute and that this is one of those cases where common sense demands some limitation. It is indeed true that restrictions on the time, place, or manner of expression can sometimes be justified, but we should be wary of relying on "common sense" to guide us in this regard. Rather, we should be careful that any such restrictions are carefully delineated and justified, and that they are neutral with regard to viewpoint.

In academic contexts, in particular, freedom of expression may justifiably be limited to matters "relevant to the curriculum" (Principle 3). A student who persistently talks about "faggots" in a calculus class, for example, might justifiably be required to stick to the topic of calculus and ultimately penalized for failing to do so. A student who persistently interrupts a calculus class to endorse gay rights, however, should be equally subject to sanction. Viewpoint neutrality is key here. Legitimate limitations on classroom speech, moreover, should not be abused by applying a stricter standard of relevance to objectionable views. The fifth student in the present case may be expressing a highly objectionable view of gays and lesbians, and may be expressing it in a rather inarticulate way (a point to which I shall return), but the student is indeed expressing a view relevant to the topic under discussion.

It might be argued that what distinguishes the fifth student from the second, third, and fourth is not viewpoint but rather the use of the epithet "faggot." Perhaps we cannot punish students for opposing gay rights but can't we punish students who use terms so offensive to others in the class that their manner of expression, as distinct from their point of view, is an act of harassment? Otherwise, some students may be so offended as to be silenced, thus denying them an equal opportunity to exercise their own academic freedom (Principle 8).

There is something to be said for this argument, but there is also great danger in it. As we will see in Case Two, it is not only sexual minorities who may be offended by their fellow students. The key to addressing this issue in a fair and consistent way, I think, is to carefully distinguish offensive speech from acts of harassment. Academic freedom protects the expression of all viewpoints, "even if those views are deemed to be false, absurd, offensive, or otherwise objectionable" (Principle 3). As noted in the Sexuality statement, however, academic freedom does not protect harassment, strictly defined as "a pattern of actions specifically directed against a particular individual with the intent of humiliating, intimidating, or otherwise harming that individual" (p. 2). If a student were to repeatedly call someone else in the class a faggot (or a bitch, kike, etc.) despite clear indication that the other student found this objectionable, that would be a serious offense not protected by norms of academic freedom. Reasonable people might disagree on exactly where one draws the line between offensive speech and harassment, but it should be clear that the comment of the fifth student in the present case falls far short of that line.

What, then, should you do in the present case? One important option for a teacher in any case involving student discussion is not to say anything at all. Peer interaction has a dynamic of its own that can be highly effective in promoting development and education and that may be undermined by pronouncements from a teacher or other authority (Moshman, 1998, 1999). It is possible in the present case that if you hold your tongue for a moment, other students, perhaps even including those opposed to gay rights, will criticize the use of the term "faggot" and, precisely because they are peers, have more impact than you could possibly have had.

There is no guarantee that this will happen, however. It is possible that there will be a stunned silence as students wait to see your reaction and that if you do not react this will be taken as acquiescence. It is also possible that if you do not step in, the discussion will move on to something else and your opportunity to use the present situation for educational purposes will be lost. Your own academic freedom as the teacher to decide how to proceed is based on the assumption that you are in the best position to judge what will be most educational for your students.

One excellent option, I suggest, is to ask the fifth student to clarify and justify his or her view. More specifically, you might, with seeming innocence, ask what is meant by "faggot" and why individuals in this category do not qualify as people. This response is, to be sure, a bit disingenuous. You are not directly accusing the student of making a snide and ignorant remark that fails to advance the discussion but you have no objection if the student or others make this inference. The student may be unpleasantly surprised to be asked to justify a comment that was not meant to be taken seriously, at least not in any academic sense. If the student has no meaningful response to your query, others in the class may conclude that comments of this sort are unjustifiable and some may go on to question the earlier facile rejections of gay rights. They may also come to see that intellectual discussions are more than just serial statements of diverse opinions. They may see that in your classroom they are free to say whatever they wish but that they should be prepared to explain and justify whatever they say.

It is possible, of course, that the student will indeed have some response. You can then proceed from there to state your own views about the use of terms like "faggot" and/or about the nature and scope of fundamental human rights. Respect for a student's right to hold a particular opinion does not entail agreement with, or even respect for, that opinion. On the contrary, respect for students is fully consistent with the presentation of alternative views and with efforts to convince students to change their opinions. The key is that such efforts must not be, and must not be perceived to be, coercive. It should be clear both to you and your students that, in the end, they "have a right to believe whatever they believe and to maintain or change their beliefs as they deem appropriate" (Principle 2).

Case Two. A class is discussing the psychological impact of discrimination on various groups. A student says that the major problem for gays is the psychological impact of Christian biases and bigotry. Another student says these remarks offend him as a Christian. Other students agree with the first that Christians are indeed, for the most part, homophobic bigots whose hateful rhetoric causes ongoing violence against gays and lesbians. The Christian student gets up to leave. What should you do as the teacher?

Two seemingly contradictory points are key in addressing this issue. First, the student has a right to leave. And second, you should try to convince him to stay.

With regard to the first point, you do have general authority as the teacher to set reasonable standards, including standards of class attendance, for passing, or receiving high grades in, your course. You have no obligation to devise criteria that will enable a student who finds your course offensive to receive an A without ever attending class. Students sometimes do have good reasons for missing class, however, and all teachers should make provisions for accommodating at least a few justified absences. In the present case, the student may be angry and upset about what he perceives as a personal attack and/or an assault on his religious beliefs. He may have learned from past experience that it is important for him to get away and cool down when he feels too angry to maintain his composure. You do not have to excuse him from whatever work he misses, but you should not forbid him to leave.

Even as you acknowledge his right to leave, however, you can and should try to convince him to stay, even if you believe that he is indeed a homophobic bigot and that his departure would help the class achieve a consensus consistent with your own views. There are at least three reasons for this. First, the departure of any student will obviously limit the education of that student. Your obligations to your students are not limited to those students who share your beliefs (Principle 8). Second, if your specific intent is to educate students about sexual orientation and alleviate homophobia, homophobic students are precisely the audience you most need to reach. The departure of an apparently homophobic student, and the consequent alienation of other Christian and/or homophobic students, thus undermines the achievement of your pedagogical goals. Finally, given that the Christian student appears to represent a minority view in this class, his departure will decrease the diversity of views in your classroom. If other students perceive it as best not to share what they see as a disfavored view, moreover, the opportunity for productive discussion is greatly compromised.

What will it take to convince the Christian student to stay? Quite possibly, he might like to see you show your support for him personally and/or for civil discussion in your classroom by punishing those who have called him a homophobic bigot.

On a continuum from offensiveness to harassment, the present circumstances arguably fall a bit closer to harassment than those of Case One. As offensive as the term "faggot" may be, no particular person was called a faggot in Case One, whereas the Christian student in the present case heard Christians denounced as homophobic bigots immediately after he identified himself as a Christian. He might believe the statements he found so offensive were aimed at him in particular with the intent to humiliate and silence him.

On the present facts, however, you have no reason to doubt that the students who said most Christians are homophobic bigots genuinely believe this, and you must be clear with all your students that they have a right to hold and express this view. Even if students were to say that *all* Christians are homophobic bigots, an assertion that is demonstrably false, you must be clear that students have a right to believe this and a right to say what they believe. If some of your students follow the Christian student back to his dorm room and continue to berate him for his views after he has made it clear that he no longer wishes to discuss the issue, they may be guilty of harassment. Wherever the line separating offensiveness from harassment may be, however, it clearly is not reached in the present case.

Unless the present case is part of a larger picture of targeted abuse, then, there is no question of harassment. Without singling anyone out for punishment, however, there is much you can do to simultaneously support the offended student, support the students who have offended him, and turn the present situation to educational advantage. For a start, you can assure the Christian student as he heads for the door that you understand why he is upset, that you intend to seriously address what has just happened in the class, and that you believe his presence will enhance the discussion to follow. You should be clear that you are not *telling* him to stay but *asking* him to stay, and that you are requesting this not just because he has a right to be in the class but because you believe his potential contributions will enhance the educational value of the class.

How you proceed from this point will depend not only on whether the Christian student decides to stay but also on what you know of the class and on how your students react to the situation. At the very least, however, you have an opportunity to encourage your students to avoid stereotyping, to express themselves in a civil manner, and to respect and value ideological diversity. You can and should promote these dispositions and values without censorship or punishment. In the short run, the most efficient way to ensure civil discussions in which no one is offended may be to set strict rules students must follow to avoid penalties. The resulting discussions, however, are likely to be not only civil but bland. In the long run, you want students to engage in civil and productive discussions out of respect for each other rather than due to fear of your power to censor and punish.

It is quite possible, I should add, that in a case of this sort the offended student might be out the door before you have time to decide what to do and gone before you can go after him. You should not berate yourself for failing to devise Solomonic responses to difficult circumstances in the blink of an eye. Even if the offended student is gone, however, the considerations raised above can direct you in discussing what just happened with the remaining students in the class, letting them know that you hope to restore relations with the offended student, explaining why, and inviting them to assist you. Following through with the offended student may not only be the right thing to do for his sake but may also provide the rest of the class with a useful model of maintaining dialogue and community in the face of deep disagreements.

Case Three. A graduate teaching assistant teaches a class of psychology students that homosexuality is a psychosexual disorder than can be reversed through reparative therapies. As the instructor responsible for the course, you think this is false and you know it is contrary to the views of most psychologists and psychological organizations. What should you do? Would it matter if the teacher were a colleague, rather than a graduate student under your supervision?

Cases One and Two both involve students' expression of their own ideas. Teachers also have a right to express their own ideas, but there is nevertheless an important difference between teachers and students. Teachers have a responsibility to organize their classes around an academically defensible curriculum. Correspondingly, those responsible for hiring, supervising, and/or evaluating teachers have the dual responsibility of (a) respecting the academic freedom of individual teachers, and (b) protecting the educational interests and academic freedom of students. The question of what is taught thus raises issues of curriculum that are in some ways more subtle than the question of what an individual has a right to say.

One preliminary consideration in the present case is the nature and scope of the course. If this were a course in calculus, it would be immediately obvious that sexual orientation and psychotherapy are at best tangential, and likely irrelevant, to what students are there to learn. The right of students and teachers to express their views in class is limited to matters "relevant to the curriculum" (Principle 3). Under some circumstances a teacher of calculus might reasonably deem it relevant to note the sexual orientation of a prominent mathematician or to comment on the effectiveness of psychotherapy for math anxiety. For a math teacher to devote substantial class time and attention to issues of sexual orientation and psychotherapy, however, regardless of what viewpoint she or he expresses about these matters, is an abuse of authority. Recognizing that students are a captive audience, teachers must not exploit their position by systematically subjecting their students to personal opinions on matters outside the scope of the course.

These considerations of relevance apply to some extent even in a psychology class. Suppose in the present case that the course for which you are the instructor is a large course in introductory psychology and that the graduate teaching assistants (GTAs) you supervise are responsible for weekly recitation sections intended to assist students in understanding material from the lecture and textbook. Students in this case have a legitimate expectation that their recitation sections will be devoted to the relevant material. GTAs should be free to provide examples and applications that go beyond those provided in lectures and text but they must not simply replace course topics with others that reflect their own idiosyncratic interests and personal agendas. Thus forbidding a GTA to devote an entire session to sexual orientation might be legitimate, providing the ban applies to all GTAs regardless of what point of view they wish to teach about this issue.

To the extent that the topic of sexual orientation is relevant to the course, however, it would infringe on the academic freedom of the GTA to forbid or punish the expression of particular views about this. Students and teachers, including GTAs, "have a right to express their views on any matter relevant to the curriculum even if those views are deemed to be false, absurd, offensive, or otherwise objectionable" (Principle 3)

That's not the end of the analysis, however. As the instructor responsible for the course, you can require that the curriculum include certain content. Thus you can present, or require the GTA to present, whatever information or ideas about sexual orientation and psychotherapy you believe ought to be included in the curriculum. This might include relevant research results, your own interpretations of these results, relevant theories and expert opinions, and/or policies of the American Psychological Association or other organizations.

Note that this approach, consistent with concern for the right of students not to be indoctrinated, instantiates a bias for inclusion, for expanding the curriculum rather than contracting it (Principle 6). You can see to it that students are exposed to whatever information or ideas you deem relevant and appropriate, but you cannot restrict the expression of alternative views by either the GTA or students in the class.

It should be noted that this bias for inclusion is not a requirement that all information and ideas relevant to a topic be included in the curriculum. If you convince the GTA that certain ideas are wrong and should not be presented, she or he is free to delete them, and vice versa (Principle 6, last sentence). It is almost never possible for a curriculum to include all perspectives, hypotheses, arguments, evidence, and interpretations on a given topic and it would thus be absurd to argue that students have a right to a curriculum that encompasses everything. But a GTA should be permitted to go beyond the curriculum you have devised, and students in turn have a right to add additional ideas of their own.

Suppose now that the teacher in question is not a GTA under your supervision but a colleague in your department. Obviously you have no personal authority to require your colleague to teach or not teach anything in particular, nor should your Chair, your Dean, another administrator, or the governing board of the institution have such authority. To the extent that responsibility for a course goes beyond the individual instructor it should be vested in a curriculum committee consisting of faculty and other professionals with relevant expertise. In order to protect the right of students to a curriculum devised on academic rather than political, religious, or other grounds, "[c]urriculum should be determined by teachers and other professionals on the basis of academic considerations" (Principle 5).

What if there is disagreement between a curriculum committee and an individual teacher? As in the relation of a supervisory instructor and a GTA, the resolution of such disagreement should not consist of vesting ultimate authority at one level or the other. Rather, the structure of authority should reflect a bias toward inclusion rather than exclusion (Principle 6). A curriculum committee might, for example, require that a particular course that serves as a prerequisite for others include particular topics, ideas, and information, but must permit individual teachers the flexibility to add additional topics, ideas, and information relevant to the course.

It is worth adding that colleagues are free to discuss their courses with each other and to recommend and consider modifications. Students and others should also be free to make suggestions. In general, faculty should be more open to "changes that expand the curriculum" than to "changes that contract or restrict it" (Principle 6). With regard to voluntary modifications of the curriculum, however, this bias toward inclusion is not absolute. Faculty should resist additions that "cannot be justified academically" and should be open to deletions if they are convinced that "what is deleted was not academically justifiable" (Principle 6). Open discussions of curriculum in noncoercive contexts are themselves an important aspect of academic freedom.

CONCLUSION

Restrictions on education about sexual orientation are pervasive throughout elementary and secondary education and all too common in higher education as well. Given this state of affairs it is understandable that in those circumstances where sexual minorities, and those sympathetic to sexual minority viewpoints, find themselves in power they will be tempted to compensate by indoctrinating students in their own views. A better approach, I have suggested, regardless of who has the power to devise and administer the curriculum, is to educate students in accord with principles of academic freedom such as those proposed by AFCON.

The proposed principles permit advocacy, rather than requiring neutrality, but do not permit indoctrination. That is, instructors may express and justify their own ideas relevant to the curriculum and try to convince students to adopt those ideas and/or to abandon alternatives, but must not coerce or require belief, censor or punish students who remain unconvinced, or restrict access to alternative views. Adherence to these principles will, I suggest, permit effective education about matters of sexual orientation that is fully consistent with the rights of all involved.

REFERENCES

American Association of University Professors (2001). 1940 Statement of Principles on Academic Freedom and Tenure, with 1970 interpretive comments. In *Policy documents and reports* (9th ed., pp. 3-10). Washington, DC: AAUP.

Hazelwood School District v. Kuhlmeier (1988). 484 U.S. 260

Kors, A. C., & Silverglate, H. A. (1999). *The shadow university: The betrayal of liberty on America's campuses*. New York: HarperPerennial.

Moshman, D. (1998). Cognitive development beyond childhood. In W. Damon (Series Ed.), D. Kuhn & R. Siegler (Vol. Eds.), *Handbook of child psychology: Vol. 2. Cognition, perception, and language* (5th ed.) (pp. 947-978). New York: Wiley.

Moshman, D. (1999). *Adolescent psychological development: Rationality, morality, and identity*. Mahwah, NJ: Erlbaum.

O'Neil, R. M. (1997). *Free speech in the college community*. Bloomington: Indiana University Press.

APPENDIX

Principles of Academic Freedom adopted by the Academic Freedom
Coalition of Nebraska (AFCON) on September 11, 1999

1. *Nature and Purpose of Academic Freedom.* Academic freedom refers to intellectual freedom in educational and research contexts, including freedoms of belief, expression, discussion, and inquiry. A commitment to intellectual freedom respects the rights of students and teachers and creates an educational context that promotes learning, development, and original research.

2. *Freedom of Belief.* All individuals, including students and teachers, have a right to believe whatever they believe and to maintain or change their beliefs as they deem appropriate. Educational institutions may present alternative views but may not require belief in those views. Students may be evaluated and graded with regard to their understanding of curricular material but not on the basis of their agreement with particular viewpoints.

3. *Freedom of Expression.* All individuals have a right to express their views privately and publicly and to discuss them with others. In academic contexts, students and teachers have a right to express their views on any matter relevant to the curriculum even if those views are deemed to be false, absurd, offensive, or otherwise objectionable. Some restrictions on expression are justifiable in cases where individuals are speaking in an official capacity on behalf of the institution.

4. *Freedom of Inquiry.* Educational institutions should encourage individuals to pursue their own interests and ideas and should promote access to relevant sources of information. Inquiry should not be suppressed by restricting access to controversial topics or viewpoints or by hindering the formulation of conclusions that may be deemed objectionable.

5. *Formulation of Curriculum.* Curriculum should be determined by teachers and other professionals on the basis of academic considerations. It is a responsibility of administrators and school boards to support justifiable curricular decisions and to educate their constituencies about the educational importance of an inclusive curriculum and the critical role of respect for academic freedom.

6. *Challenges to the Curriculum.* Suggested modifications of the curriculum should not be accepted merely to resolve a complaint, but neither should such suggestions be automatically rejected as illegitimate. In general, changes that expand the curriculum are more likely to be appropriate than changes that contract or restrict it. On the other hand, additions

may be illegitimate if what is added cannot be justified academically, and deletions may be appropriate if what is deleted was not academically justifiable.

7. *Parental Rights.* Parents have a right to discuss their views with their own children and to communicate with the school if they have suggestions or concerns about what they perceive the school to be teaching. Schools should accept the responsibility of explaining and justifying their curricula. In general, parents have the authority to direct their own minor children's education, subject to the responsibility of the school to provide an adequate education and to respect the rights of the student.

8. *Equal Opportunity.* Students and teachers have a right to academic freedom regardless of individual, biological, cultural, religious, theoretical, ideological, political or other characteristics, backgrounds, or viewpoints.

9. *Privacy.* In seeking information about potential or current employees and students, academic institutions should avoid making official inquiries that target personal expressive activities or that are so broadly or vaguely defined as to chill intellectual freedom. With regard to academic assignments, students may be encouraged to speak or write about their lives, and may choose to do so, but may not be required to reveal personal information that they wish to keep private.

10. *Due Process.* Academic institutions should ensure that their judicial and quasi-judicial procedures provide sufficient due process to protect intellectual freedom.

From Homophobia and Heterosexism to Heteronormativity: Toward the Development of a Model of Queer Interventions in the University Classroom

Gust A. Yep

SUMMARY. By examining homophobia and heterosexism within the larger context of heteronormativity at the intersections of race, class, and gender, I propose, in this article, a model of queer interventions in the university classroom. The article is divided into three sections. First, I describe the conceptual terrain of homophobia, heterosexism, and heteronormativity, and their potential limitations. Second, I present an integrative model, using heteronormativity as the central site of violence, to examine homophobia at the intersections of race, class, and gender within the larger social and cultural domain (macroscopic level) and interpersonal context (microscopic level) and illustrate this model with specific classroom activities. Finally, I discuss the implications of the model for teaching and theorizing about homophobia, heterosexism, and heteronormativity. *[Article copies available for a fee from The Haworth Document Delivery Service: 1-800-HAWORTH. E-mail address: <getinfo@ haworthpressinc.com> Website: <http://www.HaworthPress.com> © 2002 by The Haworth Press, Inc. All rights reserved.]*

Gust A. Yep, PhD, is Professor of Speech and Communication Studies and Human Sexuality Studies at San Francisco State University, 1600 Holloway Avenue, San Francisco, CA 94132 (E-mail: gyep@sfsu.edu).

[Haworth co-indexing entry note]: "From Homophobia and Heterosexism to Heteronormativity: Toward the Development of a Model of Queer Interventions in the University Classroom." Yep, Gust A. Co-published simultaneously in *Journal of Lesbian Studies* (Harrington Park Press, an imprint of The Haworth Press, Inc.) Vol. 6, No. 3/4, 2002, pp. 163-176; and: *Addressing Homophobia and Heterosexism on College Campuses* (ed: Elizabeth P. Cramer) Harrington Park Press, an imprint of The Haworth Press, Inc., 2002, pp. 163-176. Single or multiple copies of this article are available for a fee from The Haworth Document Delivery Service [1-800-HAWORTH, 9:00 a.m. - 5:00 p.m. (EST). E-mail address: getinfo@haworthpressinc.com].

KEYWORDS. Gay, heteronormativity, heterosexism, homophobia, lesbian, pedagogy, queer

In my life I have experienced the effects of homophobia through rejection by friends, threats of loss of employment, and threats upon my life; and I have witnessed far worse things happening to other lesbian and gay people: loss of children, beatings, rape, death. Its power is great enough to keep ten to twenty percent of the population living lives of fear (if their sexual identity is hidden) or lives of danger (if their sexual identity is visible) or both. And its power is great enough to keep the remaining eighty to ninety percent of the population trapped in their own fears.

–Suzanne Pharr (1988, pp. 1-2)

During the 1970s and 1980s political lesbians of color have often been the most astute about the necessity for developing understandings of the connections between oppressions [based on race, class, gender, and sexuality]. They have also opposed the building of hierarchies and challenged the "easy way out" of choosing a "primary oppression" and downplaying those messy inconsistencies that occur whenever race, sex, class, and sexual identity actually mix. Ironically, for the forces on the right, hating lesbians and gay men, people of color, Jews, and women go hand in hand. They make connections between oppressions in the most negative ways with horrifying results.

–Barbara Smith (1998, pp. 112-113)

Educators, academic researchers, policymakers, activists, and individuals in the helping professions have become more attentive to understanding the dynamics and effects of homophobia and heterosexism in recent years (e.g., Anzaldúa, 2000; Blumenfeld, 1992; Pharr, 1988; Sears & Williams, 1997; Smith, 1998; Yep, 1997, 1998). Such body of work has generally focused on combating homophobia and heterosexism in various settings (e.g., school, work, church, etc.) and with various groups and populations (e.g., high school students, ethnic populations, etc.). Anti-homophobia education typically identifies the effects of homophobia and names individual acts of violence against lesbians and gay men (Eyre, 1997). The harmful effects of homophobia and heterosexism range from the less visible (e.g., queer youth experiencing a deep sense of shame about their sexuality) to the extremely visible (e.g., gay bash-ing). They affect both lesbians and gays (e.g., living lives of fear, shame, and danger) and non-gays (e.g., homophobia inhibits an individual's ability to form close and meaningful relationships with members of one's own sex) in different ways and with various degrees of intensity (Blumenfeld, 1992). However, an exclusive focus on homophobia "diverts attention away from larger social forces that support and maintain the *normalization of heterosexu-ality* as well as away from the growing collective political activism of gay and lesbian groups" (Eyre, 1997, p. 199, my emphasis). Although anti-homopho-bia work has focused on communities of color, it generally does not address how homophobia operates when race, ethnicity, social class, and gender actu-ally mix and intersect (Smith, 1998).

By proposing a model of queer interventions in the university classroom, I attempt in this essay to partially fill these two gaps in the homophobia litera-ture by examining homophobia and heterosexism within the larger context of heteronormativity, or the normalization of heterosexuality, at the intersections of race, class, and gender. To accomplish this, I first describe the conceptual ter-rain of homophobia, heterosexism, and heteronormativity, and their potential limitations. Second, I present an integrative model, using heteronormativity as the central site of violence, to understand homophobia at the intersections of race, class, and gender within the larger social and cultural domain (macroscopic level) and interpersonal context (microscopic level). I illustrate and apply this model with specific classroom activities that I designed and tested in several uni-versity courses. Finally, I discuss the implications of the model for teaching and theorizing about homophobia, heterosexism, and heteronormativity.

THE CONCEPTUAL TERRAIN OF HOMOPHOBIA, HETEROSEXISM, AND HETERONORMATIVITY

Homophobia, as a popular term and a psychological construct, has been around for over three decades (Blumenfeld, 2000; Fone, 2000). For a thorough discussion of this concept and its history, see Fone (2000). Although a range of definitions of homophobia exists in the literature, it generally refers to irratio-nal fear, abhorrence, and dislike of homosexuality and of those who engage in it. More recently, heterosexism and heteronormativity have appeared in aca-demic and popular discourse. In this section, I discuss some of the problems with the concept of homophobia and the need to address larger, more inclu-sive, and underlying issues of heterosexism and heteronormativity in our so-cial and cultural landscape.

Although it is of paramount importance to name violence–physical, psychological, or symbolic–directed at lesbians and gay men, there are several problems with the notion of homophobia. According to Plummer (1998), these problems include: (1) it reinforces the idea of mental illness; (2) it neglects women; (3) it ignores how sexuality intersects with other vectors of oppression, namely, race, gender, and social class; (4) it directs attention away from the larger landscape of oppression of sexual minorities in general, and (5) it ignores the underlying structural and social conditions leading to sexual oppression by focusing on individuals rather than the larger social and cultural system.

First, the concept of homophobia reinforces and ratifies the notion of mental illness. While extreme expressions of homophobia–violent hate crimes against lesbians and gay men, for example–can be viewed as psychopathological, discomfort with homosexuality and inability to get along with lesbians or gay men may be, according to Plummer (1998), "better viewed as problems in living rather than sickness" (p. 89).

Second, homophobia, as a term, generally refers to male homosexuality. As such, it contains misogynistic overtones as it neglects and ignores women and female homosexuality (Plummer, 1998). When we hear terms like homophobia, "the homosexual threat," and "the homosexual agenda," male homosexuality is invoked. Much less attention is paid to lesbians and the "lesbian threat" and this process perpetuates the male bias in gay research (Plummer, 1998). Ignoring women leads to erasure of female experiences and agency as Adrienne Rich (1983) reminds us, "Lesbians have historically been deprived of a political existence through 'inclusion' as female versions of male homosexuality. To equate lesbian existence with male homosexuality because each is stigmatized is to deny and erase female reality once again" (p. 193).

Third, the concept of homophobia ignores how individuals of different social locations–based on race, ethnicity, social class, and gender–might experience their sexuality and sexual difference in ways that are distinct from European American, gay, middle-class, and physically able men. Can we assume that the experience of homophobia for a poor European American lesbian is identical to an affluent European American gay male? Similarly, does a working class, heterosexually married, Latina lesbian face homophobia in the same way as a middle-class, immigrant, Asian American man who has sex with men? A number of writers (e.g., Anzaldúa, 2000; hooks, 2000; Lim-Hing, 2000; Smith, 1998) argue that the experience of homophobia is different for people from different social locations or, to put it another way, homophobia cannot be meaningfully understood without attention to the dyamics of race, class, and gender. For example, hooks (2000) notes that homophobia directed at some African American lesbians is rooted in a religious belief that women defined their womanness through child-bearing and the assumption that to be lesbian meant no child-bearing. On the other hand, homophobia expressed toward some African American men is mediated by material privilege (e.g., money).

Fourth, homophobia, as a term, directs our focus to hatred, oppression, and attack of homosexuals at the expense of attention on sexual oppression in general (Plummer, 1998). What about oppression of individuals who choose celibacy or are in polygamous relationships? Homophobia, in this sense, can become a myopic view of sexual negativity in society.

Finally, the notion of homophobia, by focusing mostly on the individual (such as homophobic attitudes and traits), diverts attention away from the larger underlying social and cultural conditions that maintain the fear, hostility, and hatred toward human sexual difference. At the core of such underlying conditions is heterosexism and heteronormativity. Although these terms are related, heterosexism generally refers to the belief and expectation that everyone is or should be heterosexual. Heteronormative thinking assumes that heterosexuality is the indisputable and unquestionable bedrock of society; heterosexuality appears as a "given"–natural, coherent, fixed, and universal (Richardson, 1996; Warner, 1993; Wittig, 1992). It presumes that "heterosexuality is the original blueprint for interpersonal relations" (Richardson, 1996, p. 3) and in Western political thought, the heterosexual couple has come "to represent the principle of *social union itself*" (Warner, 1993, p. xxi, my emphasis). More simply stated, heteronormative thinking, in theory and in practice, assumes that heterosexual experience *is synonymous with* human experience. The equation "heterosexual experience = human experience" renders all other forms of human sexual expression pathological, deviant, invisible, unintelligible, or written out of existence.

Focusing on heteronormativity as a foundational source of human oppression (Warner, 1993, Wittig, 1992), I propose a framework for understanding daily acts of violence against individuals and groups who do not conform to the "mythical norm" (Lorde, 1990, p. 282) of heterosexuality. I now turn to a discussion of this model.

TOWARD THE DEVELOPMENT OF A MODEL OF QUEER INTERVENTIONS IN THE UNIVERSITY CLASSROOM

Based on the assumption that "to reduce public hostility to homosexuality [or other 'deviant' forms of human sexual expression] cannot simply be seen as a matter of more education or more information" (Plummer, 1998, p. 90), I propose a model that is both affective and cognitive. In other words, the model provides people with an opportunity to feel and experience (affective) and to think and understand (cognitive) daily, unrelenting acts of violence against individuals or groups assumed or perceived to be outside the "charmed circle" (Rubin 1993, p. 13) of normative heterosexuality. The "charmed circle," according to Rubin (1993), refers to U.S. societal conceptions of "good," "normal" and "natural" sexuality characterized by heterosexual, married, monogamous, procreative, non-commercial, "non-kinky" (without using sex toys or pornography) and private sexual activity involving two individuals, of the same generation, in a committed relationship. My model attempts to identify, label, and name these acts of violence, and it resonates with the spirit of Kathleen Barry's words (cited in Rich, 1983, p. 189), "Until we name the practice [of violence against non-heteronormative individuals], give conceptual definition and form to it, illustrate its life over time and space, those who are its most obvious victims will also not be able to name it or define their experience."

At the core of the model is the interrogation of heteronormativity, the presumption and assumption that all human experience is unquestionably and automatically heterosexual. Heteronormativity is a form of violence deeply embedded in our individual and group psyches, social relations, identities, social institutions, and cultural landscape. Monique Wittig (1992) reminds us that "to live in society is to live in heterosexuality" (p. 40) and "heterosexuality is always already there within all mental categories. It has sneaked into dialectical thought (or the thought of differences) as its main category" (p. 43). The power of heteronormativity as an ideology is its invisibility disguised as "natural," "normal," "universal"–its "it-goes-without-saying" character. Interrogating heteronormativity demystifies its mechanisms of power by making it visible and bare for critical analysis (for excellent discussions of heterosexuality, see: Jackson, 1999; Richardson, 1996; Wittig, 1992). The model identifies heteronormativity as a central site of psychological, psychic, social, cultural, discursive, physical and material violence for individuals and groups outside the domain of Rubin's "charmed circle" (1993, p. 13). Heteronormativity creates, nurtures, maintains, and perpetuates such daily acts of violence.

This model focuses on both macroscopic (e.g., institutional heterosexism) and microscopic (e.g., individual acts of homophobia) levels of violence against individuals deviating from the heteronormative ideal, and examines homophobia at the intersections of race, class, and gender. Borrowing from Wilber (2000), the model consists of two interdependent dimensions: (1) interior-exterior, and (2) individual-collective. Interior-exterior, the first dimension, focuses on affect, cognition, and sensations that are potentially experienced by the individual (interior) and those behaviors and actions that are acted out in the social world (exterior). Individual-collective, the other dimension, emphasizes the person (individual) and his or her relationship to the social group (collective). Taken together, these two dimensions form four quadrants to which I now turn. They are (1) Interior-individual, (2) exterior-individual, (3) interior-collective, and (4) exterior-collective.

Interior-Individual: Soul Murder and Internalized Homophobia

At a very young age, people learn that homosexuality is a powerfully shameful "condition," a stigma with all its associations with social deviance, cultural outcast, character defect, psychological blemish, and immorality. Individuals quickly learn that "homosexuality is a problem" from interactions with others like family members, friends, peers, teachers, and from the mass media. Messages about the stigma of homosexuality are virtually everywhere ranging from the subtle (e.g., the absence of happy, well-adjusted lesbians or gays in our high school curriculum) to the extremely visible (e.g., the conflation of HIV/AIDS with homosexuality). These pervasive messages promote and maintain the ideology of heteronormativity, that is, if "you are not heterosexual, there is something wrong with you." When such messages are internalized and incorporated into one's conception of selfhood and identity, they become internalized homophobia and they constitute soul murder.

Originally used to understand the dynamics and the traumatic nature of child abuse and torment, Shengold (1999) defines soul murder as the "apparently willful abuse and neglect of children by adults that are of sufficient intensity and frequency to be traumatic . . . [so that] the children's subsequent emotional development has been profoundly and predominantly negatively affected" (p. 1). Shengold (1989) further elaborates, "soul murder is neither a diagnosis nor a condition. It is a dramatic term for circumstances that eventuate in crime–the deliberate attempt to eradicate or compromise the separate identity of another person" (p. 2). One can immediately see how treatment and socialization of children and young adults in a heteronormative society are forms of soul murder. When children are called names like "dyke" and "sissy" regularly "to keep them in line" and to regulate and control their gender role behaviors, psychological abuse is performed. When children and adults are subtly and continuously told, either verbally (e.g., words) or nonverbally (e.g., facial expressions), that they are expected to follow the "heterosexual contract" (Wittig, 1992, p. 34) or engage in "compulsory heterosexuality" (Rich, 1983, p. 178), psychological violence is enacted. When children and adults are threatened with physical and/or psychological violence or actually beaten because they do not conform to gender role expectations, soul murder is committed. When lesbian and gay children are discovering their own attractions to members of their own sex, they become aware that "they are not OK" and "they are fatally flawed." These children's souls have been murdered; their emotional developments have been severely compromised with feelings of self-hatred, self-doubt, and self-destruction including suicide.

Exterior-Individual: Externalized Homophobia and Hate Crime

Although public expressions of racism, sexism, and classism are becoming less acceptable in U.S. American society, public pronouncements of dislike and hatred toward lesbians and gays are made daily and without much hesitation. The use of name-calling and derogatory terms toward lesbians and gays is common in everyday interaction. Fuelled by heteronormative thinking, externalized homophobia is commonplace. Externalized homophobia can be directed to any person who is perceived or assumed to be lesbian or gay and can be manifested in multiple ways: avoidance, verbal abuse, differential treatment and discriminatory behavior, and physical violence. All of these actions are harmful.

The most extreme expression of externalized homophobia can be seen in hate crimes against lesbians and gay men. Antigay violence is increasing (Fone, 2000) and homophobic murder is, as Donna Minkowitz (2000) put it, "still open season on gays" (p. 293). Reports on gay bashing appear regularly in the media. Take Matthew Shepard's murder, for example:

> On October 6, 1998, two young men lured twenty-one-year-old Matthew Shepard–a gay college student at the University of Wyoming in Laramie– into their truck and drove him to a remote spot on the Wyoming prairie, pistol whipped him, and shattered his skull. They then tied him, still alive, to a wooden fence as if he were a lifeless coyote, where he was bound for over eighteen hours in near freezing temperature. The message from his attackers seemed quite clear: to all LGBT [lesbian, gay, bisexual, and transgender] people, stay locked away in your suffocating closets of denial and fear and don't ever come out into the light of day. (Blumenfeld, 2000, p. 262)

Interior-Collective: Discursive Violence

In everyday discourse, lesbian and gay people are not only treated differently, they are talked about differently. From everyday conversation to media images, lesbian and gay experiences are represented differently from the invisible "heterosexual norm." For excellent discussions of LGBT representations in the media, see Gross and Woods (1999). The words, tone, gestures, and images that are used to differentially treat, degrade, pathologize, and represent lesbian and gay experiences is what I refer to as discursive violence.

It is not unusual in everyday conversations for seemingly lesbian and gay-affirmative individuals to ask the most intimate, intrusive, and inappropriate questions (e.g., "what do lesbians do in bed anyway?" "who is the 'man' [in a lesbian relationship]?"). While these invasive inquiries into the lives of lesbian and gay people are deemed as demonstration of interest in "the lesbian or gay lifestyle" and therefore socially acceptable, such questions are rarely considered appropriate among heterosexual couples. Similarly, references such as "her current partner" when discussing a long-term companion in a lesbian relationship presumes that such relationship has no lasting future. This is an act of violence.

Exterior-Collective: Institutional Violence

Undergirding all social institutions is heteronormative ideology (Richardson, 1996). Hegemonic heterosexuality permeates the family, domestic life, education, organizations, social policy, the mass media; in short, heteronormative thinking is deeply ingrained, and strategically invisible, in our social and collective consciousness. The process of normalization of heterosexuality in our social system methodically disadvantages and disempowers individuals who do not conform to the heterosexual mandate. For example, few institutions provide domestic partnership benefits to same-sex couples while such benefits are taken-for-granted by heterosexually married couples.

AN APPLICATION OF THE MODEL
IN THE UNIVERSITY CLASSROOM

To illustrate my model, I created, designed, and tested a classroom activity called "Beyond the charmed circle." This exercise is designed to engage the student in affective, cognitive, and behavioral learning. That is, the activity brings up potentially intense emotional responses, sensations, and thoughts that can be used to develop deeper awareness of the daily acts of violence committed against LGBT individuals. Such awareness can be the foundation for the development of a more critical consciousness regarding heteronormative ideology and potential ways to engage in acts of resistance (Yep, 1998). "Beyond the charmed circle" can be used in about any university course where the subject of (homo/hetero)sexuality is discussed. Before the activity starts, discussion of instructions and ground rules (e.g., non-judgmental responses, no ridiculing) is critical. About 4-6 students are placed in a group. The activity, borrowing from Griffin and Haro (1997), consists of four basic groups. Although the exercise is designed for classes with 16-24 students participating, it can easily accommodate more students by creating multiple basic groups. The four basic groups are designed to illustrate (1) Group A (soul murder and internalized homophobia), (2) Group B (externalized homophobia and hate crime), (3) Group C (discursive violence), and (4) Group D (institutional violence). Instructions for each one of these four groups follow.

Group A

Imagine a sixteen-year-old European American woman living in Coeur d'Alene, Idaho. She is attracted to her best friend, the most popular student in her high school and voted "most likely to succeed in college." Her family is extremely uncomfortable with discussions of sexuality in general. She is not sure whether she can trust her friends with the secret.

1. Now imagine what this young woman might be experiencing–her feelings, thoughts, sensations. Describe in detail.
2. What if the above situation involved a young man who is attracted to his best friend and teammate, the captain of the high school football team? Describe in detail.
3. What if the above situation involved an African American young woman? An African American young man? A Latino? A Latina? An Asian American young woman? An Asian American young man? A Native American woman? Add other social groups if you can. Describe your reactions in detail.

Group B

Imagine you are a lesbian, gay, bisexual, or transgender (LGBT) person living in Denton, Texas. You are the victim of a hate crime–you were called names when you were brutally beaten up and you were repeatedly told that you don't have the right to live because of your presumed sexuality. There were witnesses but no one attempted to intervene or help. You are seriously injured. What do you do?

1. Do you report it to the police? Will they take the incident seriously?
2. If you go to the hospital, how will you explain what happened if you are not "out"?
3. Will your name be in the newspaper?
4. How will your sense of freedom to move around and go places change?
5. What if the above situation involved a person of a different gender, race, or social class? Describe your reactions in detail.

Group C

Imagine you are a lesbian, gay, bisexual, or transgender (LGBT) person living in San Francisco, California. You and your partner are in a committed relationship of five years. You are out to your family who is uncomfortable about your "lifestyle." You and your partner visit your parents in Bakersfield, California, for the holidays. This is the first time that they asked you to bring your partner. They insisted that you stay with them for the entire two weeks you are visiting and you agree. Imagine what feelings, thoughts, and sensations you and your partner might experience in the following situations.

1. When you arrive, your mother shows you to the room where you will be staying. This room has two single beds separated by two night tables. Your sister and her new husband are staying in the adjacent room with a king-size bed.
2. Your sister, who is the closest to you and most accepting of your "lifestyle," introduces your partner to her new husband as your "current" girl/boyfriend.
3. When your nieces, nephews, and other family members arrive for the holiday dinner, your sister's new husband is introduced as "uncle" and your partner is introduced as a "friend."
4. After the holiday dinner, the adults sit around and talk about memorable moments in their intimate relationships–your parents reminisce about their first date, your sister and her new husband recall how she asked him out, your brother and his wife remember their first kiss, your aunt and uncle recall how he proposed to her. Everybody is taking turns to recall and re-live those memories. Although everybody knows about you and your partner, nobody asks you to do the same.
5. What would the above situation be like if your partner is of a different race and/or social class? Describe in detail.

Group D

You and your same-sex partner, living in Greenville, North Carolina, have decided to become parents. Imagine your feelings, thoughts, and sensations in the following situations.

1. How will you do it–alternative insemination, intercourse, adoption?
2. How will you tell your families?

3. Which partner will give birth (if you are women)? How will you decide? If you choose adoption, how will you deal with the agency's failure to recognize lesbian/gay couples?
4. How will you work out custody arrangements in the event of separation, death, or challenge by one partner's family?
5. Would the above situation be different if your race, class, and gender were different? What if your partner is of a different race and/or social class? Describe in detail.

After each group has completed their responses to the above scenarios, they are asked to summarize and share their reactions with the entire class. After all groups have presented their responses, a discussion of their experiences and the applicability of the model can follow. Debriefing is critical and students should be given ample time to identify, process, and share their feelings and thoughts.

IMPLICATIONS

In this essay, I discussed some of the problems associated with an exclusive focus on homophobia and I proposed a model that focuses on heteronormativity as a site of social, cultural, and interpersonal violence and oppression for LGBT persons. Developing a critical consciousness about the pervasive and oppressive nature of heteronormativity in all spheres of society necessitates educators, researchers, policymakers, counselors, and activists to interrogate, highlight, and demystify the often invisible ways that heterosexuality, as a concept and as an institution, influences and affects the daily lives of individuals and communities (Yep, 1998). For LGBT individuals, heteronormativity creates the conditions for homophobia, soul murder, psychic terror, and institutional violence. In addition, such violence is experienced and negotiated differently based on the individual's race, class, and gender. For heterosexual individuals, interrogation of heteronormativity means understanding their unearned privileges and perhaps seeing how sexual hierarchies limit personal freedom, human creativity, and individual expression. With a more complete understanding of the oppressiveness of our current sexual hierarchy, everyone can celebrate their own form of human sexual expression rather than having "LGBT Pride Day" once a year against the backdrop of "Everyday is 'Heterosexual Pride Day'" (Carbado, 1999, p. 442).

REFERENCES

Anzaldúa, G. E. (2000). *Interviews/entrevistas* (A. Keating, ed.). New York: Routledge.

Blumenfeld, W. J. (Ed.). (1992). *Homophobia: We all pay the price.* Boston: Beacon Press.

Blumenfeld, W. J. (2000). Heterosexism. In M. Adams, W. J. Blumenfeld, R. Castañeda, H. W. Hackman, M. L. Peters, & X. Zúñiga (Eds.), *Readings for diversity and social justice: An anthology on racism, antisemitism, sexism, heterosexism, ableism, and classism* (pp. 261-266). New York: Routledge.

Carbado, D. W. (1999). Straight out of the closet: Men, feminism, and male heterosexual privilege. In D. W. Carbado (Ed.), *Black men on race, gender, and sexuality: A critical reader* (pp. 417-447). New York: New York University Press.

Eyre, L. (1997). Re-forming (hetero)sexuality education. In L. G. Roman & L. Eyre (Eds.), *Dangerous territories: Struggles for difference and equality in education* (pp. 191-204). New York: Routledge.

Fone, B. (2000). *Homophobia: A history.* New York: Metropolitan Books.

Griffin, P., & Haro, B. (1997). Heterosexism curriculum design. In M. Adams, L. A. Bell, & P. Griffin (Eds.), *Teaching for diversity and social justice: A sourcebook* (pp. 141-169). New York: Routledge.

Gross, L., & Woods. J. D. (Eds.). (1999). *The Columbia reader on lesbians and gay men in media, society, and politics.* New York: Columbia University Press.

hooks, b. (2000). Homophobia in Black communities. In M. Adams, W. J. Blumenfeld, R. Castañeda, H. W. Hackman, M. L. Peters, & X. Zúñiga (Eds.), *Readings for diversity and social justice: An anthology on racism, antisemitism, sexism, heterosexism, ableism, and classism* (pp. 283-287). New York: Routledge.

Jackson, S. (1999). *Heterosexuality in question.* London: Sage.

Lim-Hing, S. (2000). Dragon ladies, snow queens, and Asian-American dykes: Reflections on race and sexuality. In M. Adams, W. J. Blumenfeld, R. Castañeda, H. W. Hackman, M. L. Peters, & X. Zúñiga (Eds.), *Readings for diversity and social justice: An anthology on racism, antisemitism, sexism, heterosexism, ableism, and classism* (pp. 296-299). New York: Routledge.

Lorde, A. (1990). Age, race, class, and sex: Women redefining difference. In R. Ferguson, M. Gever, M-H. Trinh, & C. West (Eds.), *Out there: Marginalization and contemporary cultures* (pp. 281-287). Cambridge, MA: MIT Press.

Minkowitz, D. (2000). Murder will out–but it's still open season on gays. In M. Adams, W. J. Blumenfeld, R. Castañeda, H. W. Hackman, M. L. Peters, & X. Zúñiga (Eds.), *Readings for diversity and social justice: An anthology on racism, antisemitism, sexism, heterosexism, ableism, and classism* (pp. 293-295). New York: Routledge.

Pharr, S. (1988). *Homophobia: A weapon of sexism.* Little Rock, AR: Chardon Press.

Plummer, K. (1998). Homosexual categories: Some research problems in the labelling perspective of homosexuality. In P. M. Nardi & B. E. Schneider (Eds.), *Social perspectives in lesbian and gay studies: A reader* (pp. 84-99). London: Routledge.

Rich, A. (1983). Compulsory heterosexuality and lesbian existence. In A. Snitow, C. Stansell, & S. Thompson (Eds.), *Powers of desire: The politics of sexuality* (pp. 177-205). New York: Monthly Review Press.

Richardson, D. (1996). Heterosexuality and social theory. In D. Richardson (Ed.), *Theorising heterosexuality: Telling it straight* (pp. 1-20). Buckingham, U.K.: Open University Press.

Rubin, G. S. (1993). Thinking sex: Notes for a radical theory of the politics of sexuality. In H. Abelove, M. A. Barale, & D. M. Halperin (Eds.), *The lesbian and gay studies reader* (pp. 3-44). New York: Routledge.

Sears, J. T., & Williams, W. L. (Eds.). (1997). *Overcoming heterosexism and homophobia: Strategies that work*. New York: Columbia University Press.

Shengold, L. (1989). *Soul murder: The effects of childhood abuse and deprivation*. New Haven, CT: Yale University Press.

Shengold, L. (1999). *Soul murder revisited: Thoughts about therapy, hate, love, and memory*. New Haven, CT: Yale University Press.

Smith, B. (1998). *The truth that never hurts: Writings on race, gender, and freedom*. New Brunswick, NJ: Rutgers University Press.

Warner, M. (1993). Introduction. In M. Warner (Ed.), *Fear of a queer planet: Queer politics and social theory* (pp. vii-xxxi). Minneapolis, MN: University of Minnesota Press.

Wilber, K. (2000). *Integral psychology: Consciousness, spirit, psychology, therapy*. Boston: Shambhala.

Wittig, M. (1992). *The straight mind and other essays*. Boston: Beacon Press.

Yep, G. A. (1997). Changing homophobic and heterosexist attitudes: An overview of persuasive communication approaches. In J. T. Sears & W. L. Williams (Eds.), *Overcoming heterosexism and homophobia: Strategies that work* (pp. 49-64). New York, NY: Columbia University Press.

Yep, G. A. (1998). Freire's conscientization, dialogue, and liberation: Personal reflections on classroom discussions of marginality. *Journal of Gay, Lesbian, and Bisexual Identity, 3*, 159-166.

*Trans*cending Heteronormativity in the Classroom: Using Queer and Critical Pedagogies to Alleviate Trans-Anxieties

Karen E. Lovaas
Lina Baroudi
S. M. Collins

SUMMARY. Although a growing body of work addresses heterosexism and homophobia in the classroom context, the majority of this literature neglects trans identities and issues. For various reasons, trans existence

---

Karen E. Lovaas, PhD, is Assistant Professor of Critical Theory in the Department of Speech and Communication Studies, San Francisco State University, 1600 Holloway Avenue, San Francisco, CA 94132 (E-mail: klovaas@igc.org). Her teaching, research, and consulting work are in the areas of gender, sexuality, culture, conflict, and communication.

Lina Baroudi, BA, is affiliated with the Department of Sociology, San Francisco State University, 1600 Holloway Avenue, San Francisco, CA 94132 (E-mail: lbaroudi@juno.com). She is in the midst of graduate school applications. Her political activism and research interests focus on queer theory and the contextualization of Middle Eastern/Arab-American (homo)sexuality within the realm of (post)colonial hysterographies, migrations, and diasporas.

S. M. Collins, BA, is affiliated with the Department of Theatre Arts, San Francisco State University, 1600 Holloway Avenue, San Francisco, CA 94132 (E-mail: smcshadow@yahoo.com). He holds his first BA from CSUN in Deaf Studies/American Sign Language. He graduated Cum Laude in 1998.

Address correspondence to: Karen E. Lovaas, San Francisco State University, Department of Speech and Communication Studies, 1600 Holloway Avenue, San Francisco, CA 94132.

[Haworth co-indexing entry note]: "*Trans*cending Heteronormativity in the Classroom: Using Queer and Critical Pedagogies to Alleviate Trans-Anxieties." Lovaas, Karen E., Lina Baroudi, and S. M. Collins. Co-published simultaneously in *Journal of Lesbian Studies* (Harrington Park Press, an imprint of The Haworth Press, Inc.) Vol. 6, No. 3/4, 2002, pp. 177-189; and: *Addressing Homophobia and Heterosexism on College Campuses* (ed: Elizabeth P. Cramer) Harrington Park Press, an imprint of The Haworth Press, Inc., 2002, pp. 177-189. Single or multiple copies of this article are available for a fee from The Haworth Document Delivery Service [1-800-HAWORTH, 9:00 a.m. - 5:00 p.m. (EST). E-mail address: getinfo@haworthpressinc.com].

currently poses particular challenges to many college students and professors. Foremost among these are traditional assumptions about sex, gender, and sexual identities as stable, essential, binary entities, notions that are often grounded in scientific, religious, and political ideologies.

In this essay, we first review various conceptualizations of transgenderism and explore the advantages of applying queer theory and critical pedagogical strategies to this subject. Second, based on our work together and our individual experiences, we offer suggestions for facilitating constructive classroom dialogues around "trans-anxieties" and provide examples of student responses to these methods. *[Article copies available for a fee from The Haworth Document Delivery Service: 1-800-HAWORTH. E-mail address: <getinfo@haworthpressinc.com> Website: <http://www.HaworthPress.com> © 2002 by The Haworth Press, Inc. All rights reserved.]*

KEYWORDS. Trans, transgender, transphobia, queer theory, critical pedagogy, trans-anxieties

(P)romoting gender equality in a democratic sexuality education involves expanding students' critical awareness of the wide range of ideological perspectives on the meaning of gender equality and the best means to reach it for both individuals and society. Fostering critical deliberation in this area represents a rejection of gender relations as "natural facts."

–Alexander McKay (1999, p. 171)

Our answer to the question "Who is a transsexual?" might well be "Anyone who admits it." A more political answer might be, "Anyone whose performance of gender calls into question the construct of gender itself."

–Kate Bornstein (1994, p. 121)

Like race, ethnicity, and class, issues dealing with gender and sexuality present special challenges for teachers and students, both when these subjects are the clearly marked focus of a course and when they arise in the midst of seemingly unrelated classroom discussions. The more closely one's personal profile matches that of the most privileged social categories in society, the more likely one is to be disturbed by the appearance of these subjects in the academy, a venue widely associated with the much vaunted qualities of objectivity, neutrality, and disembodied "truths." All are what are often referred to as "loaded" topics, safely handled only in narrowly defined contexts in which their political and emotional reverberations can be dampened if not erased. Yet, they do arise. And while, in the cases of gender and sexuality in particular, they trouble us, at times they also titillate us.

The authors of this article, a professor, a student who has worked with the professor as a teaching assistant in a class on sexual identity and communication, and a student in the same class who is a female to male transsexual or FTM, have had long conversations with one another about how the subject of transgenderism is met in the classroom. On a few occasions and in more than one course, the professor has been faced with students who have refused to attend a class session when informed that guest speakers who were transgendered would be present; in her many years of college teaching, this is the only situation in which students have cited the identity of the guest speakers—not even the specific subject matter of their talks—as the sole reason for nonattendance.

What is it about transgenderism that is so unnerving? And not only for students and professors who identify as heterosexual, but frequently for those who identify as lesbian, gay, and bisexual as well. Trans existence contraposes beliefs about sex and gender—along with and perhaps more so than sexual identity—as permanent, essential features of human experience. Encounters with transgendered subjects, whether via written and audiovisual course materials or face-to-face meetings with trans members of the academic community, threaten to inflict a disconcerting scrutiny of carefully constructed identity narratives of non-trans individuals, whether female, male, straight, lesbian, gay, monosexual, bisexual, pansexual, or queer.

As sex and gender are directly connected to sexuality studies, trans prejudice is also highly pertinent. Since the concept of trans bodies stems from the systematic support of gendered identities, one cannot talk about sexuality without discussing gender and sex. These constructs go hand in hand as they reinforce and maintain the basis of identities. Lesbian studies, which are connected to a construct of a "female" or "woman" identity, directly correlate to trans existence. After all, a trans person may be exploring the "continuum" of gender and sex, and assessing their position in relation to the identity of woman (or man). The fact that lesbian studies are already constructed around a "sex" reinforces the need for trans inclusion. Furthermore, these identity categories often overlap, with many trans individuals identifying as lesbian and vice versa.

In the title of this essay, the phrase "*trans*cending heteronormativity" conveys our sense that acknowledging and affirming trans existence in the classroom opens up what has been a little-explored perspective for viewing and deconstructing heteronormativity, that is, the nexus of sex/gender system that requires all constructions of gender and sexuality according to a heterosexual standard. We offer this claim from within the frameworks of queer theory and critical pedagogies, employing queer theory's premises regarding identity categories and aligning ourselves with critical pedagogy's conviction that education is an emancipatory project.

The title also bespeaks our intention to offer ways to "alleviate trans-anxieties." The noun "anxiety" refers to a troubled state of mind, "A state of uneasiness and apprehension, as about future uncertainties" (*American Heritage Dictionary*, 2000). In our experiences, individuals who have not contemplated transgenderism, whether by accident of circumstances or design, may profess a range of charged responses, including bewilderment, dismay, anger, curiosity, fascination; disinterest or immediate acceptance are unlikely. How do we create the conditions in which students and educators will risk looking at the unexamined, deeply held belief structure that trans existence upsets and trans-anxieties reflect?

We continue this essay by briefly defining transgenderism, summarizing the relevance of queer theory and critical pedagogies, and offering specific strategies for addressing trans-anxieties and transcending heteronormativity in the classroom context.

TRANSGENDER TERMINOLOGY

In a field undergoing rapid growth, discourse about trans individuals is in flux. In the past, "trans," usually "transsexual," was commonly understood to refer to a person who "felt trapped in the wrong body" and who crossed the sex and gender barriers by means of hormonal and surgical procedures. Virginia Prince may have been first to use the term "transgenderist" in reference to someone who lives full-time as the gender other than his or her biological sex without undergoing sex reassignment surgery (Prince, 1979).

A common meaning for transgender is now as an overarching word covering cross-dressers, drag queens, transsexuals, and anyone overtly transgressing traditional gender boundaries. Stryker explains that she uses transgender

> as an umbrella term for a wide variety of bodily effects that disrupt or denaturalize heteronormatively constructed linkages between an individual's anatomy at birth, a nonconsensually assigned gender category, psychical identifications with sexed body images and/or gendered subject positions, and the performance of specifically gendered social, sexual, or kinship functions. (1998, p. 149)

We adopt this interpretation of the term transgender and use it interchangeably with the word trans, which is quickly becoming a preferred term, and note its similarities with the radically reclaimed "queer."

QUEER THEORY

Juxtaposing homosexual identities with heterosexuality has been a central theme of lesbian and gay studies. Yet the categories of "gay," "lesbian," and "bisexual," abet the (binary) divisions of sex and gender classifications. In contrast, queer theory argues against the classification methodology of gay and lesbian studies, which inherently links sexual desire with sexual attraction and leaves out other potential attributes, such as sadomasochism, fetishism, butch/femme, and so on. Whereas lesbian and gay studies require gender classifications (such as lesbian = woman), queer theory moves beyond essentialist notions of sexuality and gender, breaking away from the definition of identities in relation to a dichotomous relationship with the "normal." Scrutiny of the compulsory expression of a normative sexual system refocuses the study of the "abnormal" to that which has been viewed as the standard. In queer theory, identity is an unrestrained performance, one that has no connection to an "essence" or truth. Identities, therefore, are not the production, but rather the result, of our performances. As Halperin (1995, p. 62) said, "Queer is by definition whatever is at odds with the normal, the legitimate, the dominant. *There is nothing in particular to which it necessarily refers.* It is an identity without an essence."

CRITICAL AND QUEER PEDAGOGIES

Critical pedagogy is education with the purpose of empowering and liberating individuals to transform social structures of inequity and oppression. The emancipatory project is not a single effort achieved solely in a classroom context. Rather, gaining knowledge with liberatory potential is an active, ongoing process that moves between acting and then evaluating one's action. As Freire (1972b) said, "The act of knowing involves a dialectical movement which goes from action to reflection and reflection upon action to new reflection" (p. 31). The result of reflective action is greater freedom to control one's social situation as opposed to participating in a hegemonic system that serves the dominant interests within a culture.

Numerous strains have emerged from Freire's "pedagogy of the oppressed" (1972a), all sharing an emphasis on praxis. Feminist and womanist pedagogies confront patriarchal discourse to decenter white male dominance, and recenter marginalized voices of women and people of color. Queer pedagogies involve engaging students in recognizing the paradoxes and troubles of socially constructed gender and sexual identities and critiquing hegemonic notions of normativity and deviance. Queer pedagogy views the classroom and the curriculum as sites for admiting specific perceived differences among individuals, not only among categories of individuals. The goal is not "that pedagogy become sexed, but that it excavate and interpret the ways it already is sexed—and further, that it inquire into the ways it is heterosexed" (Sumara & Davis, n.d.). In discussing the implications of their study of classroom use of literary forms to contest heteronormativity, Sumara and Davis advise that rather than making sexuality "an object of study," educators should acknowledge sexuality "as a valence of all knowing, and of all experiences and expressions of subjectivity."

In examining sex/gender/sexuality systems, it is vital that teachers recognize the formidable task of taking in knowledge, for student and teacher, especially when one's present understanding is functioning as an "entitlement to one's ignorance" or when the new knowledge "disrupts how the self might imagine itself and others" (Britzman, 1995, p. 159).

STRATEGIES FOR ALLEVIATING TRANS-ANXIETIES

No one should be surprised that classroom responses to trans existence reveal precisely the facets of possessed and encountered knowledge delineated by Britzman (1995), even in areas associated with tolerance and diversity, for example, the San Francisco Bay Area. Students and faculty often express a strong preference for their incoming opinions about transgenderism, with or without awareness of their underlying assumptions. Some students have visibly and audibly announced their rejection of opportunities to engage in dialogue with others around this subject; for example, in a class session in which two of us participated, one young woman, who identified herself as straight, displayed body language of yanking her cap down over half of her face, wrapping her arms tightly around her chest, and pushing her body down into her chair; a gay student in the same class complained aloud that the transgendered should make themselves more easily understood by others.

In this section, we address specific practices we have found helpful in establishing a classroom atmosphere conducive to self-reflection and collective dialogue about heteronormativity and trans oppression. Before we do so, we would like to make two points. First, though it is at times a temporary oasis from, and a source of renewal for returning to, other larger social settings, the classroom is not separate from those contexts. It is important to think in terms of struggle within or against the larger institutional structure and practices as well (Friend, 1998).

Second, and related to the first, is a recognition of the emotional challenges of the work, particularly when external support is lacking. Depending on economic and scheduling viability, co-teaching or facilitation greatly increases the available resources; when this is impossible, advance preparation and de-briefing with an appropriate colleague can be consoling as well as serving as a check on one's own gaps in knowledge or unresolved hot spots. On days when subjects about which one is underprepared are to be addressed, some instructors opt to bring in guest speakers with greater expertise and facilitation skills than their own, rather than avoiding the subject.

A teacher who is not aware of her own concerns and capacities relative to navigation of sex, gender, and sexuality, and their intersections with other identity configurations, may add to her own and others' confusion and rein-force her own and others' avoidance of these subjects. Counterproductive strengthening of denial, bias, embarrassment, anxiety, and/or withdrawal are potential outcomes of well-meaning attempts motivated by guilt or misplaced confidence. An example conveyed to the authors by an FTM student about his interaction with one such apparently well-intentioned instructor follows:

> On the first day of a theatre class, the instructor asked if I intended to pursue female or male activities in the context of class. I said, male, of course, because I am a transgender man and not a woman. She suggested that I should pursue gender neutral or gay identity positions in performances as the viewers and my peers would more readily accept me in a gay or gender ambiguous position rather than as a male. I said I would consider this but never did take this stance. I kept true to myself, though I could have taken up these other spaces. I preferred her pulling me aside to speak with me, rather than saying something in class or making a glaring gender/pronoun error in class. I still felt that she was hindered and biased in her feedback of my work, since she could not get past this issue that she had put there as an obstacle.

The same student reported an experience with a different instructor who, having established a ritual of greeting him with "hey, bub" or "what's up, guy?" dropped these greeting forms after discovering through another source that the student had transitioned. On occasion thereafter he referred to the student and a woman student in the class as "ladies." The student's gender presentation had not changed, only the instructor's reading of it had.

This, then, is the starting point for all who desire to integrate trans and queer issues and include trans and queer students in their classes: examining one's own attitudes, knowledge, and understanding. Homework should begin at home. Whatever their identity affiliations, instructors can become knowledgeable of shifting terminology and definitions and evolving traditions of respectful language related to the trans communities (see Appendix A).

Decisions about whether to and to what extent instructors can appropriately and constructively disclose their own sex, gender, and sexual identities is a topic that cannot be adequately addressed here. We do agree with the reasons Didi Khayatt gives for not declaring one's identity/ies definitively:

> because one's identity is continually in flux, and the act of freezing one's identity in place . . . , even for a moment, does not do justice to the teacher presenting herself or himself in class. What it does is to define the teacher's persona through an act of oppression and to encourage students to see the teacher as standing in for an entire group. Furthermore, there is nothing to guarantee how the statement will be heard by the individual student. (Khayatt, 1999, p. 108)

Regardless of self-labeling, students are apt to perceive the instructor who incorporates queer examples or materials into the class–practices that already break into the omnipresence of heteronormativity–as having "an agenda."

Of the three authors of this piece, one of us prefers not to make any verbal statements about gendered identities, and two of us typically, if not always initially, refer to ourselves as queer-identified. One of us felt complimented when told that by the time she made reference to her sexuality in a class, her credibility as knowledgeable, inclusive, and respectful was sufficiently strong that this disclosure was deemed unimportant.

We see no good substitute for careful work at the start of each course to establish the foundation for a safe space, that is, a relatively protected place for discussions of personally and socially volatile topics, whatever the purported subject matter of the class. Early on, we recommend that students learn that difficult subjects will not be shied away from but integrated into whatever else is happening in the course. With this in mind, students along with the teacher enumerate the qualities and behaviors that they have learned are most conducive to creating an environment for productive collaborative work, self-examination, and some risk taking, and from it construct a list of ground rules. Probably everyone will recall experiences of both negative and positive classroom environments. How might they now, with this new and temporary community, contribute to the latter? How might they sabotage the class? Reproduce, distribute, and confirm that the list will function as a set of working agreements for members of the class. You might find it helpful to review it periodically.

Some of the most entrenched blocks to trans acceptance are linked to prevailing scientific, religious, and political ideologies and gender models. Simple taxonomies can be reassuring, whatever their basis. Male and female reproductive biology, Adam and Eve in the Garden of Eden, the nuclear family, and any essentializing schema, including some feminisms, provide ready made rationales for going no further in one's thinking about–or even to just sit with–the conflicting truths represented by trans subjectivities. Even if a lesbian student, for example, has come to terms with her own internalized oppression, will she necessarily integrate the variability within trans communities, such as gender bending? How will she respond to the possibility of a lesbian friend's "choosing" to transition, and, if the relationship remains intact, how will she negotiate her responses to physical signs of the transition process?

Starting the examination of gender/sex construction with language and discourse is a stepping-stone for further discussion around trans existence. One question that we repeatedly raised in the course on sexual identity and communication was: "How do you know what you know?" Introduce such probes around topics less sensitive than sexual and gender identities. The aim is for the students to realize the social constructedness of belief systems.

Making connections between past and present attitudes towards a subject matter also lends itself to discussion of social conditioning and the effects of institutionalized mores. For example, while most students in the aforementioned class reacted to eugenics as something outrageous, we reminded them that the sciences that medicalized racial hierarchies were also responsible for the medicalization of gender, sex, and sexuality. This invitation to view social institutions as systems that classify certain individuals as inferior or deviant has prompted students to reconsider their own experiences and assumptions about the sources of their social identities. Again, we advocate an exploration of different perspectives on identities, but not to the point of pushing the students too abruptly or too far from their comfort zones.

Intervention strategies during class sessions are a major consideration in discussing trans identities in the classroom. As we mentioned early on, trans existence evokes in some an unusual degree of discomfort. Due to the diverse backgrounds and attitudes of students, shifting interpersonal dynamics, and ever-changing social contexts, it is impossible to fully prepare for reactions and questions. While we have found most individuals to be almost curiously polite when starting to talk about trans identities, the atmosphere we sensed in the classroom on the first day designated as related to transgenderism was uneasy and apprehensive (though the ingoing anxiousness of the instructor and teaching assistant enter into that impression). A challenging task of discussing trans identities in the classroom is making room for questions from people who are utterly unfamiliar with the matter, while maintaining respect and dignity for those who *are* "the matter." We must recognize that many students are interested in learning about the unfamiliar and come from a frame of reference loaded with misinformation, silence, and ridicule. Therefore, our approach to handling awkward remarks and inquiries generally involves hearing, checking for understanding of, and validating the student's contribution, followed by asking for clarification of the students' views, offering additional ways of looking at the issue, or reframing the question. The aim in responding to comments is to draw out the experiences of the students to better understand where they are coming from and how they have come to hold particular notions, while lessening the offensive charge that may be making the classroom feel unsafe for others to speak.

Ways of effectively responding to insulting remarks or gestures in the classroom has been a topic of ongoing discussion for us. Our experience indicates that addressing the situation depends enormously on the specific circumstances involved. Was it in a written assignment shared only with the instructor and/or teaching assistant? Was it in an interpersonal exchange, a small group discussion, or the full class arena?

The full class context is appropriate for providing a framework for discussing trans identities. Rather than singling out a student who has made a disparaging remark in the presence of the full class, it is beneficial to use the comment or language to address the group as a whole and/or to make an opportunity to meet with the student one on one. Smaller group discussions are useful in further development of thinking about trans identities, as they allow students to more comfortably try out their questions and ideas while the instructor can offer more attention and specific examples. Some students' feelings on a subject emerge primarily in their written work, read only by the instructor and teaching assistant. Feedback through this medium gives students a chance to reflect privately on their ideas and ways of expressing themselves. A face-to-face follow-up may be initiated by the student or the teacher. A great deal of helpful feedback, critical and positive, has surfaced in students' written work and course evaluations.

CONCLUSION

Overall, student responses to the methods described in this essay encourage us to think that we are on the right track. Three such examples of written feedback received from members of one class follow.

My entire idea about trans identities changed. I was under the impression that transgendered individuals were "in limbo" (for lack of better words), waiting to figure out what "sex" they wanted to be. . . . Honestly, I never realized how much I was ignorant, and so brainwashed to believe that a person had to be one or the other sex/gender. I was able to step back and reevaluate my own feelings, my own biases and my own ignorance. In doing so, I realized how much I judged and labeled, and how necessary it was that I re-examine who I am, and how I see people.

I was especially touched that many people who have never heard of terms like "transgender" and "FTM" were willing to learn and share their feelings and stay open minded–it is with the help of these students that society can change.

The articles we read on gender and the transgendered community were very important to me. My grasp of gender, despite the classes I've taken, remains weak. As a queer person, I am embarrassed that my knowledge on issues that affect transgendered individuals is so minimal. I've already started reading articles to increase my knowledge. If I want to work in the queer community, I need to have a broad base of knowledge about these topics.

Though many of the reflections shared in this essay emerge from classes that were explicitly concerned with gender and sexual identities, in which one can more easily justify focusing on transgenderism, the underlying queer and critical approaches and specific practices are used by the authors in other contexts as well. The instructor uses a variety of examples, case studies, exercises, and visual materials involving members of the trans community in her other courses, which include culture and communication, family communication, group communication, conflict resolution, and nonverbal communication. The student authors, working in the disciplines of Sociology and Theatre Arts, apply these ideas in their own interactions and coursework. We would be happy to continue this dialogue with the reader, to exchange recommendations for good resources, offer additional suggestions for materials and activities, and further each other's thinking about transcending heteronormativity in the college classroom.

REFERENCES

The American Heritage Dictionary of the English Language. (4th ed.). (2000). Boston: Houghton Mifflin.

Bornstein, K. (1994). *Gender outlaw: On men, women, and the rest of us.* New York: Vintage Books.

Britzman, D. (1995). Is there a queer pedagogy? Or, stop reading straight. *Educational Theory, 45*(2), 151-165.

Freire, P. (1972a). *Pedagogy of the oppressed.* Ringwood: Penguin Books.

Freire, P. (1972b). *Cultural action for freedom.* Ringwood: Penguin Books.

Friend, R. (1998). Undoing heterosexism and homophobia: Moving from "talking the talk" to "walking the walk." *Journal of Sex Education and Therapy, 23*(1), 94-104.

Halperin, D. (1995). *Saint Foucault: Towards a gay hagiography.* New York/Oxford: Oxford University Press.

Khayatt, D. (1999). Sex and pedagogy: Performing sexualities in the classroom. *GLQ: A Journal of Lesbian and Gay Studies, 5* (1), 107-113.

McKay, A. (1999). Sexual ideology and schooling; Towards democratic sexuality education. Albany, NY: State University of New York Press.

Prince, V. (1979). Charles to Virginia: Sex research as a personal experience. In V. Bullough (Ed.). *The frontiers of sex research* (pp. 167-175). Buffalo, NY: Prometheus Books.

Stryker, S. (Ed.). (1998). The transgender issue: An introduction. *GLQ: A Journal of Lesbian and Gay Studies, The Transgender Issue, 4* (2), 145-158.

Sumara, D., & Davis, B. (n.d.). *Interrupting heteronormativity with literary forms.* Retrieved from: http://eduserv.edu.yorku.ca/~davis&sumara/anthropologies2.html.

APPENDIX A
Recommended Resources

JOURNAL

The International Journal of Transgenderism. Available: URL: http://www.symposion.com/

BOOKS AND ARTICLES

Calfia, P. (1997). *Sex changes: The politics of transgenderism.* California: Cleis Press.

Cameron, L. (1996). *Body alchemy: Transsexual portraits.* California: Cleis Press.

Feinberg, L. (1998). *Trans liberation.* Boston: Beacon Press.

Hernandez, M. M. (1996). Boundaries: Gender and transgenderism. In P. Califia and R. Sweeney (Eds.), *The second coming: A leatherdyke reader* (pp. 63-70). Los Angeles: Alyson.

Sanlo, R.L. (Ed.). (1998). *Working with lesbian, gay, bisexual and transgender college students: A handbook for faculty and administrators.* Westport, Connecticut: Greenwood Press.

FILMS

Cram, B. (1997). *You don't know dick: Courageous hearts of transsexual men.* USA Made Film directed by C. Schermerhorn.

Davis, K. (2000). *Southern comfort.* USA Made Film.

Morse, O. (1996). *The wrong body: The decision documentary series.* Windfall Films, London: United Kingdom.

WEBSITES

FTM International Organization. (2001). Available: URL: http://www.ftm-intl.org

GenderPAC. (2001). Available: URL: http://www.gpac.org/

International Foundation for Gender Education. (2001). Available: URL: http://www.ifge.org/

National Transgender Library & Archives. (2001). Available: URL: http://www.gender.org/ntgla

Journeying Together:
Three Voices on the Process
of Making the Invisible Visible

Frédérique Chevillot
Susan S. Manning
Paula D. Nesbitt

SUMMARY. Three women faculty from different disciplines assert the necessity of initiating a process to confront silence and create voice in order to address heterosexism and homophobia in the classroom. One advocates for the feminist construct of a consciously positional and

Frédérique Chevillot is Associate Professor of French in the Department of Languages and Literatures at the University of Denver, 2000 E. Asbury Avenue, Denver, CO 80208 (E-mail: fchevill@du.edu), where she is presently directing the Women's Studies program. Her research centers on contemporary women writing in French. For the past two years, she has been the editor of *Women in French Studies*.

Susan S. Manning is Associate Professor in the Graduate School of Social Work at the University of Denver, 2148 S. High Street, Denver, CO 80208 (E-mail: smanning@du.edu). She teaches in the areas of professional ethics, mental health, qualitative research, and leadership in community practice. Her research focus includes professional ethics and empowerment of oppressed populations.

Paula D. Nesbitt is Visiting Associate Professor in Sociology at the University of California, Berkeley, 410 Barrows Hall #1980, Berkeley, CA 94720-1980 (E-mail: pnesbitt@uclink.berkeley.edu). She recently taught in Women's Studies and Sociology at the University of Denver, and has also taught at Pacific School of Religion and Iliff School of Theology. Her PhD is in Sociology from Harvard University. She also holds a MDiv from Harvard Divinity School.

[Haworth co-indexing entry note]: "Journeying Together: Three Voices on the Process of Making the Invisible Visible." Chevillot, Frédérique, Susan S. Manning, and Paula D. Nesbitt. Co-published simultaneously in *Journal of Lesbian Studies* (Harrington Park Press, an imprint of The Haworth Press, Inc.) Vol. 6, No. 3/4, 2002, pp. 191-204; and: *Addressing Homophobia and Heterosexism on College Campuses* (ed: Elizabeth P. Cramer) Harrington Park Press, an imprint of The Haworth Press, Inc., 2002, pp. 191-204. Single or multiple copies of this article are available for a fee from The Haworth Document Delivery Service [1-800-HAWORTH, 9:00 a.m. - 5:00 p.m. (EST). E-mail address: getinfo@haworthpressinc.com].

political voice to improve students' sensitivity to multiculturalism in regard to lesbian, gay, bisexual, and transgendered people (LGBT). Another proposes a process of locating sexual orientation in the wider issues of sexuality and gender constructions, in order to form different assumptions and starting points. A third one challenges faculty members and students to accept that recognizing their own heterosexism and homophobia is the first step in the process of confronting and transforming what they fear. *[Article copies available for a fee from The Haworth Document Delivery Service: 1-800-HAWORTH. E-mail address: <getinfo@ haworthpressinc.com> Website: <http://www.HaworthPress.com> © 2002 by The Haworth Press, Inc. All rights reserved.]*

KEYWORDS. Multiculturalism, heterosexism, homophobia, teaching strategies, lesbian/gay/bisexual/transgendered (LGBT), fear

Three women faculty from different disciplines (Women's Studies, Social Work, Sociology and Religion) have joined together to continue a process that is too often only begun among faculty on campus, often in Women's Studies classrooms–the process of confronting silence and creating voice. Susan Manning advocates for the feminist construct of a consciously positional and political voice to improve students' sensitivity to multiculturalism in regard to lesbian, gay, bisexual, and transgendered people (LGBT). Paula Nesbitt proposes a process of locating sexual orientation in the wider issues of sexuality and gender constructions, in order to form different assumptions and starting points. Frédérique Chevillot challenges faculty members and students to accept that recognizing their own heterosexism and homophobia is the first step in the process of confronting and transforming what they fear.

A VOICE FROM SOCIAL WORK: MAKING THE INVISIBLE VISIBLE

By Susan S. Manning

In social work, the challenge of teaching students to value diversity in all of its expressions is ongoing. Sexual orientation is particularly difficult to approach. Faculty and staff members, students, and clients collude in maintaining invisibility; the "closet" door seems locked. Age, gender, color, disability, and even national origin are more apparent, therefore more available, as experiential and contextual lessons in the classroom. There is a noticeable contradiction in teaching about diversity in regard to sexual orientation. Even as we teach about difference, we act as if we are all the same–that is, heterosexual. Teaching strategies based on my lived experience as a lesbian have been useful in promoting the value of multiculturalism.

The NASW Code of Ethics, social work curriculum, and socialization of graduate social work students, emphasize the importance of multiculturalism. Multiculturalism is the understanding of culture and its function in human behavior, as well as an understanding of social diversity and oppression (NASW, 1999). Social work faculty, then, have a responsibility to help students prepare themselves to practice ethically, competently, and sensitively with LGBT individuals and groups.

However, sensitivity and understanding require more than knowledge. Walker and Staton (2000, p. 453) argue that multiculturalism," is best framed as a perspective toward others with a particular sensitivity to the full context of the client's identity, emotions, thoughts, and history." Here, multiculturalism becomes a *value*, and an *ethical principle*, requiring "a greater emphasis in social work education on the ethical responsibility for empathy" which furthers the goals of multiculturalism. Strategies are needed that help students develop the ethical responsibility for empathy with clients who are different from themselves.

The Classroom as a Microcosm of Society

The demographic characteristics of our student body are similar to many social work graduate schools–most students are white (83%), female (90%), and younger (66% are 30 and under). LGBT students are difficult to identify because they rarely identify themselves as such. Their silence preempts their demographic contribution to diversity. The classroom, then, on the surface, appears to be fairly homogenous, i.e., heterosexual.

The classroom reflects the "deep social inequalities" of the dominant society, as well as " individuals' unawareness of them" (Maher & Tetreault, 1994, p. 160). Heterosexual students have little insight into the stigma and oppression of LGBT persons unless they have sustained involvement with a LGBT significant other–family member, friend, etc. Interaction between heterosexual students occurs across gender, friendship, and political ties, but LGBT students are often silent about their identities (Maher & Tetreault, 1994). Silence in relation to all forms of difference prevents students who are marginalized because of class, color, sexual orientation, etc., from "asserting their authority in relation to others" in the classroom; inequalities are further reinforced.

Silence prevents heterosexual students and faculty from *meaningful* involvement with LGBT faculty and students. Cultural sensitivity requires an awareness of cultural difference, heightened self-awareness about value conflicts and value judgments, and an ability to identify stereotypes, based on knowledge about the particular culture (Walker & Staton, 2000). These factors require meaningful interaction with others. Understanding the stigma and power inequity of LGBT people is also necessary to promote empathy and activism. The logical response to counter silence, then, is voice.

Voice as a Faculty Member

I had to find my own voice in order to encourage the voices of marginalized students. The first years of teaching were oppressive as a lesbian. Even as I promoted social work content and values–emphasizing culture and context, celebrating diversity, encouraging multicultural thinking–other faculty and I colluded in the silence about sexual orientation. My family, my life as a lesbian, was a secret to be kept because of the ambivalences and ambiguities of "coming out." No one knew what was acceptable to reveal; therefore, nothing was revealed. Case examples of LGBT persons are used in class, but always in relation to some unknown "others." Silence gave the impression that everyone at school was heterosexual. Thus, LGBT faculty and students were placed in a "system of compulsory heterosexuality" (Maher & Tetreault, 1996, p. 150).

"Coming out" at first was awkward and abrasive–"I am a lesbian." A more integrated approach to reveal my identity resulted from increased consciousness about motives and academic goals for disclosure. The "announcement mentality" was replaced by reference to lesbianism as central to personhood. I wanted students to hear my voice as a professor who is also a lesbian.

My feminist authority in the classroom was communicated through an integration of personal identity and professorial and academic responsibilities (Maher & Tetreault, 1994). The strategy was not to become "equal" or "sisters" with students, but to affirm my identification (the personal), then transcend it to confront compulsory heterosexuality (the political). Finding my own voice created the opportunity to integrate the abstract theories of social behavior with a lived experience–"the personal is political," re-affirming the feminist dictum as a powerful way to promote change (Fernandez, 1999).

My personal disclosure is an expression of "first voice"–self-revelation and understanding the "lived experience" of people who make up our world (Weick, 2000). First voice promotes praxis in the classroom; theoretical analysis is connected to the everyday life experience of self and others. For example, I disclosed a story about the celebration of my relationship with my partner through a commitment ceremony. The importance of rituals as benchmarks of change is demonstrated. Stereotypes about lesbian relationships are confronted, and the losses that lesbians and gays experience through a lack of celebration for their commitments (from family, friends, and associates) are introduced. Students are encouraged to think critically about the role of rituals–promoting visibility or invisibility of "family" in the fabric of society. Stories about invisible populations open the door for students to find their own voice.

Voice for Students

Social work students must find their voice for two important reasons. First, discovering their own "consciously positional voice" provides an opportunity for self-expression of the individual, within the dominant group. Voice creates a position from which to explore the multiplicity of identities in the classroom (and the world). Second, students discover the political underpinnings of a complex society through the "consciously politicized context" of the classroom (Maher & Tetreault, 1994, p. 100).

The creation of safety in a classroom, through role modeling by faculty of different identities, promotes students' "constructing or reclaiming a consciously positional voice . . . [To] see her identity 'whole,' rather than having to sacrifice some aspect of it in order to fit into the class" (Maher & Tetreault, 1994, p. 101). After all, if the professor doesn't fit, no one has to fit. The *invisible* differences of the class, sexual orientation, and other identities of self and family are made known and validated in class.

"Voice" encourages "deterritorialization"–confronting our own location and moving away from what is familiar (Kaplan, 1990). "We must leave home, as it were, since our homes are often sites of racism, sexism, and other damaging social practices" (p. 364). Two primary aspects occur. First, students acknowledge there are things they do not know, and second, they learn about what they "have been taught to avoid, fear, or ignore" (p. 364). Students confront their own stereotypes and social norms by seeking the unfamiliar. They have a more rich understanding of "what connects us as well as how we are different from each other" (Kaplan, 1999, p. 364).

In conclusion, strategies that promote multiculturalism as a value, and instill in students a responsibility for empathy with those most unfamiliar, are congruent with the essence of social work. Invisible lives that are lived through silence, rather than voice, reinforce the marginalization of LGBT people. As social work faculty, whether heterosexual or LGBT, we must critically assess our collusion with silence or our contribution to voice–for students and for ourselves.

OVER THE TOP:
JOURNEYING TOGETHER BEYOND HETEROSEXISM

By Paula D. Nesbitt, Sociology

Years ago, Reverend Carter Heyward described the hostility surrounding the 1974 irregular ordinations of women to the Episcopal priesthood (Heyward, 1988). She, a lesbian, was sharing a room with a heterosexual colleague when a reporter broke through security, called their room, and pressed her roommate about their being lesbians. She replied that it was none of his business, then slammed down the phone. Rev. Heyward described what it meant to her for this colleague to willingly take on the oppression of being lesbian. Although I had considered myself a liberal heterosexual feminist, this story was a turning point in my own commitment to address homophobia and heterosexism.

During the 1990s, I taught in a moderately liberal United Methodist seminary at a time when religious denominations were moving from issues of women in ministry to those of sexual orientation (this link has provided many teaching moments). Students came from various denominations, many seeking to prepare for ordination. Among them were lesbian, gay, or bisexual students gifted with pastoral and preaching skills, and in community building–talents sorely needed by the very churches that were denying them ordination. Some saw that even if they might survive the endless scrutiny and questions of their denomination's "spiritual formation" process, their chances of being hired by a congregation for a full-time appointment were very slight. Even in the most liberal denominations, far more lesbian and gay clergy were looking for appointments than there were congregations willing to consider them. Typically, midway through their second year, they went through a "retooling" experience, realistically looking at nonordained vocations in social service, justice, music, academia, pastoral counseling, or spiritual direction.

The Students

Students in most moderate to liberal theological schools today range from about half to two-thirds female. Overall, including conservative seminaries, the average is slightly more than one-third female. The largest age group for both men and women is age 40 to 49, although conservative seminaries have a much higher proportion of men in their 20s. Women in their fifties and early sixties form the next largest female age group (Willard, 2000). In my own research and teaching experience, I've found that second-career students typically have had first careers in the professions of education, business, or other white-collar occupations (Nesbitt, 1997). Often, a crisis would have led them to reflect on how they want to live their lives differently. Consequently, seminary often becomes a spiritual journey, with deeply personal significance related to finding out who one authentically is and living that truth in the world. Invariably this means that both women and men gather the courage to "come out." As such, the seminary environment represents a highly vulnerable community, where unintentional as well as overt homophobia can cut to the quick, and where faculty need to be especially careful in their teaching content as well as their methodology.

Methodology for Spirituality and Sexuality Reawakening

In my teaching, I choose to use what I call the "over the top" method. Despite the politically correct veneer in seminary of accepting diverse sexual orientations, I have found that both the underlying ambivalences and the polarized attitudes that students experience when interacting with their denominations make the topic of sexual orientation itself very sensitive and vulnerable to statements of fixed belief. By getting underneath it, encompassing it in wider issues of sexuality and gender construction, we can go over the top in our exploration and return to a discussion of sexual orientation with different assumptions and starting points. I have found that this process invariably expands students' creative thinking and capacity to see sexual orientation as one facet among many in understanding our humanity.

Typically we begin by exploring the literature on gender construction and the many ways that gender can be conceptualized. Kessler and McKenna's (1985) discussion of *gender assignment, gender attribution, gender identity*, and *gender role identity*, and the arbitrariness of criteria for each of these, provide an important starting point for discussion of how these relate to religious and cultural understandings that have used different criteria and definitions over time. Their ethnographical work on transsexual identity construction also has provided a comprehensive entry point for more recent work to further open students' minds and give them tools to hold more comprehensive discussions with people in their congregations about the nature of our humanity in relation to gender or gender-role presentation or identity.

Robert Connell's (1987) work similarly has been foundational for constructing my pedagogical methodology and in reminding students of the importance of *practice* and *process*. According to Connell, understandings of gender and sexuality develop historically through sociocultural practices influenced by power relations. Since they change over time, they themselves are processes rather than fixed phenomena. But to change practice and thereby affect the gendering process takes time. People must change underlying assumptions as well as the perspectives that these assumptions undergird. Pressed to change too quickly, there is a risk of "backlash," or at best a student "shuts down" to further thinking on the topic.

A seminar process I used when we studied the religious blessing of same-gender relationships illustrates this method. The students thought that the topic could be exhausted in two or three sessions. The first third of the course was devoted to intensive reading. The primary ground rule was that students could state their status (gay, lesbian, straight, etc.), but they could not state their position on the topic. They were encouraged, however, to discuss their interests in the issue, similar to Fisher and Ury's (1983) negotiation method of focusing on interests and avoiding the negotiation of positions. Students were given a core list of diverse readings. They also could bring in readings for the class to discuss.

The second part of the course was primarily experiential. Invited guests shared their stories from a range of perspectives, although the ground rule for each guest was a sincere compassion for those of all orientations. Guests included a Roman Catholic priest expert in canon law; a gay Protestant couple who had their union blessed by a minister of their denomination (risking reprimand by denominational leadership); a Metropolitan Community Church minister; and several gay, lesbian, and straight clergy and laity.

Only in the final part of the course did students begin to discuss their own perspectives on the topic; that was following the use of a stakeholder approach in identifying everyone with a perceived direct or indirect stake in the issue and discussing pastoral responses for each, on both sides of the issue. The interest of each stakeholder was discussed, along with a pastoral response to that stakeholder for either a "pro" or "con" decision. Students were then encouraged to write a short position paper, stating what they believed and why, and then to share the contents in class. While some minor differences existed, students were amazed at how close to consensus they had arrived–agreeing that blessing was a justice issue, where theology had been used in ways similar to criteria for gender construction–influenced by power relations and developed through historical practice. The prolonged process also gave them a method to work with congregations where feelings about sexual orientation ranged from ambivalence to sharp polarity.

A Final Note

Religion is a very important area for lesbian students because as a group they have been most consistently alienated from religious communities. While gay men may pass as single, celibate, or married, and be spiritually fed by the rich patriarchy that permeates all the major world religious traditions, lesbians who reject patriarchy have a far more difficult time finding nonpatriarchal, inclusive, or matriarchal religious communities. Typically, they have had to leave their religious tradition of birth or upbringing. Feminist and nontraditional religious communities either within or outside the mainline religions are still few in most cities. It is important to equip lesbians, and their bisexual and straight sisters, with tools for helping to increase the spiritual resources and communities welcoming of all orientations. Spiritual well-being affects a variety of facets from health, to work, to affirming and fulfilling relationships in one's life. Religious studies departments, theological schools, and other areas where feminist spirituality is taught can go a long way in building the kinds of integrative support that over time can help transform heterosexist traditions.

A VOICE FROM WOMEN'S STUDIES AND FRENCH: COMING OUT AS HETEROSEXIST AND HOMOPHOBIC: A PROCESS

By Frédérique Chevillot, French and Women's Studies

How one addresses heterosexism and homophobia among college students on campus–and hopefully beyond as well–depends on a set of parameters, of which I will emphasize at least three: who, where, and to whom. It seems to me that these three elements put together will undoubtedly define the "how." In other words, the message conveyed and the way it will be delivered (the two are inseparable) will be contingent upon: who the person conveying the message is perceived as being; in what class circumstances the message is being delivered; and who appears to be receiving it. Again, we must work within a context of appearances, perceptions, and assumptions, all of which will tend towards becoming more explicit.

My experience in this domain is directly derived from my somewhat strange position as a perceived academic authority (that of a faculty member), with little expertise on the subject matter at hand (Women's Studies). Indeed, I came to the directorship of our undergraduate Women's Studies program out of personal interest and commitment to the multifaceted discipline. Institutionally, I present the advantage of being tenured in my "home" department of Languages and Literatures; my domain of expertise is French; my field of scholarly interest is women writing in French. However, I came to Women's Studies through the small door, without any formal academic training. Furthermore, self-identifying as a sheltered, white, privileged in many ways, heterosexual woman, I had no particular empirical or scholarly experience with heterosexism and homophobia. To complete the picture, I am of foreign origin, from a different culture and mother tongue; I talk funny.

"Straight but not narrow," I am, as a feminist, committed to social and emotional justice on behalf of all women–women of color, white women, lesbians, bisexual women, heterosexual women, old women, young women, women with and women apparently without disabilities, women who have a foreign accent in English, women who don't, women who work outside their homes, women who work at home, women here, and women there. Although I am not an expert at what I teach, I am, against all odds, in a position of power in the classroom. Depending on the level of awareness, activism, and/or resistance at which my students stand, this assumed authority may or may not be challenged, as, indeed, I would like it to be. This is who I am and whom I am perceived to be.

The Classroom

I am not always sure who my students are, but I know that the majority of them are white, privileged enough to attend a small private institution, and as far as I can tell–or as far as I am led to believe–heterosexual. Most of my students are female.

The context is that of our "Introduction to Women's Studies" course, which the director of the program traditionally teaches. We systematically look at our cultural history through the eyes of women, all women, especially those who do not seem to be represented in the classroom. Open to Women's Studies majors and non-majors alike, the course offers some ground for alliance and plenty of opportunities for resistance. In other words, some of these mostly sophomore and junior students simply do not see the reason why "we" should be talking about "things" and "people" that do not resemble them; these students will voice their opinions.

Teaching Strategies

One of the techniques I use, as a matter of teaching principle, is that of collectively "assuming" out loud, by relying on statistical data, that one person out of ten in the class is not heterosexual, including myself as a potentially closeted bisexual. This allows me to more spontaneously use an all-inclusive language. It also gives me the opportunity to indirectly build up alliances; I am constantly speaking to the class assuming the presence of three potentially closeted LGBT persons (classes gather on average between twenty and thirty participants), at times more openly than others, i.e., when I specifically remind the class of statistics.

I used to speak of my "husband," as I thought that stating my heterosexuality in plain and conventional ways would make the majority of students feel more comfortable and, therefore, make them more receptive. It was a mistake; the Women's Studies classroom must be a space, albeit a safe space, where conformity and comfort levels are being challenged. I now always speak of my partner; I speak of my partner's children and mine, rather than only of "my" children. I candidly wear my wedding band on my right hand, in hopes that someone will just be wondering. I also share quite self-consciously my personal experiences: When did I last catch myself in the act of being heterosexist? Homophobic? How did it feel? Why did it hurt? Whom did it hurt? Why was I led to it? How did I come to terms with it? Have I come to terms with it? I strongly believe that once a certain level of trust has been established between the class and the instructor, after a few weeks of interaction, personal tales of failure, as well as of bridge building, are extremely helpful.

I believe that it positively debunks that feeling of "academic authority" to emphasize that we simply cannot always be in control of our own racism, sexism, or homophobia. To me, this is the beginning of real consciousness: accepting responsibility for what we fear because we do not control or understand it, which basically comes to the same. Still, there is so much "I," a white heterosexual female faculty member of European origin, can do, in the classroom, on behalf of minority and lesbian women.

In my experience, the best and most innovative way to sensitize college students to homophobia and heterosexism is to invite a special friend and colleague (one of the few out lesbians or gay men on campus), who will have the beautiful courage and seductive audacity to have a fifty-minute discussion with my class. "So, I am a lesbian . . . " and "Yes, I am a gay man." After a wonderfully intense listening to our guest's opening remarks, questions just burst out. I daresay that our college students let themselves be children again in awe; the unknown is literally touching them; the false sense of fear vanishing. My job, as a facilitator of consciousness strengthening, is to follow up on our students' awakening to nonthreatening differences; the rest of the academic quarter remains marked by this intense intellectual and emotional happening in our students' lives.

My goal in the "Introduction to Women's Studies" class is to get students started with a process. Addressing heterosexism and homophobia on college campuses is more about getting processes started among as many students, staff, and faculty members as possible, than it is about feeling guilty for fearing to do so. It is also about forgiveness; forgiveness of oneself for erring in fear; forgiveness from those we have hurt and offended, consciously or not. In *Women Who Run With the Wolves*, Clarissa Pinkola Estés speaks of forgiveness in the following terms: "The important part of forgiveness is *to begin* and *to continue*. The finishing of it all is a life work" (Estés, 1992, 1995, p. 400).[1] Within the context of a Women's Studies introductory class, we may well have the opportunity to create a safe place for processes of forgiveness and understanding *to begin* and *to continue*. This space is not only intended for female students and faculty members of color, lesbians and bisexual women, but also for white heterosexual women (some of whom may be questioning their own sexual orientation), and for male students as well. The safe space allows us to say that we did not know, but are willing to begin accepting, that we were, indeed, negligently and/or fearfully holding heterosexist and homophobic beliefs.

A Final Question

In lieu of a conclusion, I will simply ask the following question. To what extent may one resist explicitly addressing homophobia and heterosexism among college students? For it does appear to me that any faculty member, staff member, administrator, or student for that matter, *does* address heterosexism and homophobia, by not talking about it; to not address it is to address it negatively. I would like to envision "addressing heterosexism and homophobia on college campuses" as a *process* which, as such, derives its methods or techniques from the level of awareness at which it temporarily resides, on its way to becoming matter-of-factly second nature. So the techniques I use in my classroom derive completely from who I was, am becoming, and have become in the process of being more aware and less assuming, less resisting, more empowered and empowering, less complacent with myself and with others. By inviting our students to embrace a process, rather than a full-blown piece of "knowledge," we run a much better chance of letting them allow themselves to come out of the closet of their own homophobia and heterosexism.

CONCLUSION

All of our voices have emphasized the importance of teaching about heterosexism and homophobia through a *process* that invites faculty and students to change their perceptions and attitudes. The process begins with developing voice to challenge the silence and invisibility of LGBT orientations. Consciously positional voices in the consciously politicized context of our classrooms give students the opportunity to analyze and understand the social constructions of society, and to create a more humane and just world.

A process that goes "over the top" and encompasses sexual orientation in wider issues of sexuality and gender construction allows us to understand sexual orientation as one facet among many in the complexity of humanity. A process allows time for all to assume responsibility for what we fear.

The process also provokes many questions. How do we recharge our energies? How do we take stock of our successes and failures? How do we recognize that the process might have started elsewhere, and needs to be continued wherever we are, whatever course we teach, beyond the classroom, back home, and within our communities? As affiliated members of the Women's Studies program at our institution, we wrote this essay together, in an effort to join others in the process of answering these questions.

The process of teaching about heterosexism and homophobia is ongoing for us all. As Chevillot said so poignantly, "To not address it is to address it negatively . . . a process . . . from the level of awareness at which it temporarily resides, on its way to becoming matter-of-factly second nature."

NOTE

1. I am indebted to Patricia Raybon's highly provocative and inspiring book, *My First White Friend*, for the reference to Clarissa Pinkola Estés' work.

REFERENCES

Connell, R.W. (1987). *Gender and power: Society, the person and sexual politics.* Stanford: Stanford University Press.

Estés, C. P. (1992, 1995). *Women who run with the wolves.* New York: Ballantine Books.

Fernandez, M. (1999). Contemporary feminism: Art practice, theory, and activism–An intergenerational perspective. *Art Journal 58*(4), 15-17.

Fisher, R., & Ury, W. (1983). *Getting to yes: Negotiating agreement without giving in.* New York: Penguin Books.

Heyward, C. (1988, November 11-13). Plenary response. Presentation made at the conference, *A garden party: Explorations in feminist theology.* Episcopal Divinity School, Cambridge, MA.

Kaplan, C. (1990). Deterritorializations: The rewriting of home and exile in western feminist discourse. In A. JanMohamed & D. Lloyd (Eds.) *The nature and context of minority discourse*, 357-368. Oxford: Oxford University Press.

Kessler, S.J., & McKenna, W. (1985). *Gender: An ethnomethodological approach.* Chicago: University of Chicago Press.

Maher, F., & Tetreault, M. (1994). *The feminist classroom.* New York: Basic Books.

National Association of Social Workers. (1996). *Code of ethics of National Association of Social Workers.* Washington, DC: NASW

Nesbitt, P.D. (1997). *Feminization of the clergy in America: Occupational and organizational perspectives.* New York: Oxford University Press.

Raybon, P. (1996). *My first white friend: Confessions on race, love, and forgiveness.* New York: Penguin Books.

Walker, R., & Staton, M. (2000). Multiculturalism in social work ethics. *Journal of Social Work Education 36*(3), 449-462.

Weick, A. (2000). Hidden voices. *Social Work 45*(5), 395-402.

Willard, L.C. (Ed.) (2000). *Fact book on theological education 1999-2000*. Pittsburgh, PA: The Association of Theological Schools.

Teaching About Heterosexism and Creating an Empathic Experience of Homophobia

Patricia Little

Marcia Marx

SUMMARY. The concept of the "chilly campus climate" for students has long been used to describe women's experiences. The climate for lesbians and gays has not been assessed in this way; however, the attitudes of students toward diverse groups suggest that generally a hostile environment exists for this population. This paper discusses assessing students' attitudes and how this is essential to the process of teaching about heterosexism. Other pedagogical issues and concerns regarding teaching about heterosexism and homophobia are examined. These include examples of teaching exercises intended to create an empathic response from students that reinforces their cognitive understanding of homophobia. *[Article copies available for a fee from The Haworth Document Delivery Service: 1-800-HAWORTH. E-mail address: <getinfo@haworthpressinc.com>*

Patricia Little, PhD, is Assistant Professor, Department of Sociology, California State University, San Bernardino, 5500 University Parkway, San Bernardino, CA 92407-2397 (E-mail: plittle@csusb.edu).

Marcia Marx, PhD, is Associate Professor, Department of Sociology, Ethnic and Women's Studies, California State University, San Bernardino, 5500 University Parkway, San Bernardino, CA 92407-2397 (E-mail: mmarx@csusb.edu).

This project was a collaborative effort and the order in which the author's names are listed does not imply that one author contributed more than the other.

[Haworth co-indexing entry note]: "Teaching About Heterosexism and Creating an Empathic Experience of Homophobia." Little, Patricia, and Marcia Marx. Co-published simultaneously in *Journal of Lesbian Studies* (Harrington Park Press, an imprint of The Haworth Press, Inc.) Vol. 6, No. 3/4, 2002, pp. 205-218; and: *Addressing Homophobia and Heterosexism on College Campuses* (ed: Elizabeth P. Cramer) Harrington Park Press, an imprint of The Haworth Press, Inc., 2002, pp. 205-218. Single or multiple copies of this article are available for a fee from The Haworth Document Delivery Service [1-800-HAWORTH, 9:00 a.m. - 5:00 p.m. (EST). E-mail address: getinfo@haworthpressinc.com].

205

KEYWORDS. Homophobia, heterosexism, pedagogy, teaching, empathy

The "chilly campus climate" was first used to explain the experience of women on college campuses both inside and outside the classroom (Hall & Sandler, 1982; 1984). The campus climate project had been instrumental in gathering numerous reports and attitudinal surveys focusing on women's common experiences at colleges throughout the U.S. The various data documented the inequitable treatment that women received when compared to men. These reports had a significant effect on increasing the awareness of educators, staff personnel, and administrators regarding the sexist nature of campus cultures, and, as a result, the report proposed numerous policies that were designed to effect change on college campuses.

Since then, studies have examined the experience of other diverse groups, including African Americans and gays and lesbians. Similar to the results found in the reports undertaken by the Project on the Status and Education of Women, the climate for African American students has been characterized as unwelcoming and even hostile (Feagin, 1999). Studies that have examined the campus climate for gays and lesbians draw similar conclusions (Cotton-Huston & Waite, 2000; D'Augelli, 1989; Herek, 1984, 1986; Kite, 1994); therefore, the need to work for change on college campuses is apparent. This is the point at which our paper begins, since our focus is the classroom and how as educators we can improve what is now a "chilly campus climate" for gays and lesbians. Specifically, we examine issues of pedagogy, including various techniques to use when teaching about heterosexism and homophobia.

HOW CHILLY IS THE CLASSROOM FOR GAYS AND LESBIANS?

Our own research (Marx & Little, 2001) has documented the extent of students' prejudices, and, frankly, we had not anticipated how severe the problem was on our campus. As a result, we encourage routine assessment of students' attitudes in order to identify the climate and situate students' perceptions in the context of the course materials before beginning the discussion of heterosexism and homophobia. We include an instrument to use for assessing students' attitudes in Appendix A. The questions from the survey instrument can then be used as an effective tool to begin a dialogue about homophobia and heterosexism. We often have students break into small groups to discuss their answers; they begin with the statements that they were most comfortable answering, moving to those that they were least comfortable answering. On other occasions, we have presented summary statistics to the class and analyzed the results as a group. It is important before beginning any dialogue that students either are given guidelines for classroom discussions, or, time permitting, construct their own list of standards.

CREATING EMPATHIC AWARENESS THROUGH EXPERIENTIAL LEARNING

Fear of the "other" is one source of people's prejudices. We learn to react negatively or indifferently to those unlike us, and, as a result, segregation by race, class, and sexual orientation persists. Because prejudice alienates people from the targets of their hostility, individuals make little effort to understand the people against whom they are prejudiced. Empathy and familiarity, therefore, are critical to breaking down the barriers of prejudicial thinking and the changing of attitudes. Psychologists assert that there are two types of empathy, including emotional and cognitive empathy (Davis, 1994; Stephan, 1999). Cognitive empathy results from perspective taking or role taking, whereas emotional empathy is characteristic of sympathy or emotional responsiveness (Stephan, 1999). Because racial prejudice is rooted in out-group difference, many multicultural programs involve the use of empathy in an effort to improve inter-group relations (Banks, 1997; Stephan, 1999). Information about diverse groups is presented from their own perspectives so that individuals can increase their awareness about persons unknown to them; this reflects the use of cognitive empathy to reduce prejudice. A change in the attributes assigned to out-groups often results because individuals see that they are less different than what they had originally thought. This also reduces the fear of out-groups because individuals no longer have exaggerated perceptions of them (Green, Dixon, & Gold-Neil, 1993; Walters, 1994).

Other research suggests that information alone is not enough and that additional pedagogical techniques are necessary for homophobic attitudes to change. For example, some scholars assert that interaction with gays and lesbians is needed for attitude change to occur (Black, Oles, & Moore, 1998; Cramer, Oles, & Black, 1997; Herek, 1988; Lance, 1987). Interaction in the classroom, however, has had mixed success in dispelling students' perceptions of difference (Goldberg, 1982; Green, Dixon, & Gold-Neil, 1993; Herek, 1984; Lance, 1987; Stevenson, 1988; Walters, 1994). The success in changing homophobic attitudes when audiovisuals are used in the classroom has also been inconclusive (Goldberg, 1982). Walters (1994) found, however, that when audiovisual materials complemented lectures on heterosexism and homophobia, students demonstrated increased empathy and less prejudice compared to a class that had received only the lectures. The use of role-playing is another useful pedagogical tool used in changing attitudes, especially since it involves both cognitive and emotional empathy (McGregor, 1993; Stephan, 1999). These studies suggest that the most effective way to change homophobic attitudes and the fear of interaction with gays and lesbians is when techniques that increase students' cognitive empathic responses are combined with teaching practices that stimulate their emotional responsiveness. The use of such pedagogical tools will now be discussed.

EXPERIENCING HOMOPHOBIA

Assuming that experiential knowledge increases the likelihood that students will be more empathic and that homophobic attitudes may be changed, we encourage instructors to use the following exercises, albeit with an understanding of the ethical issues that may accompany their use. No one exercise used alone can be expected to achieve long-lasting changes in prejudicial attitudes; however, a multifaceted approach, using a variety of techniques, has yielded positive results (Black et al., 1998).

1. Locate and purchase a news magazine dealing with lesbian and/or gay issues. Examples are *Gay Community News* (men and women), *Lesbian Connection* (women), *Lesbian News* (women), *The Advocate* (men and women). Carry it home unwrapped, and read it in public. Leave it in plain sight at home.

2. Purchase and wear openly and visibly a button proclaiming or suggesting a gay/lesbian orientation. Examples include pink triangles (a symbol worn by gay men in Nazi concentration camps, now a symbol for gay liberation), interlocking male or female signs, "Don't presume I'm heterosexual," "Gay and proud," "Support gay and lesbian rights," etc. If someone asks what the button means, explain it in detail.

3. If you are a heterosexual involved in an intimate relationship with a person of the opposite sex, try to keep this relationship " in the closet" for a week. This involves at the very least having no physical contact with the person in any public area, being very careful about where and if you are even seen together, not mentioning this person or the relationship to anyone, and not being seen or heard talking on the phone to this person.

Instructors who ask students to engage in experientially based activities that are designed to increase students' empathic responsiveness are providing students with powerful learning experiences. Students experience personally the homophobic norms of the culture, both from their own awareness and also from the responses of others. Exercises such as the wearing of the pink triangles or carrying of gay/lesbian magazines in public places means that students may be perceived to be gay or lesbian. As a result, students may then directly experience the oppression based on sexual orientation that gays and lesbians routinely face when their status is known to others. The pink triangle and magazine exercise parallels other experientially based class projects, such as when white students observe firsthand the racial oppression that is directed at a student of color who is a member of the fieldwork assignment team (Pence & Fields, 1999). Whether students engage in the exercises within the confines of the classroom, conduct them on or off campus, their written or verbal responses should include the way others treated them as well as how they felt in the process. The potential for students to feel an emotional empathic response when they experience homophobic oppression personally is so great that students must be given the opportunity for debriefing as part of the process.

The next pedagogical techniques that we discuss involve the use of role-playing in the classroom. As stated earlier, role-playing engages students in both cognitive and emotional empathy because they are required to take the role of another (McGregor, 1993; Stephan, 1999). These activities are less risky than those discussed in the previous section because students are simulating and not experiencing firsthand homophobic oppression; nonetheless, what they experience during this process may produce similar effects. American culture prescribes heterosexism as normative and any deviation from this norm justifies discriminating against gay men and lesbians (Herek, 1988; Walters, 1994). Students do not even realize the extent that their assumptions of normalcy influence their attitudes; therefore, these exercises require them to confront their own heterosexism.

The third of the listed participatory exercises is the relationship role-play. This requires heterosexual students who are involved in a relationship with a member of the opposite sex to keep the relationship "in the closet" for a week. Students are instructed that they cannot have physical contact with the person in any public place, including whether they are even seen together. This exercise requires that students not mention their relationship to anyone nor be overheard talking to their partner. Since these are the challenges that gay men and lesbians face in their intimate relationships, students who participate in the exercise begin to realize the "invisible weightless knapsack" of privileges that they take for granted (McIntosh, 2001, p. 30). Students who cannot participate in this assignment because they do not have a partner can still learn from the experiences of their peers who do engage in the role-play. For example, students may work in groups on this assignment and the students who are not participating may benefit from hearing about the experiences of their peers who are involved. Again, a larger class discussion is needed after the students complete their week of role-play and have had sufficient time to discuss their daily experiences in their respective groups.

Finally, the "questioning heterosexuality" exercise encourages students to challenge their assumptions of the norm (refer to Appendix B). By answering a number of questions regarding their own heterosexuality, students must understand the issues and queries that gay men and lesbians routinely encounter. This exercise works well when students are first paired up, given the handout of questions, and then ask each other the various questions. Students can then be combined into larger groups to focus on their reactions to the questions and a discussion involving the entire class can follow.

USING VISUAL MEDIA TO CREATE EMPATHIC RESPONSIVENESS

Images of gay men and lesbians in the media are typically demeaning, as the characters are comical when present or, more frequently, simply do not exist (Gross et al., 1988, Nardi, 1991; Walters, 1994). Visual media can be used in two ways in the classroom: (1) as an educational intervention that enhances students' understanding of an issue, or (2) as a critical thinking exercise that requires students to deconstruct media representations of gay men and lesbians.

The first use of video is more traditional: instructors preview a selection that enhances the reading material or topics that have been discussed in class, the instructor briefs students regarding the content of the video, then shows it to the students and uses the video to elicit discussion. We have had positive results using videos chosen to increase students' awareness of various issues and topics critical to understanding the experience of gay men and lesbians. (See end of this collection for a listing of videos that may be used in classes.)

One of the more successful ways to change students' attitudes is to have students critically examine media images of gay men and lesbians (Walters, 1994). Most of the exercises that engage students in the deconstruction of media images require that the instructor provide the images for the students (Texeira & Marx, in press). Alternatively, instructors may have students find their own representations of gay men and lesbians in various media categories. For a complete discussion of this assignment, refer to "Critically Thinking About Race Through Visual Media" (Marx & Texeira, 2001a; 2001b). While this assignment was originally designed to examine representations of people of color, it can be easily adapted for other oppressed groups.

PANEL DISCUSSIONS

Inviting a panel of lesbians, bisexuals, and gay men to speak in classrooms is a powerful method of increasing students' exposure to the gay community. Some research has indicated that panel presentations may increase prejudice (Serdahely & Ziemba, 1984). Some studies have not supported this, finding no effects of panels on attitude change (Anderson, 1981; Stevenson, 1988), while others suggest there are significant benefits for having panel discussions (Green, Dixon, & Gold-Neil, 1993). It has been our experience in many of the classes that we have taught that students will often tell us that the panel was their first (knowing) introduction to anyone who did not identify as heterosexual. These panels have worked the best when the instructors ask the panel members to share their coming out experiences and a little bit about what their lives are like today. They are asked to reflect upon the effect of their non-normative sexuality upon their family relationships, their jobs, educational experiences, and (if appropriate) their religious expressions. They may also respond to the question, "Is sexual orientation something we are born with, or is it something that develops during socialization?" Usually each panel member (depending upon time and the number of panelists) will speak for 5 to 10 minutes, and each panel member speaks before questions are entertained. When it is time for questions, the instructor should moderate, choosing the next student to ask a question. If the class has developed guidelines for discussion at the beginning of the term, students can be reminded of these before the discussion begins. The following guidelines may be suggested, and the students may add others: (1) Set your own boundaries for sharing; (2) Speak from experience and avoid generalizations about groups; (3) Respect confidentiality; (4) Listen respectfully to different perspectives.

The difficulty inherent in this method of increasing student empathy toward gay people is that the students may respond to the panelists as though they are a kind of "freak show." For students who are devoutly homophobic, there may be no way to avoid this response. We found this to be particularly true when our panels included transgendered people. In constructing the panel, the instructor needs to be clear about the purpose of the activity: is it to discuss the range of sexual orientations or should it also include a discussion of gender identity? It has been helpful on some of our panels to include a gay-friendly heterosexual person in order to teach the concept that *everyone* has a sexual orientation. For example, instructors might consider participating in such a panel, with gay instructors using their experiences of heterosexism and straight instructors discussing their awareness of heterosexual privilege. Since research has demonstrated that people who have a relationship with someone who is gay are less homophobic that those who do not (Herek, 1988; Black et al., 1998), instructor self-disclosure has had positive results for reducing homophobic attitudes in students (Black et al., 1998, Cramer, 1997). Participation in a panel discussion is one of many ways in which an instructor might self-disclose.

Certainly, the extent to which panelists may have an effect on changing students' attitudes depends on who they are and what they say (Stevenson, 1988). It is important, therefore, to include people who are experienced in discussing these issues with groups. Often, the campus's Lesbian, Gay, Bisexual, Transgender (LGBT) or Gay, Lesbian, Bisexual (GLB) club or resource center will be helpful in providing names of speakers, or possibly a community GLB or LGBT Center. Occasionally, we have even had students in the class volunteer for the panel. For some, speaking on the panel is an important part of the process of developing their own identity as a member of the gay community; however, it is critical that they participate with more experienced speakers. Regardless of whether students' attitudes are changed by a panel discussion, providing an opportunity for gay men and lesbians to speak is a way of supporting the gay community even as it offers its resources in support of educating our students.

CONCLUSIONS

Professors who want to make a difference in the campus climate toward gays and lesbians need to be proactive in their approach to teaching about heterosexism and homophobia. It is not enough to just wait and see if it comes up in class during a discussion of some other kind of prejudice, in the topic of family structure, or the many other ways that the topic may present itself. It has been said that we will not name that which we fear, so instructors may create a safe space in the classroom for gay men and lesbians by addressing the issue, by listing it on the syllabus, and by including readings that address heterosexism and homophobia.

A final and very important factor in an overall pedagogy around heterosexism and homophobia is that of the professor. The best teacher about a topic is one who is comfortable and familiar with it. Using the pedagogical techniques described in this discussion will increase an instructor's own comfort level. For example, if a professor invites members of the gay community to participate on the sexuality panel, this will increase her or his contact with the community. Long-standing connections and familiarity may develop simply through hosting a panel in a class. The wearing of a pink triangle for a day along with one's students will help provide a professor firsthand knowledge of the dynamics she or he is trying to teach.

In addressing the "chilly climate" that gay and lesbian students face on campus, instructors must be prepared to step outside of the convention of a lecture format. The pedagogical techniques discussed in this paper provide an opportunity for students to develop empathy at both the cognitive and emotional levels (Davis, 1994; Stephan, 1999). The strategy underlying these techniques is to focus upon experiential learning, as opposed to simply providing students with information. This approach will create a classroom environment that, even on the "chilliest" of campuses, may allow students to develop respect for diverse sexual orientations. When such a safe space is created, instructors will find that the gay and lesbian students will be much more likely to participate comfortably. The increased visibility of the lesbian and gay students will then contribute to the heterosexual students' familiarity and development of empathy toward their classmates.

REFERENCES

Anderson, C.L. (1981). The effect of a workshop on attitudes of female nursing students toward homosexuality. *Journal of Homosexuality, 1,*52-79.

Banks, J.A. (1997). *Teaching Strategies for Ethnic Groups*. Boston: Allyn and Bacon.

Black, B., Oles, T., & Moore, L. (1998). The relationship between attitudes: Homophobia and sexism among social work students. *Journal of Women and Social Work, 13*, (2) 166-190.

Cotton-Husten, A., & Waite, B. (2000). Anti-homosexual attitudes in college students: Predictors and classroom interventions. *Journal of Homosexuality, 38*(3)117-133.

Cramer, E.P. (1997). Effects of an educational unit about lesbian identity development and disclosure in a social work methods course. *Journal of Social Work Education, 33,* 461-472.

Cramer, E. P., Oles, T.P., & Black, B. (1997). Reducing social work students' homophobia: An evaluation of teaching strategies. *Arete, 21*(2)36-49.

D'Augelli, A. (1989). Lesbians' and gay men's experiences of discrimination and harassment in a university community. *American Journal of Community Psychology,17*(3)317-321.

Davis, M. H. (1994). *Empathy: A social psychological approach*. Madison, WI: Brown and Benchmark.

Feagin, J. (1999). The continuing significance of racism: Discrimination against black students in white colleges. In C. Ellison and W. A. Martin (Eds.), *Race and ethnic relations in the United States* (pp. 346-355). Los Angeles, CA: Roxbury.

Goldberg, C. (1982). Attitude change among college students toward homosexuality. *Journal of American College Health, 30*, 260-268.

Green, S., Dixon, P., & Gold-Neil, D. (1993). The effects of a gay/lesbian panel discussion on college student attitudes toward gay men, lesbians, and persons with AIDS (PWA's). *Journal of Sex Education and Therapy, 19*(1)47-63.

Gross, L., Aurand, S.K. & Adessa, R. (1988). *Violence and discrimination against lesbian and gay people in Philadelphia and the Commonwealth of Pennsylvania*. Philadelphia: Philadelphia Lesbian and Gay Task Force.

Hall, S. (1995). The whites of their eyes: Racist ideologies and the media. In G. Dines and J. M. Humez (Eds.), *Gender, race and class in media: A text reader* (pp. 19-22). Thousand Oaks, CA: Sage.

Hall, R., & Sandler, B. (1982). The classroom climate: A chilly one for women? Report published by the Project on the Status and Education of Women, Washington, D.C.

Hall, R., & Sandler, B. (1984). Out of the classroom climate: A chilly one for women? Report published by the Project on the Status and Education of Women, Washington, D.C.

Herek, G.M. (1984) "Beyond homophobia": A social psychological perspective on attitudes toward lesbians and gay men. *Journal of Homosexuality, 10,* 1-21.

Herek, G. M. (1986). *Sexual orientation and prejudice at Yale: A report of the experiences of lesbian, gay, and bisexual members of the Yale community.* Unpublished report.

Herek, G. M. (1988). Heterosexuals' attitudes toward lesbians and gay men: Correlates and gender differences. *Journal of Sex Research, 25,* 451-477.

Kite, M.E. (1994). When perceptions meet reality: Individual difference in reactions to lesbians and gay men. In B. Green & G.M. Herek (Eds.), *Lesbian and gay psychology: Theory, research, and clinical application* (pp. 25-53). Thousand Oaks, CA: Sage.

Lance, L.M. (1987). The effects of interaction with gay persons on attitudes toward homosexuality. *Human Relations, 40,* 329-335.

Lutz, C. A. & Collins, J.L. (1993). *Reading National Geographic.* Chicago: University of Chicago Press.

Marx, M., & Little, P. (2001). *The construction of prejudice: Comparing attitudes toward African-Americans and attitudes toward gays and lesbians.* Unpublished manuscript.

Marx, M., & Texeira, M. (2001a). Critically thinking about race through visual media. In K. McKinney, F. Beck, & B. Heyl (Eds.), *Sociology through active learning: Student exercises* (pp. 113-118). CA: Pine Forge Press.

Marx, M., & Texeira, M. (2001b). Critically thinking about race through visual media. In McKinney K., Beck, F. & Heyl, B. (Eds.), *Sociology through active learning: Instructor manual* (pp. 68-72). CA: Pine Forge Press.

McGregor, J. (1993). Effectiveness of role playing and antiracist teaching in reducing student prejudice. *Journal of Educational Research, 86,* 215-226.

McIntosh, P. (2001). White privilege and male privilege: A personal account of coming to see the correspondences through work in Women's Studies. In Richardson, R. Taylor, V. & Whittier, N. (Eds.) *Feminist Frontiers* (5th ed.) (pp. 29-36). Boston: McGraw-Hill.

Nardi, P. (1997). Changing gay and lesbian images in the media. In T. Ore (Ed.) *The Social Construction of Difference and Inequality: Race, Class, Gender, and Sexuality* (pp. 384-396). Mountain View, CA: Mayfield Publishers.

National Organization for Women, Boston Chapter, Lesbian Task Force (1980). *Lesbians: A consciousness raising kit.* Cambridge, MA: Boston NOW.

Pence, D., & Fields, A. (1999). Teaching about race and ethnicity: Trying to uncover white privilege for a white audience. *Teaching Sociology, 27*(2) 150-158.

Serdahely, W. J., & Ziemba, G. J. (1984). Changing homophobic attitudes through college sexuality education. *Journal of Homosexuality, 10*(1/2) 109-116.

Stephan, W. (1999). The role of empathy in improving intergroup relations. *Journal of Social Issues,* 55(4) 729-744.

Stevenson, M. (1988). Promoting tolerance for homosexuality: An evaluation of intervention strategies. *Journal of Sex Research, 25* (4)500-511.

Texeira, M. & Marx, M. (In press). Encouraging critical thinking about race through media analysis.

Walters, A. S. (1994). Using visual media to reduce homophobia: A classroom demonstration. *Journal of Sex Education and Therapy, 20*(2)92-100.

APPENDIX A-1
Attitudes Toward Homosexual (Gay) People

As you were growing up: Think back to your childhood and remember the messages that you received from your family, friends, church, and community about homosexual (gay) people.

Directions: Please mark an **X** on each continuum to represent what you were taught about homosexual (gay) people *as you were growing up.*

1. attractive/...../....../...../....../......./unattractive
2. unspiritual/...../....../...../....../......./spiritual
3. rational/...../....../...../....../......./irrational
4. immoral/...../....../...../....../......./moral
5. disciplined/...../....../...../....../......./undisciplined
6. trustworthy/...../....../...../....../......./unreliable
7. healthy/...../....../...../....../......./unhealthy
   (physically)
8. healthy/...../....../...../....../......./unhealthy
   (mentally)
9. loners/...../....../...../....../......./family-oriented
10. perverted/...../....../...../....../......./sexually normal
11. disobedient/...../....../...../....../......./obedient
12. respectful/...../....../...../....../......./disrespectful
13. lazy/...../....../...../....../......./hard-working
14. goal-oriented/...../....../...../....../......./lacking goals
15. dishonest/...../....../...../....../......./honest

We developed this semantic differential scale measuring socialization effects. The reliability coefficient for this scale is .8935.

APPENDIX A-2

Today: This next questionnaire is designed to measure the way you feel **today** about working with or associating with homosexual (gay) people.
Directions: Consider each item as carefully and accurately as you can, then place the number indicating your feeling next to each item. The numbers are:

Strongly Agree   Agree   No Opinion   Disagree   Strongly Disagree
     1   2   3   4   5

_____1. I would feel comfortable working closely with a gay male.

_____2. I would enjoy attending social functions at which homosexuals were present.

_____3. I would feel uncomfortable if my neighbor was a homosexual.

_____4. If a member of my sex made an advance toward me, I would feel angry.

_____5. I would feel comfortable knowing that I was attractive to members of my sex.

_____6. I would feel comfortable if a member of my sex made an advance toward me.

_____7. I would feel uncomfortable being seen in a gay bar.

_____8. I would feel disappointed if I learned that my child was homosexual.

_____9. I would be comfortable if I found myself attracted to a member of my sex.

_____10. I would feel nervous being in a group of homosexual people.

_____11. I would feel comfortable if my minister were homosexual.

_____12. I would be upset if learned that my brother or sister was a homosexual.

_____13. I would feel that I failed as a parent if I learned that my child was gay.

_____14. If I saw two men holding hands in public, I would feel offended.

_____15. I would feel comfortable if I learned that my daughter's teacher was a lesbian.

_____16. I would feel at ease talking with a gay person at a party.

_____17. I would feel comfortable reporting to a homosexual boss.

_____18. If I saw two women holding hands in public, I would feel offended.

Note: The social distance scale was originally developed by the *Campaign to End Homophobia*, and originally appeared in "Lesbians: A Conscious-ness-Raising Kit" (1980), a document of the Boston chapter of the National Orga-nization for Women. Used with permission. The scale's reliability coefficient is .9097. Validity for both scales was confirmed through factor analysis.

APPENDIX B
QUESTIONING HETEROSEXUALITY

1. What do you think caused your heterosexuality? How did you learn what to do?
2. When and how did you first decide you were a heterosexual?
3. Does your heterosexuality stem from a fear of people of your same sex? How do you know that it does not?
4. Is your heterosexuality just a phase you will outgrow; how can you tell?
5. Isn't it possible you simply need a good gay lover?
6. If you have never been sexual with a person of the same sex, how do you know you wouldn't prefer that?
7. How can you enjoy a fully satisfying sexual experience or deep emotional rapport with a person of the opposite sex when the physical, social, and political differences between you are so vast?
8. Your heterosexuality doesn't offend me as long as you don't try to force it on me. Why do you people feel compelled to seduce others into your sexual orientation?
9. Why do you insist on flaunting your heterosexuality? Can't you just be who you are and keep it quiet?
10. To whom have you disclosed your heterosexual tendencies and how did they react?
11. If you raise children, would you want them to be heterosexual, knowing the problems they would face?
12. Why do heterosexuals place so much emphasis on sex? Why are male heterosexuals so promiscuous?
13. Does any heterosexual acting out necessarily make one a heterosexual?
14. The great majority of child molesters are male heterosexuals. Is it safe to expose your children to male heterosexual teachers?
15. Heterosexuals are noted for their assigning and acting out narrowly restricted, stereotyped sex roles. Why do you cling to such role-playing?
16. A disproportionate number of irresponsible, violent, and antisocial people are heterosexual. Don't you think that you should consider this when you hire a heterosexual for a position?
17. There seem to be very few happy heterosexuals. Techniques have been developed where you might be able to change if you really want to. Have you considered trying aversion therapy?

This set of questions is adapted from "A Heterosexual Questionnaire" by M. Rochlin, PhD, in *M*, Spring 1982.
Appendix B and the three exercises used gratefully with permission from the National Organization for Women, Boston Chapter, Lesbian Task Force.

Beyond Empathy:
Confronting Homophobia
in Critical Education Courses

Catherine Taylor

SUMMARY. Anti-homophobia education is rarely included in the anti-bias curriculum of Education faculties, a grave omission since education graduates will teach in a homophobic school system that oppresses gay and lesbian students. This article draws on my experience in using a range of anti-homophobia strategies to confront homophobia among religious students in critical education courses where the principle of respecting each and every child is foundational. I argue that strategies designed to produce empathy sometimes fail because of the extreme importance attached to homophobia in the religious discourses that structure the identities of these students. At such times we should shift our

Catherine Taylor, PhD, is Assistant Professor, BEd Program, University of Winnipeg, 515 Portage Avenue, Winnipeg MB Canada, R3B 2E9 (E-mail: taylor@uwinnipeg.ca). Her dissertation for her PhD in Cultural Studies and Critical Pedagogy from OISE at the University of Toronto was a discourse study of the development of Lesbian Studies in the Liberal Arts. She is the co-editor with Janice Ristock of *Inside the Academy and Out: Lesbian/Gay/Queer Studies and Social Action* (Toronto and London: University of Toronto Press, 1998). She is currently involved with a project to implement anti-homophobia education in the Education Faculty at the University of Manitoba. Her current research involves studying the implementation of a groundbreaking initiative that involves anti-homophobia education for all teaching and administrative staff in the secondary schools of Winnipeg School Division One.

[Haworth co-indexing entry note]: "Beyond Empathy: Confronting Homophobia in Critical Education Courses." Taylor, Catherine. Co-published simultaneously in *Journal of Lesbian Studies* (Harrington Park Press, an imprint of The Haworth Press, Inc.) Vol. 6, No. 3/4, 2002, pp. 219-234; and: *Addressing Homophobia and Heterosexism on College Campuses* (ed: Elizabeth P. Cramer) Harrington Park Press, an imprint of The Haworth Press, Inc., 2002, pp. 219-234. Single or multiple copies of this article are available for a fee from The Haworth Document Delivery Service [1-800-HAWORTH, 9:00 a.m. - 5:00 p.m. (EST). E-mail address: getinfo@haworthpressinc.com].

219

pedagogical efforts to confront the ethical conflicts between homophobia and the principle of respect. I describe how I focus on the discursive production of both the forms and limits of personal identity, feelings, and beliefs to handle the confrontation productively. Although confronting homophobia sometimes involves hearing hurtful speech, it usefully problematizes the ethical status of homophobic students who are otherwise committed to classroom democracy, often provoking them to adopt less oppressive behaviors. It also usefully exposes the existence of homophobia for other students who might have underestimated it. Both groups end up better prepared to fight homophobia in their work as teachers. *[Article copies available for a fee from The Haworth Document Delivery Service: 1-800-HAWORTH. E-mail address: <getinfo@haworthpressinc.com> Website: <http://www.HaworthPress.com> © 2002 by The Haworth Press, Inc. All rights reserved.]*

KEYWORDS. Empathy, discourse analysis, critical pedagogy, teacher education

Under the pressure of an increasingly diverse society and civil rights movements mobilized along lines of race and gender, contemporary educators have developed various teaching methods designed to promote social harmony by reducing bigotry, and anti-bias education of some sort is now commonplace from kindergarten through university. Yet forty years into the lesbian and gay rights movements, anti-heterosexism/homophobia education is rarely included in these efforts. One of the most consequential sites of omission is Bachelor of Education programs, and not only because B.Ed. students need to learn how to address all forms of bigotry in their own classrooms. The omission matters because we need future teachers to confront and unlearn their own homophobia (or apathy about others' homophobia) before they assume their influential places in that notoriously homophobic site, the public school system (Baker & Fishbein, 1998; McCaskell, 1999). For schools to be transformed from sites where homophobia is learned and practiced into ones where students can unlearn homophobia, teachers must act as "change agents" who recognize and confront the homophobia of school culture.

Since homophobia is a form of prejudice that still enjoys a robust social acceptability in many mainstream communities, this takes courage and commitment on the part of teachers, and most, unless provoked, choose not to undertake the challenge. In many school districts, classroom teachers cannot address homophobia or make a positive reference to lesbians or gays without fear of losing their jobs; if teachers there can summon the courage to intervene in cases of homophobic bullying, that is perhaps all we can ask of them. But even in districts where there is explicit administrative support for anti-homophobia education, the prospect is so intimidating that few teachers attempt it. Those who do are often lesbian or gay themselves.

In this article I discuss an approach to provoking education students to become teachers who identify as change agents committed to fighting homophobia. I focus here on negative attitudes to homosexuality that prove resistant to methods developed by anti-bias educators to dislodge bigotry. In particular, I focus mainly on homophobia, which I am defining as an aggressive, passionate hostility to homosexuality on moral grounds, rather than its more passive, though no less harmful, counterpart, heterosexism, which can be defined as an assumption, occurring in both conscious and unexamined forms, of the rightful dominance of heterosexuals in the social order. (In so defining homophobia, I am not restricting the category to those who have feelings of fear or hatred towards gays and lesbians [Pharr, 1988]; many religious homophobes, for example, would deny they fear or hate anyone.)

While my experience of university student attitudes generally reflects recent survey studies that show the majority of Canadian young people are far from homophobic ("Canadians back," 2000), virulently anti-homosexual attitudes persist in various cultural pockets, and notably, among adherents to various fundamentalist and orthodox religions (though not, of course, uniformly; some fundamentalist and orthodox believers are not homophobic). My own experience involves confronting adamant homophobia in Christian students, and in particular among evangelical students who believe that their views are scripturally-grounded. The same evangelical devotion that inspires such students to imitate Christ by helping others and working for social justice, often drawing them to the field of education in the first place, can carry with it a conviction that homosexuality is a sin. This conviction seems impervious to a whole range of anti-bias pedagogies, including corrective information, critical analysis, and empathic experience. It can be argued that a strategically sound response to such determined homophobia is to accept the impossibility of reaching everybody, and to focus our efforts where they are more likely to succeed. However, the prospect of these committed homophobes becoming educators changes the calculation exponentially and makes it important to persist. Homophobic teachers harm children by contributing to a hostile school culture that has been tied to depression, teen suicide, and victimization by bullies (Hershberger & D'Augelli, 2000). As much as I believe anti-homosexual faith traditions are in grave error, as much as I would prefer that homophobes not become teachers, I am therefore convinced that it is in our best interests that we keep striving with them.

My experiences of encountering deep homophobia among future teachers and of recognizing its extreme resistance to change, even in these otherwise loving, generous people, leads me to ask, "When we cannot dislodge homophobia, how can we motivate people not to act on it? Further, how can we motivate passive supporters of lesbian and gay rights to become active allies in the struggle?" These questions suggest a move away from moral territory, where attitudes to homosexuality vary widely and are often constituted within deeply cherished value systems, and a move into ethical territory, where we can focus on the professional obligation of all teachers to respond to the needs of all children entrusted to their care.

To explore this territory I reflect on my own experience of working with a diverse group of student teachers to dislodge homophobia. I draw on scholarship on psychological and discursive structures of identity that offers insights into the formidable social apparatus that fortifies individual psyches, showing us in a very concrete way what we are up against when we work for social change in homophobic contexts. Specifically, I consider evangelical Christian identity as an example of profound attachment to a discourse that can make homophobia almost inevitable. In so doing I am using "discourse" not in the broad linguistic sense that denotes any stretch of text or dialogue, but in the sociological one that denotes instead the whole system of interrelated and mutually supportive concepts, terms, and attendant social practices that are involved in adherence to a particular belief system. I argue that the usual methods of fighting bigotry are structurally doomed to fail in cases of deep investment in a homophobic discourse, and articulate an ethical stance that offers hope of moving past this failure.

For many years progressive educators have attempted to fight bigotry by promoting tolerance and encouraging empathy. In tolerance pedagogies, educators try to overcome bigotry through methods that focus on promoting a liberal principle of coexistence and erasing inaccurate negative stereotypes about marginalized groups such as lesbians and gay men in order to make them less objectionable. Critical educators informed by a Cultural Studies perspective on social power now see tolerance as a weak, ultimately conservative, notion that merely recirculates problematic notions of *noblesse oblige* among members of dominant culture, leaving normalcy undisturbed. Tolerance persists, however, as a plank of mainstream liberal organizational policies in government, business, and social services, where it is demanded in the interests of "diversity management," not of social change. Tolerance is a popular goal for mainstream institutions because it keeps existing power structures of dominance and subordination intact while asking little of the privileged beyond forbearance in the face of foreign bodies. In a tolerance pedagogy, members of dominant culture are the subjects of education, and members of subordinated ones are its subject matter. Homophobes are never asked to consider their common humanity with lesbians and gay men, much less reassess their ethical obligations to us.

As increasingly diverse classrooms have made such monocultural approaches to working across social differences less viable, educators working for social change have turned their attention from tolerance to empathy (Angell, 1994; Greene, 1995; Holm & Aspegren, 1999; Kanpol, 1999; Macedo & Bartolome, 1999; Morrison, 1995). Having long recognized that information alone is not enough to produce empathy (Steward & Borgers, 1986), attitudinal changes from bigotry to compassion are sought through such devices as exposing students to positive representations of marginalized groups, providing access to the voices of silenced populations, facilitating role-playing experiences that let students of dominant culture simulate marginalized people's oppressive experiences, and providing students with corrective information about the oppressive experiences of the members of such groups. The goal of such lessons is for students to project themselves into the difficult social situations of others unlike themselves, recognize their common humanity, and move in the process from disrespect to solidarity. To avoid slippage out of empathic identification into pity and to encourage a commitment to social change, the provocation to empathy is often coupled, particularly in the higher grades, with critical analysis of dominant culture's role in making the lives of others miserable. Much of the literature on education for social change now leans on critically informed empathy.

Where tolerance leaves people divided, empathy demands that we see ourselves in each other. Yet empathy often proves to be as troubled a strategy for seeking social harmony as is tolerance, and its limits became acutely evident in my teaching context, a Canadian faculty of Education where I teach critical education courses that draw largely progressive student teachers who easily identify as social activists. Evangelical Christians are disproportionately represented in these courses, which is perhaps surprising to those of us accustomed to associating them with right-wing political movements (the Republican Party and, currently, the Canadian Alliance). They, like most students who have enrolled in my courses, tend to be intensely committed to doing good in the world, and when I propose that we work at building a democratic community in our own classroom to put to the test both progressive theories of education and our own commitment to working across differences, students have been intrigued and enthusiastic. We strive together to create the type of democratic classroom central to the practice of critical pedagogy (Shor, 1992), where social power is problematized and learning is animated by an ethics of respect for one another.

As we have explored the troubled terrain of mutual obligations ensuing from that respect, I have been deeply impressed by their commitment to doing the hard work involved.

In this enviable teaching context, students can be, if anything, almost *too* easily convinced they are in harmony with the socially progressive project of critical education. They tend to be very confident of their own ability to empathize with others of different races, ethnicities, and socioeconomic levels, and equally confident of the adequacy of empathy as a strategy for teaching multicultural citizenship in their own classrooms. They easily agree that racism is wrong and are invested in seeing themselves as needing only to learn appropriate teaching techniques in order to become effective anti-racist educators. I take the approach that while empathy-producing pedagogies can increase positive attitudes to social diversity, empathy is prone to failure in cases of cultural conflict. But that proves to be a tough sell; most of my students place great hope in their own and others' power of empathy and resist critical views of it. However, the limits of empathy become obvious when sexual identity is on the table. When the occasion involves a collision between the rights of lesbians and gays, and the anti-homosexual convictions held by some evangelical Christians, I have witnessed eruptions of hostilities so deep that empathy is either not forthcoming at all, or insufficient to overcome homophobia. Indeed, far from lessening hostilities, attempts to arouse empathy can backfire, triggering passionate assertions of God's law.

Since I want students to experience and reflect together on various pedagogical approaches to creating unoppressive classrooms where everyone is respected, I employ a whole range of progressive strategies for deflecting homophobia, including the ones like empathy that I know will fail to move some students. When students argue that "Sex doesn't belong in elementary schools," or "Sex is a private matter; just keep quiet about it," I respond with corrective information they lack: statistics about suicide rates and suicide attempt rates by gay and lesbian teenagers, the high percentage of runaways, the ubiquitous use of "fag" and "gay" as the ultimate schoolyard insult, the 1 in 10 estimate, and so on. I provoke critical analysis of the connection between these incidents and maintaining a "don't ask, don't tell" policy of teacher nonintervention, and I ask for critical reflection on the uses of homophobia (what kinds of interests are served by it, and whose). I include children of same-sex families and lesbian and gay teenagers in my litany of those likely to suffer discrimination at school in various forms. I sometimes come out as lesbian myself. (And sometimes not. For an interesting discussion of the pedagogical benefits of not coming out, see Khayatt, 1998.) I show a documentary film called *It's Elementary!* about teaching young children about homophobia (Chasnoff, 1996). In a perfect pitch for empathy, the film includes a little girl reading an earnest speech to her classmates about how much she loves her two mommies and how much she has been hurt by other children's anti-gay comments. This and other segments, including a first-grade lesson about gay and lesbian issues, show that homophobia is meaningless and easily shed among six-year-olds, who talk easily about such topics as gay parenting and lesbian couples.

Among education students, however, the film generates intense and mixed responses, and I believe those responses expose the limits of empathy in a useful way. Most students in my courses have been open to differences of sexuality. They easily identify with the little girl with two mommies and are pleasantly surprised to see how easily first-graders could talk about gay and lesbian topics without talking about sex. The majority go so far as to acknowledge their own responsibility to intervene in cases of homophobic, gender-normative schoolyard harassment, moving along the scale from merely accepting homosexuality to actively opposing homophobia, and they often describe the experience of empathy as the provocation for their change of heart. Some describe the film as having enormous impact on them as human beings and as teachers.

But other students remain committed not only to the personal belief that homosexuality is deeply wrong, but that it must be actively discouraged, explaining their attitudes in terms of religious identities that are powerfully structured in homophobia. In this group, I see two types of failure of empathy. First, some are able to empathize with gay and lesbian individuals such as the little girl with two mommies but their empathy is overruled by the stronger force of their commitment to following the word of God. Contemporary understandings of the structures of identity drawn from psychoanalysis and Cultural Studies would account for this failure of empathy as one of weakness in the face of self-interest, specifically an interest in fulfilling the demands of the religious discourse that constitutes a believer's sense of Self. The second type of failure is one of total refusal of empathy, something I have most often seen in men who express both religious condemnation of homosexuality and gut-level disgust at sex between men. For them, homophobia is extravagantly overdetermined by their allegiance to discourses of both religion and masculinity. In psychoanalytic terms, in such cases the "Other" is so much in conflict with an extremely rigid spiritual and social identity structure that homosexual behavior means the death of "Self." Where their own empathic capacities fail them, it makes perfect sense then that homophobes justify their disrespect for the Other by appealing to the high court of gut feelings (Nature) or religious convictions (God), case closed. The moral authority of the normative discourses in which these feelings and convictions develop easily trumps the ethical authority of empathy.

Such refusals of empathy are entirely predictable from Foucauldian discourse analysis, which shows that successful discourse systems reinforce their powerful hold on their adherents by delegitimizing any contradictory utterance as insane or immoral (Foucault, 1982). The insight that individuals can recognize the authority only of utterances consistent with the discourse in which they are invested, provides a rationale for the strategy used by some anti-homophobia educators of challenging homophobes on their own discursive grounds, in this case by countering religious homophobia with lesbian and gay-positive interpretations of scripture. (See, for example, McNeill, 1993.) If students have had no previous exposure to interpretations that challenge the position that the New Testament unequivocally condemns homosexuality, the strategy might be thought-provoking. My own experience has been that many evangelical students take Bible study very seriously and are interested in interpretive dialogue. However, whether such dialogue can become an occasion for conceptual shifts in homophobic students, and a turn towards the possibility of developing empathy, depends not only on how skilled the instructor is in biblical interpretation, but once again on how crucial it is within the student's religious discourse system to condemn homosexuality, and on how elaborately the condemnation is fortified within the discourse, not only by church leaders and congregational convention but by key elements of the belief system itself.

And fortified it is. For example, the challenge constituted by feeling moved at the plight of a little girl with two mommies is neatly deflected by the admonition to "love the sinner but hate the sin." By mobilizing this consistent element of Christian discourse, believers can experience empathy for lesbians and gays as suffering human beings without budging from the position that homosexual desire is a temptation akin to gambling or drunkenness which one can and must resist. Other discursive elements repeated continually in church services and bible study are also at the ready to defend against any challenges to the authority of homophobia: these elements include a description of their own version of Christianity as the one true faith, and of Christians as the most loving and caring people on earth; an evangelical obligation to convert others to their belief system; lifelong instruction in resisting the persuasive appeals of other religious and secular perspectives on moral issues; and, of course, continual repetition of the messages that heterosexual couplings are pleasing to God and that homosexual ones are abominable.

All of these features of religious discourse help to fortify the believer against any transformative effect that critical reflection and empathy might otherwise have had. Yet such pedagogical strategies are still effective to the extent that they strip away the wildly inaccurate beliefs about lesbians and gays (typically as hedonistic sexual predators incapable of sustained commitment) with which students may have begun the course, leaving only the stark force of their own religious discourse, unsupported by any rationally plausible evidence, to justify their homophobia. This clarification reveals individuals committed to anti-homosexual religious discourses as incapable of, and impervious to, any other perspective on lesbians and gays. In Emmanuel Levinas' terms (1993), they have refused the ethical obligation to listen to the Other before they know the Other at all.

Empathy, then, is mainly achievable in those cases when there is no very deep psychic investment in demonizing the Other. Historical and psychological studies (Blumenthal, 1999; Milgram, 1974; Young-Bruehl, 1996) that reveal the banality of evil show that there is often little antipathy involved in collaborating with genocidal leaders or participating in gang assaults; lessons in empathy can probably reduce the incidence of cruelty where there is no profound self-interest at stake in cruelty. Such lessons can also be an effective provocation to social advocacy among passive sympathizers who would otherwise have remained idle in the face of injustice (Shor, 1992). Empathy is probably sturdy enough to deal with social *diversity*, and crudely put, it's a device easily pulled out of the teacher's desk in the form of guest speakers and role plays. But like tolerance, empathy ultimately fails when the Other is unable to bypass the rigid psychic defences on which the rigorously self-monitored identity structures of some religious discourses depend. When we encounter such an intensely proscribed Other as some evangelical Christians encounter in a gay or lesbian person, even the illusion of empathy can be impossible. The conflict with key discoursal structures of identity–what one needs to believe and who one needs to be–would be too great, amounting, in psychoanalytic terms, to a suicidal move.

What do we do here? Having reached beyond tolerance to empathy, to what can the progressive educator appeal beyond empathy when confronted with the obdurate homophobia that is demanded and fortified by some religious discourses?

Recognizing that the strategies of teaching tolerance and empathy fail us in cases of extreme hostility, educators working in Cultural Studies frameworks have taken a different tack: instead of hoping for changes of heart, we have tried to disrupt the overwhelming force of dominant discourses by denaturalizing them to expose their "awesome materiality" (Foucault, 1982, p. 216) as socially constructed systems of meaning that have concrete effects on our lives. The aim is to show that the gut-level disgust often cited as proof that homosexuality is unnatural is in fact a product of powerful socially constructed discourses such as medicine, law, capitalism, and religion that thoroughly pervade the perceptions of homophobes, leaving them in no position to discern any pre-discursive message from God or Nature. However, understanding that discourses structure even our most intensely personal thoughts and feelings does not undermine their authority: other people's religious convictions may be mere discursive productions, but not our own.

In any case, even deconstructive classrooms often maintain the bifurcated tradition of Western scholarship which shoos matters of religious faith off-stage into the personal arena, leaving them unscrutinized. In practical terms, the academic avoidance of discussing personal religious beliefs lets homophobic Christians complete Education degrees and arrive in classrooms with their prejudices intact, never having experienced the conflict between their faith and a commitment to just teaching practices. It also lets passive anti-homophobes grossly underestimate the continuing prevalence of homophobia in their future teaching colleagues, confirming our likeliest allies in a complacent attitude that homophobia is extinct when, for the sake of lesbian and gay students and the children of lesbian and gay parents, we need teachers to be alarmed at the damage homophobes continue to do.

In a critical classroom where people have committed to doing the work involved in learning to respect each other, I therefore believe it is important that gays and lesbians be prepared to hear hurtful homophobic statements. This is not to say that I believe critical classrooms ought to be microcosms of society, with all its bigotry ushered raw into class discussion. On the contrary, the casual racism, sexism, and homophobia of mainstream culture are extremely unlikely to be expressed in a critical classroom, given how committed the students are to social justice and how thoroughly power and oppression are scrutinized there. However, if casual homophobia is unlikely to be expressed or even implicit in such a context, the conscientious, deadly serious variety is almost certainly there; our choice is only whether to hear it or not. It is easy enough to declare any expression of homophobia out of bounds in a democratic classroom; religious students are accustomed to minding their tongues at school. But I believe it is important that homophobic faith-based speech not be disqualified so that religious students who have committed to an ethics of respecting everyone get a chance to face up to their failure to do that. When students break their academic silence about their religious opposition to homosexuality, they can begin to struggle with the conflict between their faith and their ethical obligations as teachers. I have been hurt and appalled by what has been said on such occasions, and I have worried about exposing lesbian and gay students to it, but the alternative route of shutting down homophobic speech would leave homophobic beliefs intact within their own self-legitimating discourse system, ready to authorize future homophobic acts (and failures to act) in teaching situations. Students have sometimes approached me to debrief after particularly harrowing occasions, when religious students have declared in deadly earnest that they are not homophobic but that they must teach children that homosexuals must repent or be damned: shaken lesbian and gay students, shocked nonhomophobic heterosexual students who had not understood the depth of homophobia out there, and troubled or indignant religious students who have had the academically rare experiences of having their convictions recognized and challenged as unethical. No student has ever suggested it would be better not to have experienced these occasions.

I have been impressed by religious students' very evident struggle to resolve the conflict between their beliefs and their ethical obligations (not by the courage they must summon to utter their beliefs publicly; testifying is amply rewarded in Christian culture). Their own commitment to social justice and urgent need to find resolution act as motivation to continue the struggle. Most realize, when confronted with the conflict, that they are not entitled to act on personal beliefs in ways that violate other people's human rights, even if they are wholeheartedly convinced that they are in possession of the truth. In most provinces of Canada, including Manitoba where I teach, critical educators are able to provide additional motivation to resolve the conflict between beliefs and ethical obligations by pointing out that discrimination on the grounds of sexual identity violates provincial human rights codes and the Canadian Charter of Rights. Although school authorities are often reluctant in practice to enforce anti-homophobic policies, official documents such as rights legislation and professional ethics codes can provide a legitimizing support for lesbian and gay students (a counterpart to the higher authority religious students cite in the form of Bible passages they believe legitimize their homophobia) and an important recourse for teachers who need to remind students of their contractual obligations to protect the dignity of all students when their enthusiasm for the project of democracy dims (Kiselica, 1999).

In my experience, only a few students remain adamant in withholding respect, but the intensity of their opposition involves everyone present in an important experience of how deeply motivated and egocentric discrimination can be, how much it has to do with maintaining the identity structure of the Self and how little with actual qualities of the Other. The strong commitment to community building through mutual respect around which the class is organized from the start makes the experience of homophobia an occasion for sorrow that seems to involve everyone, including the homophobes. It becomes the fulcrum around which it is possible to ask anti-homosexual students to "turn the uninvited Othering look back on itself" (Ellsworth, 1991, p. 9) by imagining themselves, in their own social locations, as Other, lodged in what Judith Butler (1993) call the "uninhabitable zone" of someone else's psyche.

My purpose in asking this is not to take another run at empathy, but to take a run at the Self, provoking the recognition that each one of us is the object of someone's disgust, that we are all equally abject occupants of other people's discourse; that everyone makes *some*body sick. Christians, of course, are familiar with a version of this encounter with the self as demonized other; the admonition to bear up steadfastly in the face of persecution by nonbelievers is axiomatic to evangelical faith. However, in my experience most seem genuinely not to realize that the characteristics of their experiences of deep conviction (intense certainty, a sense of fellowship or divine presence, etc.) are not unique signs of God's will, but are basically identical to those of people with radically different beliefs and prejudices. Nor have they grappled with the knowledge that equally loving, kind, socially progressive people can have radically different beliefs; they seem to have been taught that only people who share their own are truly loving. Because many religious students adhere to discourse systems that are structured in extremely polarized notions of Self and Other, I press students hard to realize that they and nonbelievers have much more in common than they had assumed, that the boundaries between those inside and those outside the uninhabitable zone are much more permeable than they might have imagined.

In pressing for this recognition, I am not fantasizing that individuals will abandon homophobic belief systems; however, I am inviting them to reach the self-subversive understanding that intense feelings of religious conviction or gut-level certainty are not certain proofs that one's prejudices are justified. Rather, such feelings are common as muck, associated with discourses centered in mutually contradictory versions of truth, and target a wide range of human beings including themselves. I point out that depending on the discourse system involved, the object of deep disgust might be a lesbian, or an orthodox Muslim family; an independent professional woman unaccompanied by a male relative, or a single mother on welfare; any American, or a Christian fundamentalist. Clearly it would be dangerous for all of us if people felt entitled to act on the authority of religious conviction and disgust. As Isaiah Berlin (2001) explains, "Few things have done more harm than the belief on the part of individuals of groups (or tribes or states or nations or churches) that he or she or they are in sole possession of the truth: especially about how to live, what to be & do–& that those who differ from them are not merely mistaken, but wicked or mad: & need restraining or suppressing." In this spirit I have pointed out that while I have a deep conviction that homophobic beliefs are ethically wrong and contribute to the misery of the world, I am not entitled to interfere with the human rights of homophobic people, only to oppose their oppressive behavior.

My attempt to provoke a sense of common danger is not the normalizing, homogenizing fellow-feeling aspired to in empathy that allows us to dream we are all the same. Instead, this move towards common ground takes as its predicate that Self and Other can be similar in ethical status and still be radically incompatible if one person's identity is deeply structured in hostility to another's, as in my example of religiously mandated homophobia. Much as we might fantasize about other people becoming the same as us, we must therefore live with others in our differences. I in my corner had to learn that some anti-gay Christians are deeply loving people who agonize over ethical questions and are genuinely committed to doing good in the world–but that I am still not going to make them see the error of their homophobic beliefs. The usual strategies of multiculturalist educators are not going to work.

This discouraging conclusion usefully widens the net of abjection but throws us back onto the rocks of asking, how can we proceed when empathy fails, as Freud says it inevitably must? If we cannot always dislodge homophobia, given the strength of some identity structures, how can we at least challenge the feeling of entitlement to act on it? What aren't we doing that we might do in progressive education?

I have tried to use the shared experience of failed democracy described above as an opportunity to explore what is required of us when empathy fails at the rigid outer limits of our own discourse systems, where we are literally unable to know the Other on any but our own oppressive terms. What, we ask together, does this failure require of people committed to building a democratic community in which everyone is respected? This is not a question that we pose and answer in one or two classes: rather, because the curricula of critical education courses focus on issues of student diversity and social justice, it can become a continuing theme to which we return throughout the course. While it may sound unrealistic to suggest that adherents to extremely dogmatic faith traditions could apprehend the concept of there being limits on their abilities to know, the concept of ignorance can in fact resonate quite profoundly for Christian students with the sense of humility in the face of mystery that is found in most religions. We cannot expect individuals to foresake their most cherished structures of identity, but if they know that they do not know, perhaps we can expect them to learn to move on from a naive attachment to the notion that religious conviction authorizes them to oppress other human beings.

If so, gays and lesbians would not be any more genuinely understood or liked by homophobes, but failure to empathize could be understood as a sign of having reached the limits of one's earthly knowledge (in Biblical terms); of one's own structures of identity (in Foucauldian ones); of one's own openness to knowing (in psychoanalytical ones)–rather than as a call to action against us. Otherness would be centered as an expected condition and persistent experience of relations between individuals in a diverse population where people are deeply invested in conflicting discourse systems. We would not be in a position, then, of striving to create a community of consensus (that is impossible in a community of deeply motivated hostilities): we would strive to learn how to live together in a community not just of diversity but of "dissensus" (Readings, 1996, p. 167). The failure of empathy would be understood as the moment signifying the presence of someone beyond our discursive ken. In such a peda-gogy, we would be thrown back in this moment on a critical examination of our own structures of feeling (such as the extravagantly overdetermined social grounds of "natural" aversions to homosexuality) and an ethical recognition of our obligations to learn from the Other what our ignorance, and perhaps fixed antipathy, requires of us. As Bill Readings (1996) puts it, "We have to lis-ten, without knowing why, before we know what it is that we are to listen to" (p. 162). Such a premise of ignorance of our obligations to each other seems to me an entirely appropriate goal for critical classrooms like mine where people tend to self-select on the basis of commitment to working against the oppres-sive effects of social differences. While homophobic students might be ex-pected to have little motivation to examine their ethical obligations to lesbians and gays, they do have a personal stake in finding an ethical position from which they can fulfil their ethical obligation as teachers without violating their beliefs.

Further encouragement for homophobes to accept an ethical stance when they've already refused an empathic one derives from the same interest in pre-serving the Self that makes empathy impossible in the first place. When ethical obligation to others cannot arise from a sense of common bond, sometimes it can from a vivid apprehension of the sense of the common danger of being cast into the uninhabitable zone of other people's discourses. What my experience of confronting discursively obdurate homophobia suggests is not that homo-phobic students need new knowledge of the Other to tackle that formidable im-passe; when the wall of religious conviction rises up to guard against the provocation to empathy, the teacher relying on empathic strategies has no re-course but to offer more of the same, provoking the same result. Instead of new knowledge, sometimes we need a new strangeness. Classroom experiences such as the ones I have described can nurture such strangeness: classes in which homophobic speech is uttered in a context of democratic commitment to respecting others can be the springboard to an appropriately unsentimental un-derstanding of what respect requires of us.

Two important things can happen when empathy fails and intensely reli-gious students who would normally keep silent about their homophobic beliefs are instead asked to explain their positions. First, they are confronted by their peers and by the challenge to their own self-concept as people who respect hu-man dignity, they agonize over what to do, and in many cases they change their outlooks on their future careers. Sometimes they decide that they need not teach their students that homosexuality is wrong, that it would be sufficient to model a loving Christian way of life for them. Some go further, to actively in-tervene in playground harassment and teach against discrimination in their classes. A few go further still, to include gay and lesbian people in the curriculum without judgment, just as they include people of different religions without judging them. And a few decide not to teach in the public school system, because the conflicts are too great. Without room in ethically demanding classrooms to speak from their faiths, all would otherwise have been certified as teachers with their prejudices intact and operated out of them with clear conscience in their teaching careers. The second important lesson here was for other students who had assumed that intense homophobia was almost obsolete and nothing they needed to fight against in their own teaching careers. Many were shocked at the depth and obduracy of anti-gay religious sentiments expressed in the classroom, and became committed to actively fighting homophobia in their work as teachers.

For me the lessons of homophobia are that we had better work from an ethical position informed by knowledge of our empathic limits rather than from one that relies on empathy: we might remain certain that we know our God, but we need to learn that we certainly do not know each other. In particular, given the murderous projects that religious homophobia has demonstrated itself to be capable of fueling, people whose sense of Self is strongly invested in homophobic religious discourses need to learn that they are profoundly closed to listening to lesbians and gay men, and hence to acting ethically towards us. Such lessons can be learned in democratic classrooms where respect is worked at and hostilities are nevertheless invited to surface, exposing the materiality of discourse. Students who have suffered, witnessed, or themselves demonstrated the limits of empathy in such a context (whatever their own abiding religious convictions) might then become teachers who are prepared to respect all their students–and who are very alarmed that some of their colleagues do not.

REFERENCES

Angell, D. (1994). Can multicultural education foster transcultural identities? In K.M. Borman and N.P Greenman (Eds.), *Changing American education: Recapturing the past or inventing the future?* (pp. 297-309). Albany, NY: State University of New York Press.

Baker, J.G., & Fishbein, H.D. (1998). The development of prejudice towards gays and lesbians by adolescents. *Journal of Homosexuality, 36* (1), 89-100.

Berlin, I. (2001, Oct 18). Notes on prejudice. *The New York Review of Books.* Retrieved October 25, 2001 from the World Wide Web: http://www.nybooks.com/articles/14625

Blumenthal, D.R. (1999). *The banality of good and evil: Moral lessons from the Shoah and Jewish tradition.* Washington, DC: Georgetown University Press.

Butler, J. (1993). *Bodies that matter: On the discursive limits of "sex."* New York: Routledge.

Canadians back same-sex rights, federal poll finds (2000, February 10). *The Guardian* (Charlottetown), Final Edition, p.B5.

Chasnoff, D., dir. (1996). *It's elementary!: Talking about gay issues in school* [video-recording]. Produced by Helen S. Cohen and Debra Chasnoff. San Francisco, CA: Women's Educational Media.

Ellsworth, E. (1991). Teaching to support unassimilated difference. *Radical Teacher, 42,* 4-9.

Foucault, M. (1982). *The archaeology of knowledge and the discourse on language.* New York: Pantheon.

Greene, M. (1995). *Releasing the imagination: Essays on education, the arts, and social change.* San Francisco, CA: Jossey-Bass.

Hershberger, S.L., & D'Augelli, A.R. (2000). Issues in counseling lesbian, gay, and bisexual adolescents. In R.M. Perez, K.A. DeBord, & K.J. Bieschke (Eds.), *Handbook of counseling and psychotherapy with lesbian, gay, and bisexual clients* (pp. 225-48). Washington, DC: American Psychological Association.

Holm, U., & Aspegren, K. (1999). Pedagogical methods and affect tolerance in medical students. *Medical Education, 33* (1), 14-18.

Kanpol, B. (1999). Multiculturalism and the politics of a democratic imaginary. In *Critical pedagogy, an introduction* (2nd ed). (pp. 111-36). Westport, CT: Bergin & Garvey.

Khayatt, D. (1998). Parodoxes of the closet. In J.L. Ristock & C.G. Taylor (Eds.), *Inside the academy and out: Lesbian/gay/queer studies and social action* (pp. 31-48). Toronto and London: University of Toronto Press.

Kiselica, M. (1999). Reducing prejudice: The role of the empathic-confrontive instructor. In M. Kiselica (Ed.), *Confronting prejudice and racism during multicultural training* (pp. 37-54). Alexandria, VA: American Counseling Association.

Levinas, E. (1993). *Outside the subject.* Trans. M.B. Smith. Stanford, CA: Stanford University Press.

Macedo, D. & Bartolome, L.I. (1999). *Dancing with bigotry: Beyond the politics of tolerance.* New York: St. Martin's Press.

McCaskell, T. (1999) Homophobic violence in schools. *Orbit, 29* (4), 20-21.

McNeill, J.J. (1993). *The Church and the homosexual* (4th ed.). Boston, MA: Beacon Press.

Milgram, S. (1974). *Obedience to authority: An experimental view.* New York: Harper & Row.

Morrison, H.B. (1995). Multiculturalism: Intersubjectivity or particularism in education? *Thresholds in Education, 22* (3-4), 34-37.

Pharr, S. (1988). *Homophobia: A weapon of sexism.* Little Rock, AR: Chardon Press.

Readings, B. (1996). *The University in ruins.* Cambridge, MA: Harvard.

Shor, I. (1992). *Empowering education.* Chicago: University of Chicago Press.

Steward, R. & Borgers, S.B. (1986). Multicultural counseling: Knowledge is not enough. ERIC Document 303758.

Young-Bruehl, E. (1996). Adolescence and the aims of hatreds. In *The anatomy of prejudices* (pp. 299-339). Cambridge, MA: Harvard University Press.

The Family Lecture

Nancy E. Rose

SUMMARY. This paper describes a lecture about my extended family, in which I discuss a variety of configurations consisting of lesbian, gay, and bisexual adults, and our children. It raises an array of issues, including alternative insemination, biological and nonbiological parentage, donors and birthmothers, adoption, co-parenting and blended families, significant others, and gay marriage and domestic partnership. It helps many students obtain both a more expansive sense of family and a deeper understanding of homophobia. *[Article copies available for a fee from The Haworth Document Delivery Service: 1-800-HAWORTH. E-mail address: <getinfo@haworthpressinc.com> Website: <http://www.HaworthPress.com> © 2002 by The Haworth Press, Inc. All rights reserved.]*

KEYWORDS. Lesbian and gay families, family values, homophobia

This essay is a contribution to the project of teaching about homophobia. In it, I describe what I have come to call the "family lecture," a discussion of my

Nancy E. Rose, PhD, is affiliated with California State University, San Bernardino, Economics Department, 5500 University Parkway, San Bernardino, CA 92407 (E-mail: nrose@csusb.edu).

Author note: I would like to thank my family members for discussions about parts of this essay. Everyone has given their permission to use their first names. For permission to use "The Family Lecture" in your own classroom with my family as an example, contact the author directly.

[Haworth co-indexing entry note]: "The Family Lecture." Rose, Nancy E. Co-published simultaneously in *Journal of Lesbian Studies* (Harrington Park Press, an imprint of The Haworth Press, Inc.) Vol. 6, No. 3/4, 2002, pp. 235-241; and: *Addressing Homophobia and Heterosexism on College Campuses* (ed: Elizabeth P. Cramer) Harrington Park Press, an imprint of The Haworth Press, Inc., 2002, pp. 235-241. Single or multiple copies of this article are available for a fee from The Haworth Document Delivery Service [1-800-HAWORTH, 9:00 a.m. - 5:00 p.m. (EST). E-mail address: getinfo@haworthpressinc.com].

own extended family that I have been developing over the past decade. It encompasses descriptions of a range of groupings consisting of straight and lesbian, gay, and bisexual adults, and our children. At each step I ask students how they view the constellation–whether they consider it to be a family. Introducing these configurations raises an array of issues, including: alternative insemination; biological and nonbiological parentage; the role of donors and birthmothers in children's lives; adoption issues, including second-parent adoption, adoption by single adults and lesbian, gay, bisexual, transgender (LGBT) couples, and transracial adoption; co-parenting, stepparenting, and blended families; the role of significant others (sometimes called fictive kin) and community; and gay marriage and domestic partnership.

It works! Most students obtain a more expansive conception of what constitutes a family, and have a broader understanding of a range of other LGBT issues as a result. As the discussion unfolds, students see that most of the issues affect both heterosexual and LGBT parents; indeed, the only issue in this list that solely affects LGBT adults is gay marriage and domestic partnership. As a result, LGBT families become more normalized. Further, students generally can understand gay marriage and domestic partnership as civil rights issues even if they remain stuck about what they perceive to be religious implications.

My main purpose in writing this essay is to motivate others to include discussions of LGBT families, including their own, in teaching about homophobia. Many students wedded to idealized notions of family and "family values" do not see us as having real families. If our families are acknowledged at all, they are often seen as oddities, sometimes represented by Hollywood celebrities, but not by "ordinary folks." I realize that I am lucky in this regard. Both my sister and I are bisexual and my brother is gay, and a variety of configurations exist within my own extended family, making it productive and instructive to use us as a case study. However, increasingly, many of these, and other, situations can be found within our individual networks of family and friends.

The family lecture is presented at least halfway through Women's Studies courses. Thus by the time of the lecture students should have a thorough understanding of sexism and patriarchy, including the importance of homophobia in maintaining gender oppression. Just before the family lecture, I present statistics of changing household configurations in the U.S. over the past few decades. This generally includes: "traditional nuclear" families, i.e., mom, dad, and one or more children under age 18; married couples without children; single adults, both female and male, with and without children; and unmarried adult households, with and without children.

Several points emerge in this discussion. One is that the nuclear family is declining while all of the other types of households are increasing. Another is that we do not have reliable statistics on LGBT families. The substantial increase in female-headed households is explained by the increase in divorce and in never-married women having children. Along these lines, I also present statistics on the decline in teenage pregnancy and talk about the increase in professional women choosing to have children outside marriage (the Murphy Brown scenario). It is in this context that I first discuss the lesbian baby boom–it is simply one of the ways in which (legally) unmarried women have been becoming mothers. A similar, though much less pronounced, trend exists for unmarried fathers, both heterosexual and gay, who are family heads.

Now for the lecture itself. (Imagine this as a power point presentation–each person appears on the screen as a circle and is then connected to the others in their immediate household.) For my purposes in this essay, I will describe the groupings, along with a sociogram of the resultant diagram (Appendix A), and the questions and discussions that arise throughout the lecture.

I begin with a (seemingly) heterosexual unmarried couple: myself (Nancy) and then-partner (Heath). Then I add one child (Jesse) and another (Zach). Along the way Heath and I got married. This leads to a brief discussion about cohabitation, and why or why not people choose to marry. I point out that in many countries marriage is not as common as it is in the U.S., and that a couple is considered legally partnered after a given amount of time (e.g., seven years in Australia). This is rather straightforward, however, and everyone agrees that we were a family, especially after we married.

Next, Heath and I divorced, with joint physical and legal custody of the boys, who had homes with each of us. Most students continue to see each grouping as a family, although many view the two families as "broken," reflecting the strength of the idealized notion of the nuclear family. Heath then became unmarried partners with Haile, a situation that can lead to a usually brief discussion of stepparenting. (I've remained blessedly single.)

I then introduce my sister (Jill), who was partnered with another woman (Annie) when they had their son (Joshua). Asking students whether they see this grouping as a family raises a multitude of issues. However, before we get to those, someone inevitably asks how my sister became pregnant, a question that opens up a far-ranging discussion about alternative insemination. Students are reminded of the increase in infertility and the variety of treatments for it, including sperm and/or egg donors as well as surrogate mothers. Students generally associate infertility with heterosexual couples, in line with its attention in the media over the past few decades; yet it is fairly easily seen as an issue common to both heterosexual and LGBT adults. Returning to the question of how my sister conceived becomes quite easy; it involved no high-tech interventions since she was inseminated at home using a syringe. This sounds relatively uncomplicated by this point.

Other questions are predictable as well. One is whether it is "fair" to conceive, and parent, a child without a father. There are several responses. The first, quick one is a reminder of the statistics showing the increase in families headed by single mothers, and the much slighter rise in families headed by single fathers, as a result of divorce or never having been married. It is simply a fact that increasing numbers of children are being raised by one parent. Yet this is typically not the case for children of LGBT adults, as there are often two parents. I also ask the students whether it is fair for children to be raised by abusive parents, and note that these are the children about whom they should be concerned.

The most important response to the concern about "fairness" to the children raised by LGBT adults regards how they are doing. Here I discuss the growing body of literature on children raised in LGBT families. The studies show several things, most importantly, that psychologically the children are turning out to be relatively well-adjusted. First, they are wanted and loved; indeed, often elaborate planning goes into their conception and/or adoption. Further, compared to other children, they tend to be more accepting of a range of differences–racial, abilities, as well as sexual orientation. The problems that they encounter with their parent's sexual orientation are primarily caused by other people's negative reactions.

Another question that often arises has to do with the sexual orientation of children raised by LGBT adults. I respond that the children raised in LGBT families are no more or less likely than anyone else to be LGBT themselves. (Most LGBTs were raised by heterosexual parents, yet this did not affect our sexual orientation.) However, it is likely that our children will be encouraged to explore their sexual orientation, rather than feeling that they need to hide it from their parents.

Finally, this segues into a discussion about whether or not the child knows the biological father. I respond that a spectrum of options exists for mothers–from anonymity via a sperm bank, to knowing the father, who can have varying degrees of involvement with the child. Indeed, this decision typically involves a great deal of thought, and sometimes changes after the child's birth. Further, many children in LGBT families have significant others–"aunts" and "uncles"–who are an ongoing part of their lives.

This strand of thought, in turn, moves into a discussion of the importance of family networks in the LGBT community. Indeed, in part since it is not legally sanctioned, there is more purposive creation of extended families. Often we consider each other as kin; for example, Annie has been my sister-in-law since she and Jill were partners. In fact, these extended families, or "family webs," were the topic of a research project proposed with another sister-in-law, Lynn, who became partners with Annie after she and my sister split up (Bravewomon & Rose, 1998). As was the case with my children, Joshua had homes with both my sister and with Annie and Lynn. By this point, it becomes more difficult for students to view the situation of my children, but not that of Joshua, as being part of two families.

Eventually we return to the family constellations and the sociogram. After several years, Lynn gave birth to another child (Sam), and Annie subsequently adopted both Joshua and Sam. This leads to an informative discussion of second-parent, same sex adoptions, in which the birthmother is not required to relinquish custody in order for another adult of the same sex to adopt the child. Many students become so eager to understand these machinations that they cease to be as concerned about a child having two women as legal mothers. I then tell them that Annie and Lynn filed as domestic partners, and are as married as possible in California. This leads to a discussion of domestic partnership and gay marriage, during which many students gain some understanding of their implications and importance as civil rights issues, often seeing them as protection for the child.

Next we look at my sister's current partner (Larry) and his two daughters (Chelsey and Simone). This is a modern blended family: all of the children have two homes, as Chelsey and Simone live with Larry and Jill, and with their biological mother and her current husband and their biological child. By this point, many students see this situation as just as complicated as that of Joshua. They often relate to it easily as they know others in similar circumstances, which helps further normalize Joshua's families.

Finally we come to a gay male couple, my brother (Avi) and his partner (Ron). In the early 1980s, Avi was a donor for a lesbian couple (Nan and Lisa, more sisters-in-law), who had a daughter (Aarin). By now the idea of a lesbian couple having a child seems less strange, and does not become the focus of the ensuing conversation. Instead, this leads to a discussion of how much more difficult it is for gay men to parent than it is for lesbians, and of the various ways in which gay men, as well as other adults, both gay and straight, can parent and/or become significant others in the lives of children. Someone often asks about adoption, which leads to the last situation, as Avi and Ron are in the process of adopting a child, or siblings, through the foster care/adoption program. After extensive home visits and certification, they are eagerly awaiting placement. Most likely this will be a transracial adoption, a subject that can lead to a discussion of such adoptions in general. Again, students see that these issues affect both gay and straight adults.

CONCLUSIONS

I hope that this essay will encourage others to talk about LGBT families when teaching about homophobia, and to incorporate their own situations in these discussions. It seems to soften students somewhat, and to see LGBT families as more real, rather than as something that only affects people who they don't know. Although it obviously does not work for everyone, it helps many students further understand homophobia, changing their hearts as well as their minds.

REFERENCE

Bravewomon, L. & Rose, N.E. (1998) Family webs: A study of extended families in the lesbian/gay/bisexual community. *Feminist Economics, 4(2)*, 107-109.

APPENDIX A

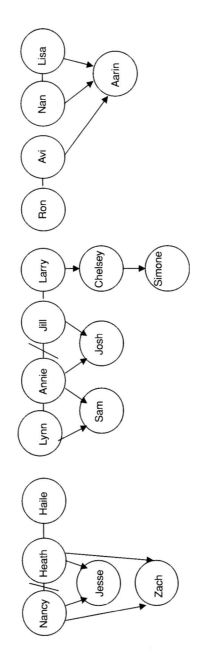

Teaching the Teachers:
Confronting Homophobia and Heterosexism in Teacher Education Programs

Anne Zavalkoff

SUMMARY. This paper presents a conceptual tool designed to help teacher education students think critically about the roots and consequences of personal, parental, community, and institutional resistance to diverse sexual identities and behaviours. To explore the roots of sexualized and gendered prejudice and ground the conceptual tool theoretically, it begins with a careful examination of Judith Butler's work on performativity. The paper then describes and illustrates the conceptual tool. The Continuum of (Subversive) Drag Performance helps stimulate critical thinking about the power implications of people's sexed and gendered performances through its six ranges: Radical, Stealth, Commercial, Passing, Mainstream, and Privileged. Because these ranges are independent of common considerations of "normalcy," they offer teacher education students a relatively unthreatening framework for analyzing conceptions of sexuality and gender that, left unexamined, can contribute to sexism, heterosexism, and homophobia. *[Article copies available for a fee from The Haworth Document Delivery Service: 1-800-HAWORTH. E-mail address: <getinfo@haworthpressinc.com> Website: <http://www.HaworthPress.com> © 2002 by The Haworth Press, Inc. All rights reserved.]*

Anne Zavalkoff, BA, is a PhD candidate at the University of British Columbia, 3024 West 10th Avenue, Vancouver, BC V6K 2K8 (E-mail: annez@attglobal.net).

[Haworth co-indexing entry note]: "Teaching the Teachers: Confronting Homophobia and Heterosexism in Teacher Education Programs." Zavalkoff, Anne. Co-published simultaneously in *Journal of Lesbian Studies* (Harrington Park Press, an imprint of The Haworth Press, Inc.) Vol. 6, No. 3/4, 2002, pp. 243-253; and: *Addressing Homophobia and Heterosexism on College Campuses* (ed: Elizabeth P. Cramer) Harrington Park Press, an imprint of The Haworth Press, Inc., 2002, pp. 243-253. Single or multiple copies of this article are available for a fee from The Haworth Document Delivery Service [1-800-HAWORTH, 9:00 a.m. - 5:00 p.m. (EST). E-mail address: getinfo@haworthpressinc.com].

KEYWORDS. Sexuality, gender, performativity, drag performance, education

Countering the heterosexism, homophobia and sexism sometimes found among teacher education students is of vital importance, because teachers greatly influence the moral development of their students. Moreover, they interact daily with students, parents, and the children of parents who identify as lesbian, bisexual, gay, or transgendered (LBGT). If straight children are to grow up without biases against other, often marginalized, sexualities, they need teachers who will help them to explore their personal, familial, cultural, and institutional assumptions and prejudices about difference. If LBGT students, or students who love LBGT people, are to feel safe at school and develop healthy identities, they need teachers who do not tolerate homophobic name-calling in the classroom, the halls, or the playground. But elementary, junior high, and high school teachers can only do their part if they are first taught to see both institutional heterosexism and their own homophobia.

This paper grows out of my experiences both as a sexual health educator in Canadian high schools and as a lecturer in the teacher education program at the University of British Columbia. It presents a conceptual tool designed to help teacher education students think critically about the roots and consequences of personal, parental, community, and institutional resistance to diverse sexual and gendered identities and performances. To explore the roots of sexual and gendered prejudice and also ground the conceptual tool theoretically, the paper begins with a careful examination of Judith Butler's work on performativity. To explore the consequences of labeling some sexualities and genders "deviant," it then describes and illustrates the conceptual tool I have developed called The Continuum of (Subversive) Drag Performance (The Continuum). The Continuum helps stimulate critical thinking about the power implications of people's sexed and gendered performances through its six ranges: Radical, Stealth, Commercial, Passing, Mainstream, and Privileged.

Although The Continuum can be used successfully with many different populations, its often humorous, practical illustrations make it particularly well-suited for use in teacher education programs. Unfortunately, space limitations prevent me from elaborating both on the reasons for this good fit and on why I contend that many current teacher education students don't understand well the workings and resulting injustices of institutional heterosexism or their own homophobia.

BUTLER ON PERFORMATIVITY:
THE CONSTRUCTION AND SUBVERSION OF THE "NORMAL"

Homophobia, heterosexism, and sexism are partially rooted in the belief that some displays of sexuality and gender are "normal" and thus acceptable, while other "deviant" displays are not. According to Judith Butler, different communities' expectations of normalcy and goodness are constructed through a "performative" process. Action, speech, and meaning are performative when practiced frequently and consistently, thereby creating cultural ideals that virtually compel compliance (1990; 1993). Although these ideals actually originate in the fairly uniform repetition of patterns of dress, behavior and speech, individual and institutional conformity to them makes them appear "natural" and "essential." Through this spiraling, performative process, communities' dominant ideals of gender, sexuality, and the other facets of identity are constructed and valued as normal.

Butler's argument is perhaps more easily grasped when spelled out in concrete terms. For example, North American understandings of the performative category "woman" are created and perpetuated in part by North American females who fairly consistently dress and behave as "women." That is, when North American women wear high heels and push-up bras, they have a part in actually producing the gendered assumption that normal, desirable women have shapely legs and big breasts. Of course, individual females are not solely responsible for their communities' gendered expectations of what it is to be a woman. Pop culture performances of femininity in magazines, in movies, and on television play a large part in shaping a community's beliefs about what constitutes appropriate displays of gender. Also worth noting–conceptions of gendered and other normalcies vary greatly across North American communities: sexuality, race, income level, and religion being only some of the complicating factors.

Butler's understanding of the production of normalcy allows enormous potential for altering oppressive gendered and sexed roles and their unjust material consequences. As Butler asserts, "the ideal that is mirrored depends on that very mirroring to be sustained as an ideal" (1993, p. 14). That is, because the performative construction of meaning relies on consistent performances, an incongruous act can throw meaning into question. So, for example, although exceedingly difficult to disobey, if enough women perform "womanhood" differently than expected, the corresponding gendered, sexed, and sexualized assumptions of others may be undermined. Thus, the very performative dynamic that constructs gender and sexuality as seemingly coherent and innate can also reconfigure them altogether.

THE CONCEPTUAL TOOL–
THE CONTINUUM OF (SUBVERSIVE) DRAG PERFORMANCE

My conceptual tool, The Continuum of (Subversive) Drag Performance, (Figure 1) builds on Butler's idea that normalcy is socially constructed through a performative process. I argue that the habitual sexed and gendered roles of women and men should be placed along a continuum of drag performance, because they are no more "natural" or "essential" than the roles adopted by those commonly understood as drag queens. I also argue that because every display of gender and sexuality is a performance, people's dress, behavior, and speech should only be condemned if, and to the extent that, they contribute to social injustice.

The Continuum of (Subversive) Drag Performance provides an analytical lens through which to evaluate the material consequences of people's gendered and sexualized performances. In particular, it makes explicit those patterns of dress, behavior, and speech that parody and break down social inequalities, as well as those patterns that reinforce them. By making teacher education students aware of the power implications of their own and others' performances, The Continuum has the potential to help them question the personal and community understandings of sexuality and gender that sometimes contribute to prejudice and social inequality.

There are six different ranges along the continuum: Radical, Stealth, Commercial, Passing, Mainstream, and Privileged. I will discuss each form of drag performance in terms of two factors: its *emancipatory potential*, i.e., its potential to disrupt unjust power structures, and its *flamboyance*, i.e., the extent to which it falls outside of the norms of the majority of people who perceive it. I justify the placement of the various types of drag on the basis of their emancipatory potential–proceeding from those with the most potential to those with the least–and not on the degree to which the dress, behavior, or speech in question differs from the expected. As a social justice educator, I consider a

FIGURE 1.

The Continuum of (Subversive) Drag Performance

| Maximally Subversive | Radical Queen | Stealth Queen | Commercial Queen | Passing Queen | Mainstream Queen | Privileged Queen | Maximally Oppressive |

strategy's likelihood of emancipation to be more important than its potential to surprise and amuse, although the two are not entirely separate.

For many individuals, the term "drag performance" conjures attire-based images that highlight the visual, adorned body. On some level, there is an expectation of being able to *see*–by examining people's clothing, make-up, or any other of a number of gender signifiers–who is "in drag." Indeed, examining how we present ourselves visually and, more importantly, how others interpret those representations is an essential part of any analysis of performance.

However, to fully understand the scope and implications of drag performance as I discuss it, people's speech and actions must also be considered. In Excitable Speech, Butler discusses the power of language and speech to shape people's conceptions of gender, sexuality, and race, as well as their general realities (1997). In an effort to more fully investigate the multiple dimensions of performance, I will explore below the relative flamboyance and emancipatory potential of the sartorial, behavioral and verbal aspects of drag.

One final note–in advocating that future teachers explore the production of sexuality and gender through an analysis of drag performance, I am not advocating that they abandon most of the "artificial" norms that serve as the contours of their lives. That would not be practical. I am more concerned that future teachers become culturally literate. Only then might they hope to successfully fight homophobia, heterosexism, and sexism in their classrooms and schools.

Radical Queen

On one end of the drag continuum is the Radical Queen whose performances are both emancipatory and flamboyant. This type of drag intentionally and explicitly caricatures dominant conceptions of what is considered normal and appropriate. "Drag queens are a mockery of 'normal' men as much as of women . . . Drag queens play up the absurd, ambiguous and contradictory in our lives" (Ibañez-Carrasco, 1995, p. 11). The Radical Queen throws seemingly coherent meaning into question by displacing gendered, sexed, and sexualized patterns of dress, behavior, and speech from their naturalized contexts. In doing so, she threatens the status quo.

To be truly Radical and subversive, this type of performance should not be flawless. Flawless imitation increases the risk of reinforcing power differentials instead of disrupting them. Luce Irigaray's conception of mimesis/mimicry develops this idea. For a woman to enact Irigaray's mimicry, she must "resubmit herself [to the terms of the dominant discourse] . . . so as to make 'visible,' by an effect of playful repetition, what was supposed to remain invisible" (1977/1985, p. 76). To effectively mimic an established discourse, and thus potentially alter it, people must not be wholly reabsorbed by that discourse. They must imitate it, but differently.

Similarly, in order for a drag performance to be emancipatory, it cannot be a perfect repetition of its gendered or sexed "foundation." As Marjorie Garber remarks, "the radical drag queen . . . wants the discontinuity of hairy chest or moustache to clash with a revealingly cut dress" (1992, p. 49). Irony is the element that piques curiosity and engages reflection.

> So the edge is when you see someone who is not perfect, who shouldn't be doing that. A fat man dressed as Madonna . . . It's not offensive, but it makes you uncomfortable. And that's the parodic edge, the sarcastic edge of drag that I think can be used. Anything that makes the audience uncomfortable and elicits or provokes some response in terms of saying "Why is this bothering me?" (F. Ibañez-Carrasco, personal communication, November 11, 1997)

Because the Radical Queen's attire is so often visually flamboyant, it is important to emphasize that it is possible for only the behavior or speech of the Radical Queen to be outrageously transgressive. For example, a friend "John" once commented that a particular woman would be quite beautiful if not for her tiny breasts. Appalled at John's reduction of this woman's appearance and humanity to her potential to sexually arouse him, I replied, "Oh, but you haven't seen her thighs. They're luscious–the kind you'd really like to get between." By mimicking John's performance in such a Radical, over-the-top way, I made explicit the sexist and heterosexist assumptions behind his comment in a way that John understood. In this case, parodic speech alone served as an amply effective educational tool.

Radical Queens who combine the visually, behaviorally, and verbally flamboyant aspects of drag are perhaps the most likely to subvert established meaning, because they challenge norms on many levels simultaneously. For example, lesbian or gay commitment ceremonies that take up an ironic tone can successfully reveal the artifice of both conventional heterosexual weddings and the institution of marriage itself. As Butler explains,

> The replication of heterosexual constructs in non-heterosexual frames brings into relief the utterly constructed status of the so-called heterosexual origin. Thus, gay is to straight *not* as copy is to original, but, rather, as copy is to copy. The parodic repetition of "the original," . . . reveals the original to be nothing other than a parody of the *idea* of the natural and the original. (1990, p. 31)

As long as the Radical Queen's flamboyant imitation of the "original" is not flawless, it has the potential to undermine the original's otherwise taken-for-granted status.

Stealth Queen

Whereas flamboyant, Radical drag achieves change by confronting people's assumptions about the world, performances that conform to broader social expectations can also be effective political tools. Less flamboyant than the Radical Queen, but also ripe with emancipatory potential, is the Stealth Queen. She is so named because others may not even notice her presence/performance until she has achieved her goal. The Stealth Queen enters and appears to accept the very system she is trying to change, adopting its customary codes of behavior, speech, and dress. Using the tools of the relatively powerful, she reduces social inequalities from within.

This type of drag is often in evidence when marginalized groups and their advocates lobby political bodies and fundraise successfully. Stealth Queens construct funding proposals for lesbian community centers or health programs according to official guidelines. They network effectively and call traditional press conferences. When marginalized groups and their advocates control their image and the media in this way, they Stealthily become subversive.

The attire, behavior, and speech of the Stealth Queen are not commonly read as drag, because her performances are not visually flamboyant. Since she blends so effectively into existing power structures, the Stealth Queen is usually only identifiable through the subversive effects of her carefully staged performances. Along The Continuum, the emancipatory image/media manipulation and role-playing of the marginalized Stealth Queen fall between the Radical Queen and the next range: the Commercial Queen.

Commercial Queen

The goal of the Commercial Queen is to repeat, as exactly as possible, the expectations of a community with which she would not typically be associated. For example, those who perform in commercial drag shows strive to achieve perfection in their visual, behavioral, and verbal gender imitations of the opposite sex. While still in some sense flamboyant, this type of drag lacks a biting, Radical edge. Commercial drag show audiences are more likely to question how female (or male) performers make themselves look so much like men (or women) than they are to question the artificiality and absurdity of the constructs of masculinity or femininity.

The extreme dilution of Commercial drag's emancipatory potential is even more in evidence when people who are not performing commercially cross-dress so effectively that they literally "pass" as the opposite sex. In these circumstances, without the artifice of the stage, nothing remains to underline that it is a female (or male) who is adopting traditionally masculine (or feminine) conventions. Without some overtly readable gendered or sexed discontinuity, not only is the absurdity of the visual, behavioral, and verbal regulatory codes lost, but so is the potential for piquing critical thought.

The performances of the Radical Quentin Crisp highlight the political shortcomings of Commercial Queens. Motivated by a desire to engage others in an analysis of gender codes, Crisp refused to remain culturally invisible. He dressed in a way he described as "effeminate" which was "signified for him by a deliberately disconcerting mélange of stylistic tropes (hair, makeup, jewelry, walk, gesture)" (Garber, 1992, p. 140). Crisp had no interest in what I describe as Commercial drag, where, using Irigaray's terminology, performers enter into the discourse so completely that they are reabsorbed by it. The less identifiable and readable the performance of the Commercial Queen becomes, the more she resembles the Passing Queen.

Passing Queen

The Passing Queen has the explicit, depoliticized intention of disappearing into dominant cultural expectations in order to escape oppression. The "normalcy" of this type of drag makes it the antithesis of flamboyance. However, because the Passing Queen aims to be accepted by the status quo without the goal of later subverting it, her role-playing also lacks emancipatory power. Ibañez-Carrasco points to this type of drag when describing the performances of some gay men.

> We demurely speak about "partners"; we want, among other things, to exercise our right to adopt children, get legally married, obtain same sex benefits, and participate in the culture of violence of the military. We know how to "pass" as decent and normal men. (1997, p. 11)

Adolescent girls who stop raising their hands in class, young boys who reluctantly stop playing with their favorite doll, as well as closeted S/M players and homosexuals, are all Passing Queens. They are so placed along the Continuum, because their role-playing grows out of their desire to avoid gendered or sexual discrimination. However, quite ironically, their passing performances unintentionally reinforce the very same inequalities from which they are trying to escape.

Mainstream Queen

Moving even further away from an emancipatory drag is the Mainstream Queen, who manipulates her image and the media with the intention of buttressing power differentials. Like the Stealth and Passing Queens, she attempts to limit her flamboyance by adopting the accepted codes of behavior, dress, and speech of the communities into which she blends. However, only the Mainstream Queen strategizes in this way with the goal of maintaining the status quo.

The media products of advertising agencies and the entertainment industry are usually Mainstream. In featuring dominant gendered, sexed, sexualized, classed, and racialized codes–for example, conventionally handsome, white, heterosexual men engaging in moneyed activities–they reinforce the seemingly natural alignment of these characteristics. Most politicians are also Mainstream Queens who try to hide the political machinations and spin doctoring behind their public appearances.

One of the most common exhibitions of Mainstream drag in North America is a mass compliance with dominant gender expectations. Most females act like "women" and most males act like "men." While the norms of femininity and masculinity vary across many North American communities, the ubiquitous repetition of "approved" gender codes tends to limit those that are widely socially acceptable. As Steven Cohan comments:

> "Masculinity" does not refer to a male nature but instead imitates a dominant regulatory fiction authorizing the continued representation of certain types of gender performances for men (like the breadwinner), marginalizing others (like the momma's boy), and forbidding still others (like the homosexual). (1995, p. 57)

The gendered dress, behavior, and speech of most women and men is perhaps the most frequently repeated, normalized, and concealed form of drag there is.

Privileged Queen

The drag of the Privileged Queen has the least emancipatory potential of the categories along The Continuum. It is performed flamboyantly by those with relative privilege who have the intention of reinscribing the power dynamic from which they derive their privilege. These visual, behavioral and verbal performances are so over-the-top that in an important sense they cannot be taken seriously. Take, for example, the Privileged performances of supermodels and Hollywood actors or the decadent surroundings portrayed on the television show *Lifestyles of the Rich and Famous.* These outrageous spectacles depict absurd lifestyles that are difficult to read as normal. Regardless, they are still very successful in naturalizing power differentials.

For the "average" heterosexual who does not fit dominant codes of beauty, wealth, or race, to become a bride is often to become the Privileged Queen, at least temporarily. The customary trappings of Western weddings–veils, trains, bridesmaids, flower girls, ring bearers, extravagant cakes, and on and on–are highly flamboyant, artificial, and costly. Yet, every time this elaborate scene is performed, the socially constructed ideals that it represents–not the least of which are heterosexuality, marriage and wealth–are strengthened and normalized.

Male bodybuilders are also fine examples of the Privileged Queen. Through drugs, extreme diets, and hours at the gym, bodybuilders begin to embody the musculature that gender codes construct as the natural male physique. Even while male bodybuilders are viewed as part freak, they reinforce gender expectations by writing an exaggerated masculinity on their physical bodies. The female bodybuilder, however, should be understood as Radical, because her extreme adoption of the "masculine" body crosses gender expectations.

I have tried to clarify through explanation and example what distinguishes the different types of performance that are located along The Continuum of (Subversive) Drag Performance. There are many nuances to The Continuum that, because of space restrictions, I cannot explore in detail here. However, I will briefly mention three. First, there exist no strict divisions between the different categories of drag. Second, the performances of individuals forever shift among, and sometimes exist concurrently in, different drag categories. Last, even communities with relatively little social capital have the moral responsibility to reexamine those expectations that become normalized within their own communities.

CONCLUSION

The conceptual tool presented in this paper outlines a framework for understanding and evaluating gender and sexuality that does not depend on common considerations of normalcy. As such, The Continuum's six ranges of drag performance offer teacher education students another perspective from which to explore their personal, parental, community, and institutional assumptions about sexuality and gender. Setting aside time to help future teachers investigate these preconceptions should be an integral part of every teacher education program, as such unexamined assumptions often form the foundation for homophobic, heterosexist, sexist and other prejudiced beliefs and behaviors.

Teachers who better understand both the workings and the injustices of institutional heterosexism and their own homophobia will likely be more sensitive to the needs of students, parents, and the children of parents who identify as LGBT. They will also be better teachers to all their students–equipped to deal with prejudice and social injustice in their own classrooms, schools, and school systems.

REFERENCES

Butler, J. (1990). *Gender trouble: Feminism and the subversion of identity*. New York and London: Routledge.

Butler, J. (1993). *Bodies that matter*. New York and London: Routledge.

Butler, J. (1997). *Excitable speech: A politics of the performative*. New York: Routledge.

Cohan, S. (1995). The spy in the grey flannel suit: Gender performance and the representation of masculinity in North by Northwest. In A. Perchuk & H. Posner (Eds.), *The masculine masquerade: Masculinity and representation* (pp. 43-62). Cambridge, Massachusetts: The MIT Press.

Garber, M. (1992). *Vested interests: Cross-dressing & cultural anxiety*. New York: Routledge.

Ibañez-Carrasco, F. (1995). Art on high heels, art that heals. *front: alternative arts magazine, 7* (2), 10-13.

Ibañez-Carrasco, F. (1997). The happy hour: AIDS drug cocktails. *front: alternative arts magazine, 9* (2), 11-15.

Irigaray, L. (1977/1985). *This sex which is not one*. (Catherine Porter with Carolyn Burke, Trans.). Ithaca, New York: Cornell University Press. (Original work published 1977.)

PART V
FEATURE FILMS AND DOCUMENTARIES

Feature Films and Documentaries List

Compiled by Patricia Little and Marcia Marx

FEATURE FILMS DEALING WITH GAY AND LESBIAN ISSUES

(Rent at most video stores. Also available through moviesunlimited.com or Amazon.com.)

Antonia's Line (1995)
This film centers on an elderly woman who recalls her life in a small Dutch village on the day of her death. Her remembrances involve five generations of women and some of their men, including her artist (lesbian) daughter.
102 min. In Dutch with English subtitles.
Rated: R
Disrector: Marleen Gorris

Bar Girls (1995)
A Los Angeles lesbian bar is at the center of the action in a refreshingly honest look at alternative relationships in the 1990s. Cartoonist Loretta meets Rachael, an unhappily married actress, at the Girl Bar, but soon finds that jealousy, ex-lovers and other bar patrons complicate their developing relationship.
95 min.
Director: Marita Giovanni
Rated: R

[Haworth co-indexing entry note]: "Feature Films and Documentaries List." Little, Patricia, and Marcia Marx. Co-published simultaneously in *Journal of Lesbian Studies* (Harrington Park Press, an imprint of The Haworth Press, Inc.) Vol. 6, No. 3/4, 2002, pp. 257-264; and: *Addressing Homophobia and Heterosexism on College Campuses* (ed: Elizabeth P. Cramer) Harrington Park Press, an imprint of The Haworth Press, Inc., 2002, pp. 257-264. Single or multiple copies of this article are available for a fee from The Haworth Document Delivery Service [1-800-HAWORTH, 9:00 a.m. - 5:00 p.m. (EST). E-mail address: getinfo@ haworthpressinc.com].

257

The Birdcage (1996)
A gay Miami nightclub owner is forced to play it straight and asks his drag-queen partner to hide out when his son invites his prospective–and highly conservative–in-laws and fiancée to a meet-and-greet dinner party.
119 minutes
Director: Mike Nichols
Rated: R

Bound (1996)
Intense, erotic crime thriller. An ex-con, after having a sexual liaison with her woman neighbor, joins forces with her to dupe the neighbor's gangster boyfriend out of $2 million of laundered loot. Explicit lesbian sex scenes portrayed. Violent scenes are intense.
105 min.
Director: The Wachowski Brothers
Rated: R

Boys on the Side (1995)
Focuses on the developing connections between three women heading on a cross-country car trip. Whoopi Goldberg plays a lesbian lounge singer, Mary-Louise Parker a real estate salewoman, and Drew Barrymore a flirtatious young woman invested in her interactions with men.
117 min.
Director: Herbert Ross
Rated: R

The Color Purple (1985)
The award-winning drama about a black woman's struggles to take control of her life in a small Southern town in the early 20th century, based on Alice Walker's novel. (Woman to woman love and sexuality explored.)
152 min.
Director: Steven Spielberg
Rated: PG-13

Coming Out (1989)
Philipp has known that he's been gay since he was very young but has struggled to ignore his feelings and live a "normal" life, even dating and moving in with a woman. But when a chance meeting with a young man turns into a loving relationship, Philipp must finally come to terms with who he is. This is the first gay-themed film to come from East Germany.

108 min.
In German with English subtitles.
Director: Heiner Carow
Rated: NR

Desert Hearts (1986)
The repressed wife of a teacher moves to Nevada for solitude and to consider divorce, but finds herself becoming attracted to her landlady's openly lesbian daughter. Set in the 1950s.
91 min.
Director: Donna Deitch
Rated: R

Fried Green Tomatoes (1991)
A frustrated housewife is transfixed by the tales spun by an elderly woman living in a nursing home. The stories involve two independent women who ran a popular cafe in Alabama in the 1930s and whose friendship (which some view as a love relationship) survived extraordinary hardships.
130 min.
Director: Jon Avnet
Rated: PG-13

In & Out (1997)
Popular and about-to-be-married, a high school teacher is "outed" by a former student during an Academy Award acceptance speech, turning his small Indiana town into a center of national attention. Now he is trying to convince everyone–from his parents and fiancee to his students and a tabloid TV reporter–that he's straight . . . but is he?
92 min.
Director: Frank Oz
Rated: PG-13

The Incredibly True Adventure Of 2 Girls in Love (1995)
Sensitive, funny and sensual comedy of a lesbian love affair involving two high school students. Randy, a defiant white tomboy working at a gas station, shares a mutual attraction to Evie, an affluent African-American girl confused about her sexuality.
94 min.
Director: Maria Maggenti
Rated: R

Ma Vie en Rose (My Life in Pink) (1997)
Seven-year-old Ludovic enjoys playing dress-up with lipstick and high heels and plans to marry a male classmate . . . which would be fine, except that Ludovic is a boy. His gender-bending play is met with bemusement at first by his parents, but the family soon faces scorn and ostracism by their suburban Belgian community.
89 min. In French with English subtitles.
Director: Alain Berliner
Rated: R

Serving in Silence: The Margarethe Cammermeyer Story (1994)
Emmy-winning true story of Col. Margarethe Cammermeyer, the Army nurse with over 20 years of service whose fight to remain in the service, after admitting she was a lesbian, threatened her career and family life and threw her into the national media spotlight.
92 min.
Director: Jeff Bleckner
Rated: NR

The Twilight of the Golds (1997)
When an expectant couple learns through genetic testing that their unborn son will probably be gay, they debate whether or not to abort the pregnancy with the wife's family, including her gay brother.
90 min.
Director: Ross Kagan Marks
Rated: PG-13

When Night Is Falling (1995)
In this lesbian re-telling of the myth of Cupid and Psyche, Camille, a professor at a Calvinist college engaged to marry a fellow teacher of religion, falls for Petra, an uninhibited circus performer. The film includes scenes of circus erotica.
94 minutes
Director: Patricia Rozema
Rated: R

DOCUMENTARIES

(Most available through moviesunlimited.com, videoflicks.com, or Amazon.com, in addition to the specific contact information provided.)

All God's Children
Provides a look at the experiences of several African-American gay men and lesbians. Offers a glimpse of the double oppression of racial discrimination

and homophobia. Deals with the issue of religion, so central to the communities in which the film's interviewees are involved.
(800) 343-5540 or fax (201) 652-1973 (to order)
Woman Vision (415) 273-1145 (message)
3145 Geary Blvd., Box 421, San Francisco, CA 94118

Before Stonewall: The Making of a Gay and Lesbian Community (1984)
(The Cinema Guild)
A groundbreaking look at the birth of the gay and lesbian movement, this award-winning documentary follows the history of the homosexual experience in America, from social experimentation of the 1920s to McCarthy-era scapegoats to the beginning of the gay rights crusade. Includes interviews with Allen Ginsberg, Audre Lorde, Barbara Gittings and others.
87 min.
Director: Robert Rosenberg
Rated: NR
Available through http://moviesunlimited.com

Coming Out, Coming Home: Asian and Pacific Islander Family Stories (1998)
Features 4 families talking about their processes of coming back together after someone came out as lesbian or gay.
30 minutes
Director: Hima B.
A/PI-PFLAG Family Project
P.O. Box 640223, San Francisco CA 94164
http://www.geocities.com/WestHollywood/Heights/5010/films.html

Forbidden Love: The Unashamed Stories of Lesbian Lives
At once touching, sexy and funny, this camp salute to the lesbian pulp novels of the 1950s and 1960s mixes documentary interviews of women fighting to live their own lives during the "sexual dark ages" with a fictional drama of a young girl's coming out.
90 min.
Director: Aerlyn Weissman, Lynne Fernie
Rated: NR
Available through Amazon.com

The Gay Gene (1992)
The science behind the controversial genetic research into the so-called "gay gene" is the focus of this program. A geneticist explains how the study was carried out, from initial interviews with gay men and their families, to the plotting of family trees, the extraction of DNA, and the analysis of samples in the

lab. The program also considers the findings of the research: that homosexuality is, in part, genetically determined. It discusses whether these finds will advance the cause of gay rights and promote tolerance and understanding in society at large.

30 minutes

Available from Films for the Humanities and Sciences

(800) 257-5126

P.O. Box 2053, Princeton, NJ 08543-2053

http://www.films.com

It's Elementary: Talking About Gay Issues in School (1999)

The film addresses the issue of whether and how gay issues should be discussed in schools. It features elementary and middle schools where (mainly heterosexual) teachers are challenging the prevailing political climate that attempts to censor any dialogue in schools about gay people. The film makes a compelling argument that anti-gay prejudice and violence can be prevented if children have an opportunity to have these discussions when they're young.

78 minutes

Director: Debra Chasnoff

(201)652-6590 www.newday.com (to order)

Women's Educational Media

2180 Bryant Street, Suite 203, San Francisco, CA 94110

(415) 641-4616; E-mail: wemfilms@womedia.org

Off the Straight and Narrow: Lesbians, Gays, Bisexuals, and Television (1998)

How are we to make sense of the transformation in gay representation–from virtual invisibility before 1970 to the "gay chic" of the 1990s? Off the Straight & Narrow is the first in-depth documentary to cast a critical eye over the growth of gay images on TV. Leading media scholars provide the historical and cultural context for exploring the social implications of these new representations. *Off the Straight & Narrow* challenges viewers to consider the value and limits of available gay images. The video is an invaluable tool for all educators interested in introducing students to issues of representation and diversity in the media.

63 minutes

Director: Kathryn Sender

Media Education Foundation

26 Center St., North Hampton, MA 01060

Tel: (800) 897-0089/(413) 584-8500

Fax: (800) 659-6882/(413) 586-8398

E-mail: media@mediaed.org

Out of the Past (1998)
Set against the true story of 17-year-old Kelli Peterson, who ignited a nationwide controversy when she tried to start a gay and lesbian student group at her Utah high school, this award-winning documentary opens a long-neglected chapter in American history as it profiles key figures in the struggle for inclusion by homosexuals.
70 min.
Director: Jeffrey Dupre
Rated: R
From GLSEN (Gay, Lesbian, and Straight Education Network)
A-PIX Entertainment, Inc.
200 Madison Ave., 24th floor, New York, NY 10016

The Question of Equality–a series of 4 films (1995 Production
Values, KQED Video) *(From Rage to Respect: The Gay and Lesbian Struggle Since Stonewall)*
This public television series documents the hard-fought gains and heartbreaking losses in the struggle for lesbian and gay equality. The Question of Equality weaves together rarely seen archival footage and firsthand accounts to reveal some of the movement's most dramatic moments, from the Stonewall riots of 1969 to the visionary efforts of today's youth.
Part One, *Out Rage '69*–Revisiting key historical moments that sparked the formation of the gay and lesbian rights movement.
Part Two, *Culture Wars*–Probes the violent anti-gay backlash in the midst of the AIDS crisis.
Part Three, *Hollow Liberty*–Focusing on the federal laws and policies that effectively restrict the rights of gay and lesbian Americans.
Part Four, *Generation Q*–Highlights the challenges and triumphs of today's lesbian and gay youth.
Available through http://videoflicks.com

You Don't Know Dick (2000)
Focuses on the issue of gender identity by providing honest and riveting portraits of six men who once were women. They are a diverse group: one gave birth to three children; another is a longtime mechanic and bodybuilder. Michael, Ted, Stephan, Max, Loren, and James share the joy and the pain of their journey from female to male. Through their commentary and the experiences of their partners, friends, and family members emerges an unforgettable story of self-discovery. There also emerges a remarkable series of reflections on the differences between male and female sexuality, on social perceptions of gender, and on the relationship of one's personal history to one's present life.

Directors: Candace Schermerhorn and Bestor Cram for Northern Light Productions.
University of California Extension Center for Media and Independent Learning
2000 Center Street, Fourth Floor
Berkeley, CA 94704
http://www-cmil.unex.berkeley.edu/media/
cmil@uclink.berkeley.edu
phone: (510) 642-0460 fax: (510) 643-9271

Index

Australia, study of attitudes
toward sexuality issues
among
Sexuality reawakening, methodology
for, 197-198
Shengold, L., 169
Shepard, M., 22,170
Singer, B., 49
Smith, B., 164
Social work students, homophobia and
heterosexism among, holistic
approach to addressing,
121-132. *See also*
Heterosexism; Homophobia
Society, classroom as microcosm of,
193-194
Spielberg, S., 258
Spirituality reawakening, methodology
for, 197-198
Staton, M., 193
Stokes, T., 75
Stolorow, R., 136
Story Monkey, 148
Stowe, A.M., 99
Strader, S., 114
Stryker, S., 180
Sullivan, G., 4,73
Sumara, D., 182

Tarver, D.E., II, 47
Taylor, C., 219
Taylor, L., 60-61,63-64,66,68,70
Taylor, S., 31
Teacher education programs,
confronting homophobia and
heterosexism in, 243-253.
See also Heterosexism;
Homophobia
The Advocate, 208
The Birdcage, 258
The Color Purple, 258
The Gay Gene, 261-262
*The Incredibly True Adventure of 2
Girls in Love,* 259

*The Journal of Counseling and
Development,* 90
The Question of Equality, 263
The Twilight of the Golds, 260
Thompson, N., 88
Toomey, B.G., 90
Tozer, E., 89
Trans
defined, 44
described, 45
Trans staff and faculty
creating a safe environment by,
50-51
current needs and concerns of,
47-49
establishing resources by, 52
increasing awareness and providing
educational training by,
51-52
meeting needs of, 43-55
updating policies and forms for, 50
using appropriate language by, 50
working conditions for, 48-49
Trans students
creating a safe environment by,
50-51
current needs and concerns of,
47-49
described, 45
establishing resources by, 52
increasing awareness and providing
educational training by,
51-52
meeting needs of, 43-55
in our schools, 47-48
updating policies and forms for, 50
using appropriate language by, 50
Trans-anxieties, alleviation of
queer and critical pedagogies in,
177-189. *See also*
Heteronormativity,
transcending of, in classroom
strategies for, 182-186
Transgender, terminology related to,
180-181